S0-BIH-443

Master Student Reader

A MASTER STUDENT TEXT

Master Student Reader

Catherine F. Andersen
Gallaudet University

HOUGHTON MIFFLIN COMPANY
Boston   New York

i

Publisher: Patricia A. Coryell
Executive Editor: Mary Finch
Sponsoring Editor: Shani B. Fisher
Assistant Editor: Andrew Sylvester
Editorial Assistant: Amanda Nietzel
Project Editor: Nan Lewis-Schulz
Editorial Assistant: Katherine Roz
Senior Production/Design Coordinator: Jill Haber
Composition Buyer: Chuck Dutton
Manufacturing Manager: Karen Banks
Manufacturing Coordinator: Brian Pieragostini
Marketing Manager: Elinor Gregory
Marketing Associate: Evelyn Yang

Cover Image: Ladder image © Robert Schoen Photography, Collage by Walter Kopec.

Printed in the U.S.A.
Library of Congress Control Number: 2006922756

ISBN - 10: 0-618-60603-3
ISBN - 13: 978-0-618-60603-0
123456789-EB-10 09 08 07 06

Acknowledgements

This book could not have been completed without the help, work and inspiration from many people. First, I would like to acknowledge the authors of the original works that are included. Obviously, they have inspired me with their writings. I also want to acknowledge and thank a number of individuals, especially Shani Fisher and Andrew Sylvester for their feedback, encouragement and support. Thank you to my colleagues at Gallaudet University, Judith Termini and Maria Waters, for their part in identifying important readings for first-year students and those in transition and for being my friends.

I thank my husband Lloyd, and my mother, Adelaide Finneran, for their encouragement and help always, but especially when I needed to meet deadlines.

This book is dedicated to my daughters, Julia and Anna, their friends and the thousands of students I have taught. You have taught me more than I have taught you.

I would also like to thank the members of our reviewing panel who provided valuable comments and feedback that helped to shape many aspects of this text throughout development:

David Campaigne, University of South Florida

Ginny Curley, Nebraska Methodist College

Ellen A. Hay, Augustana College, IL

Tracy Agnes Hooper Gottlieb, Seton Hall University, NJ

Kathryn K. Kelly, St. Cloud State University, MN

Patsy Krech, The University of Memphis, TN

Cindy Lowe-Adams, Pima Community College, AZ

AnnMarie Marlier, Bryant and Stratton College, WI

Susan L. Neste, Angelo State University, TX

Margaret Puckett, North Central State College, OH

Karla Sanders, Eastern Illinois University

Lori Schlicht—SUNY Cortland, NY

Mahara Sinclaire, Langara College, BC

Jane Speer, Alpena Community College, MI

Christel Taylor, University of Wisconsin

Mary Todd, Ohio Dominican University

Carol A. Van Der Karr, SUNY Cortland, NY

Jodi E. Webb, Bowling Green State University, OH

Contents

Preface

Dear Student,

Welcome to a journey during your first semester in college that I hope will conclude with you well on your way to being a successful college student. There is no question that to get the most out of your education, you must work hard. The harder you work and the more you challenge yourself, the more you will learn. But it is up to you. Take advantage of this time when you are guided by a knowledgeable instructor and surrounded by peers who can enrich your life by providing unique perspectives on class discussions, readings and activities.

The *Master Student Reader* will help you on this journey by providing a starting point for your discussions. The readings you find here cover a range of topics: career prospects and obstacles you will face in joining the work force, the development of thinking skills, ways to promote sound health, the importance of memory, the impact of illiteracy on society, the power of language and how it has been affected by technology, strategies to combat stress and performance anxiety, civility and cultural awareness, the dangers of debt, and the impact of our choices. Before you begin, I want to share some tips about how you might make the best use out of this text.

The text is built around thirteen Power Processes, which are articles that encourage you to take charge of your college experience. These thirteen Power Processes will begin each chapter and set the stage for the readings. Eldon L. McMurray, Director of the Faculty Center for Teaching Excellence at Utah Valley State College, suggests that when you read the Power Processes consider the following: (1) **Why** a Power Process might matter to you (or to your children, family, coworkers, etc.); (2) **What** the transition to college means with regard to this Power Process; (3) **How** will you make this transition work for you; and (4) **What** do you risk by not making this transition now.

The *Master Student Reader* is structured in a way that exposes you to a variety of writing styles and mediums. Readings are excerpted from student writing, textbooks, magazines, newspapers, web sites, essays, and speeches. Journal writings in each chapter stress self-assessment, along with more traditional approaches such as persuasive essays, fact or opinion papers and research papers. Specific techniques for reading, writing, vocabulary development and critical thinking are important skills to develop.

In the section "Mastering This Reader" below, you will find tips for reading, writing and thinking critically, and mastering vocabulary. By using these techniques, you can truly enrich your understanding of the material you read–not just in this text, but in any readings that you encounter in and out of an academic setting. However, it is truly up to you. The more effort you put forth the more you question yourself and why you are doing something in a particular way, the more you try to see another person's point of view, and the more you are willing to try new behaviors, the greater the likelihood that you will emerge at the end of the semester as a stronger student. Whether you are a first time college student or a non-traditional student who put your life on hold and are now ready to begin, you can do it.

Mastering This Reader

Learn to Know Yourself

As you think, read, and write, constantly relate what you are doing to your own experiences. Ask yourself, how might I respond in this situation? Is it an appropriate response? Are there ways I can change? Am I giving this assignment my all? If I cannot, are there good reasons why I can't? Do I need help with something? Am I afraid to ask for help? Why?

Some of the fundamental ideas behind getting to know yourself are reinforced by a growing body of research that links college student success with emotional intelligence. Emotional intelligence refers to our ability to recognize our emotions and those of others, and manage them in such a way that allows for clearer thought and sound personal decisions. Unlike an intellectual quotient (I.Q.), Emotional Intelligence (E.I), can be enhanced. In fact, in a study by Schutte and Malouff (2002) in the Journal of the First Year Experience, students who read about emotional coping strategies and self-efficacy skills, and wrote about their own emotions, had higher grade point averages (GPA's) at the end of the semester than students enrolled in traditional first- year seminar courses.

Among the many skills that emotional intelligence encompasses is optimism; an "I can do" attitude. Other important skills include problem solving, independence, flexibility, assertiveness, reality testing (am I seeing things accurately?), social responsibility, interpersonal skills, the ability to handle stress, emotional self-awareness, empathy and general happiness. As you read, think, write, and act, continue to ask yourself how you might measure up in these areas.

Read to Understand

First, always read with a pencil, pen or highlighter. Mark on the books, ask questions. If you cannot write on the reading, use a notebook to write comments, questions, and a summary.

Second, make note of any word you don't understand. Write it down in a book. Use a dictionary to help you find the meaning of words. There are many online dictionary and vocabulary resources. Each chapter in this text has a section on Mastering Vocabulary. Use it. Create word lists using a notebook or index cards to practice words that are unfamiliar to you. My father had a little notebook where he put down any word he did not understand as he came across them during the day. At night, he would look up the word and think of ways he could use it in context. His mother, who only completed 8th grade, was the most prolific reader I have ever met and a champion Scrabble player. She too made every effort to learn words that she did not understand. Both of these individuals believed that the more they understood, the more they could gain in life and contribute. For them, knowledge was power.

Third, use a strategy like the SQ3R to become actively involved in your reading and fine tune your critical thinking skills. The SQ3R technique is simply a before, during and after reading approach.

SQ3R

SURVEY Quickly look over the material you are supposed to read. What will this reading be about?
- What is the title?
- What is the purpose of the reading?
- What is the main idea?
- What are the subheadings?
- Are there graphics, charts, maps or diagrams?
- Are there any reading aids like bold or italics?

QUESTION Actively question and search for answers as you read. Keep your mind active. Don't wander.
- What does the author mean?
- Why would they bold or italicize something?
- What do illustrations such as graphics mean?

READ Find the answers to your questions.
- Read sections keeping your questions in mind.
- Pose new questions.

RECITE Answer your questions in your head or out loud.
- Go section by section and answer your questions.
- Pretend as if you are teaching someone. Ask your question and answer it.
- Don't go to the next section until you can answer previous sections.

REVIEW When you are finished summarize the reading.
- Summarize the reading according to the headings and sub headings (use these as your guide).

While you are reading—question, question and question. What is the main point? How does this apply to me? Do I agree with this author? Why or why not? Is there another way to think about this? Is the author biased in his or her viewpoint? Why? These kinds of behaviors are what educators call *critical reading.* Most of us have heard these words, but do we really know what it means? Arthur Chickering (1981) states that a good liberal arts education prepares students in a variety of areas and should develop the skill of critical thinking, "To see things as they are, to go right to the point, to disentangle a skein of thought, to detect what is sophisticated and to disregard what is irrelevant."* He suggests that this skill is necessary to be successful in the workforce, as workers must be able to analyze and synthesize information, learn from experience to generate new ideas and behaviors, and to understand many sides of a controversial issue.

Basically, someone with good critical thinking skills understands the main points, takes a position on an issue drawing from personal experience and support from credible sources, and considers other's point of view when taking a stand. They identify and question assumptions, distinguish between fact and opinion, and understand how values influence judgments. How can you do this? Can you draw conclusions from what the author is saying? Is it logical? Does the information conflict with what you believe? Does the conflict stem from a lack of background information that inhibits your ability to fully understand the argument, or does the argument go against your own ethical or moral beliefs? Learn to know yourself. Discuss what you are reading with someone else. When we teach or explain something to another, our learning is greatly enhanced.

When you are finished reading, review what you just read. What did I read? If you only had five sentences to sum up the reading, what would they be? Are there any things in the reading you want to know more about?

---

*Chickering, Arthur. "Integrating Liberal Education, Work and Human Development," American Association for Higher Education, Vol. 33, No.7.March 1981, pp.1,11-13,16.

Look it up. Ask questions. As a faculty member, I can tell which students are prepared for class by the way they ask questions and contribute to class discussion. In fact, there is plenty of research that indicates that students who engage in their own learning learn more and are more satisfied with their education. It makes perfect sense.

In addition to the strategies associated with the SQ3R, there is a much more basic aspect to successful reading: your environment. Try to read in a place that is comfortable and where you have the best chance of comprehending. Sometimes finding the ideal location is not possible. You may be in between classes, or sitting in a motor vehicle office waiting for a new license, but when possible, read in an environment that will help you remember what you read. Again, "learn to know yourself." When do you work best and where?

Write to Relflect, Assess, Summarize, and Convince

Follow the criteria stated when responding to writing assignments. Writing assignments have specific criteria to follow. Assignments have a purpose. A particular assignment may ask you to describe, argue, define, critique, compare, contrast or persuade. Keep in mind this purpose, and make sure your writing answers the question that has been posed to you.

As a writer, you will need to support your writing with a variety of techniques, depending on the assignment. When you write you will be answering the same kinds of questions you posed when you were reading, but this time you will be developing a persuasive argument that includes evidence to back it up. Write about the "how's and why's" by analyzing, not just summarizing. Use the critical thinking techniques described in the "Read to Understand" section above to make sure that you are approaching your argument from all sides and basing your writing on sound reasoning supported by experience and credible sources.

As you are composing your writing, make sure that it includes the following elements:

Introduction: In any writing, it is important to let your reader know where you are headed from the beginning. Your introduction should identify the central argument, and give an outline of the position you will be taking. A key component of the introduction is the *thesis statement,* which is a concise sentence that clarifies the central argument of your paper: "Harriet Tubman's activities with the Underground Railroad led to a relationship with the Union army during the Civil War."

Body: This is where you will explain in depth the main points supporting your thesis statements. You will explain all aspects of the argument, and provide evidence in support of your claims.

Conclusion: This will be the summation of your paper, in which you reiterate your position.

Another important aspect of writing is *audience;* instructors, peers, parents, prospective students, or members of a college governing board. How you approach your writing will depend very much on your reader. If you are writing a paper discussing new rules in college basketball, even though your conclusions may be the same, your actual writing will differ greatly if your reader is a high school student than if the reader is a college coach. As you are writing, remember to ask yourself who will be reading this? How much do they know about the subject? Are they likely to agree or disagree with my conclusions?

The writing assignments included in this text will allow you to practice your skills at developing persuasive and informative writing.

Keep a journal. In addition to responding to specific writing prompts at the end of each reading, students are encouraged to keep a journal.

The purpose of the journal is to think and write about ones own behavior. For example, students can write about academic behavior ("I wish I could memorize easily" or, "I am such a slow reader and my mind wanders") or a response to a specific event ("My roommate doesn't seem to be homesick, so I don't want to tell her or anyone that I am"). Journal writing should be relaxing and enjoyable, and will provide you with a means to bring thoughts and feelings to the surface. Instructors may request weekly journal entries, but at a minimum, a journal entry should be done in the first, mid and last week of the semester. Journal writing can be an excellent way to "learn to know yourself."

Each chapter in this text includes Journal Entries using *Discovery and Intention Statements.* The *Discovery and Intention Statement System* is a tool for developing your emotional intelligence: an instrument for knowing yourself. Discovery Statements are declarations of your goals, descriptions of your attitudes, statements of your feelings, transcripts of your thoughts, and chronicles of your behaviors. Intention Statements can be used to alter your

Discovery Statements:
1. Record the specifics about your thoughts, feelings, and behavior.
2. Use discomfort as a signal and let your emotions direct you.
3. Suspend judgment about yourself.
4. Tell the truth.

Intention Statements:
1. Make intentions positive.
2. Make intentions observable.
3. Make intentions small and keepable.
4. Set timetables that include rewards.

course. They are statements of your commitment to do a specific task or take a certain action. The questions that comprise the Journal Entries in each chapter ask you to reflect on both your discoveries and intentions in your writings. Here are some guidelines as you complete these assignments:

Writers write, re-write, re-write, re-write and then submit their work. Ask any English teacher or journalist and they will tell you that it is rare that a good work is accomplished without re-writing. You must continually question your work, question your assumptions, and analyze your conclusions to ensure that your writing is clear and persuasive to others. At times, specific help on *how and what* to revise will be needed. Take advantage of willing professors, friends and family members who are good writers, and your college writing center. In addition, there are many online tools available for suggestions on how to write. Tools include suggestions for writing thesis statements, topic sentences, summaries, and how to identify common grammatical mistakes.

Some of your professors may ask you to use writing conventions such as the Modern Language Association (MLA) or the American Psychological Association (APA) tools for citing work. Basically, MLA and APA documentation techniques help readers understand that you are summarizing or quoting someone else's work but documenting where you got it. Also, MLA and APA give specific rules for how to list a work in your bibliography or works cited. To give you an idea of how this works, each reading selection has been listed using both the MLA and APA documentation format.

In addition to the strategies listed above, additional activities are included in each chapter that encourage group work, presentations, and research. These supplemental activities help to develop skills for successful college students. The readings and the assignments that accompany them are intended to encourage self-reflection and analysis; the foundation for student success.

Again, welcome to this journey of self-discovery. You are well on your way to knowing yourself better; improving your thinking, reading and writing skills; and understanding the views and perceptions of others. You are well on your way to a life of learning, and to becoming a truly educated person. Congratulations.

Sincerely,
Dr. Catherine Andersen

Discover What You Want

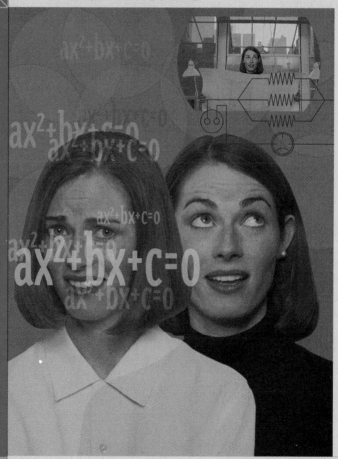

What kind of college student do you want to be? Can you picture yourself in December, at the end of one year, and at your graduation? Successful college students get to know themselves, understand their strengths, their weaknesses, and the way they learn. They also set goals. They move from "discovery to action." As you read this Power Process, envision yourself.

The Power Process: Discover What You Want

Imagine a person who walks up to a counter at the airport to buy a plane ticket for his next vacation. "Just give me a ticket," he says to the reservation agent. "Anywhere will do."

The agent stares back at him in disbelief. "I'm sorry, sir," he replies. "I'll need some more details. Just minor things—such as the name of your destination city and your arrival and departure dates."

"Oh, I'm not fussy," says the would-be vacationer. "I just want to get away. You choose for me."

Compare this with another traveler who walks up to the counter and says, "I'd like a ticket to Ixtapa, Mexico, departing on Saturday, March 23, and returning Sunday, April 7. Please give me a window seat, first class, with vegetarian meals."

Now, ask yourself which traveler is more likely to end up with a vacation that he'll enjoy.

The same principle applies in any area of life. Knowing where we want to go increases the probability that we will arrive at our destination. Discovering what we want makes it more likely that we'll attain it. Once our goals are defined precisely, our brains reorient our thinking and behavior to align with those goals—and we're well on the way there.

Mastery lies in the details

The example about the traveler with no destination seems far-fetched. Before you dismiss it, do an informal experiment: Ask three other students what they want to get out of their education. Be prepared for hemming and hawing, vague generalities, and maybe even a helping of pie-in-the-sky à la mode.

That's amazing considering the stakes involved. Our hypothetical vacationer is about to invest a couple weeks of his time and hundreds of dollars—all with no destination in mind. Students routinely invest years of their lives and thousands of dollars with an equally hazy idea of their destination in life.

Suppose that you ask someone what she wants from her education and you get this answer: "I plan to get a degree in journalism with double minors in earth science and Portuguese so that I can work as a reporter covering the environment in Brazil." Chances are you've found a master student. The details of a person's vision offer a clue to mastery.

Discover the benefits

Discovering what you want greatly enhances your odds of succeeding in higher education. Many students quit school simply because they are unsure of their goals. With well-defined objectives in mind, you can constantly look for connections between what you want and what you study. The more connections you discover, the more likely you'll stay in school—and the more likely you'll benefit from higher education.

Having a clear idea of your goals makes many decisions easier. Knowing what you want from your education helps you choose the school you'll attend, the courses you'll take, the major you'll declare, and the next career you'll pursue.

Discovering what you want also enhances your study skills. An example is memorizing. A skydiver will not become bored learning how to pack her parachute. Her reward for learning the skill is too important. Likewise, when information helps you get something you want, it becomes easier to remember.

You can have more energy when your daily activities lead to what you want. If you're bogged down in quadratic equations, stand back for a minute. Think about how that math course ties in with your goal of becoming an electrical engineer—how your philosophy course relates to your aim of becoming a minister or how your English course can help you become a better teacher.

Succeeding in higher education takes effort. When you follow the path of getting what you truly want, you can enjoy yourself even if the path is uphill. You can expend great energy and still feel fresh and eager to learn. When you take on courses that you care about and prepare for a career that you look forward to, you can play full out. You can work even to the point of exhaustion at times, and do it happily.

That's one purpose of discovering what you want. Your vision is not meant to be followed blindly; it's meant to pull you forward.

Put it in writing

For maximum clarity, write down what you want. Goals that reside strictly in your head can remain fuzzy. Writing them down brings them into sharper focus.

As you write about what you want, expand your imagination to many different time frames. Define what you want to be, do, and have next week, next month, and next year. Write about what you want five years from now—and five minutes from now.

Approach this process with a sense of adventure and play. As you write, be willing to put any option on the table. List the most outrageous goals—those that sound too wonderful to ever come true.

You might want to travel to India, start a consulting business, or open a library in every disadvantaged neighborhood. Write those goals down.

You might want to own a ranch in a beautiful valley, become a painter, or visit all of the hot springs in the world. Write those down too.

Perhaps you want to restore the integrity of the ozone layer or eliminate racism through international law. Or perhaps you simply want to be more physically fit, more funny, or more loving. Whatever you want, write it down.

Later, if you want, you can let go of some goals. First, though, live with them for a while. Goals that sound outlandish right now might seem more realistic in a few weeks, months, or years. Time often brings a more balanced perspective, along with an expanded sense of possibility.

Move from discovery to action

Discovering what you want can be heady fun. And it can quickly become an interesting but irrelevant exercise unless you take action to get what you want. Most discoveries come bundled with hints to *do* something—perhaps to change a habit, contact someone, travel, get educated, or acquire a new skill. Dreams that are not followed with action tend to die on paper. On the other hand, dreams that lead to new behaviors can lead to new results in your life.

To move into action, use this book. It's filled with places to state what you want to accomplish and how you intend to go about it. Every Journal Entry and exercise exists for this purpose. Fill up those pages. Take action and watch your dreams evolve from fuzzy ideals into working principles.

With your dreams and new behaviors in hand, you might find that events fall into place almost magically. Start telling people about what you want, and you'll eventually find some who are willing to help. They might offer an idea or two or suggest a person to call or an organization to contact. They might even offer their time or money. The sooner you discover what you want, the sooner you can create the conditions that transform your life.

Readings

What is it that you want to accomplish at the end of the semester or your time in college? Is it really worth it to you to go to college? The readings in this section are about getting to know oneself better and setting goals, as well as the details needed to accomplish them. The readings are chosen to encourage you as a student to think long term and to see the success of individuals who set goals and what one might do to overcome hurdles and to understand both the psychological and monetary rewards of getting what you want.

Reading One

Three young men from the poverty-ridden streets of Newark, New Jersey, decided to make a pact with each other to succeed and make something of their lives. While the odds were against them, two became doctors and one a dentist. How did they do it? Read on.

The Pact: Three Young Men Make a Promise and Fulfill a Dream

Drs. Sampson Davis, George Jenkins, and Rameck Hunt

We treat them in our hospitals every day.

They are young brothers, often drug dealers, gang members, or small-time criminals, who show up shot, stabbed, or beaten after a hustle gone bad. To some of our medical colleagues, they are just nameless thugs, perpetuating crime and death in neighborhoods that have seen far too much of those things. But when we look into their faces, we see ourselves as teenagers, we see our friends, we see what we easily could have become as young adults. And we're reminded of the thin line that separates us—three twenty-nine-year-old doctors (an emergency-room physician, an internist, and a dentist)—from these patients whose lives are filled with danger and desperation.

We grew up in poor, broken homes in New Jersey neighborhoods riddled with crime, drugs, and death, and came of age in the 1980s at the height of a crack epidemic that ravaged communities like ours throughout the nation. There were no doctors or lawyers walking the streets of our communities. Where we lived, hustlers reigned, and it was easy to follow their example. Two of us landed in juvenile-detention centers before our eighteenth birthdays. But inspired early by caring and imaginative role models, one of us in childhood latched on to a dream of becoming a dentist, steered clear of trouble, and in his senior year of high school persuaded his two best friends to apply to a college program for minority students interested in becoming doctors. We knew we'd never survive if we went after it alone. And so we made a pact: we'd help one another through, no matter what.

In college, the three of us stuck together to survive and thrive in a world that was different from anything we had ever known. We provided one another with a kind of positive peer pressure. From the moment we made our pact, the competition was on. When one of us finished his college application, the other two rushed to send theirs out. When we participated in a six-week remedial program at Seton Hall University the summer before our freshman year, each of us felt pressured to perform well because we knew our friends would excel and we didn't want to embarrass ourselves or lag behind. When one of us made an A on a test, the others strived to make A's, too.

We studied together. We worked summer jobs together. We partied together. And we learned to solve our problems together. We are doctors today because of the positive influences that we had on one another.

The lives of most impressionable young people are defined by their friends, whether they are black, white, Hispanic, or Asian; whether they are rich, poor, or middle-class; whether they live in the city, the suburbs, or the country. Among boys, particularly, there seems to be some macho code that says to gain respect, you have to prove that you're bad. We know firsthand that the wrong friends can lead you to trouble. But even more, they can tear down hopes, dreams, and possibilities. We know, too, that the right friends inspire you, pull you through, rise with you.

Each of us experienced friendships that could have destroyed our lives. We suspect that many of the young brothers we treat every day in our hospitals are entangled in such friendships—friendships that require them to prove their toughness and manhood daily, even at the risk of losing their own lives. The three of us were blessed. We found in one another a friendship that works in a powerful way; a friendship that helped three vulnerable boys grow into successful men; a friendship that ultimately helped save our lives.

But it wasn't always easy. There were times when one of us was ready to give up, and times when we made bad decisions. Some of that is ugly and difficult to admit, and we suffered pain and other consequences. But we have laid it all out here nonetheless.

We did this because we hope that our story will inspire others, so that even those young people who feel trapped by their circumstances, or pulled by peer pressure in the wrong directions, might look for a way out not through drugs, alcohol, crime, or dares but through the power of friendship. And within our story are many others, of mentors, friends, relatives, and even strangers we met along the way, whose goodwill and good deeds made a difference in our lives. We hope our story will also demonstrate that anyone with enough compassion has the power to transform and redirect someone else's troubled life.

If we have succeeded at all in helping to turn even a single life around or in opening a window of hope, then this book was well worth our effort.

"Introduction", from THE PACT by Sampson Davis, George Jenkins and Rameck Hunt, with Liza Frazier Page, copyright c 2002 by Three Doctors LLC. Used by permission of Riverhead Books, an imprint of Penguin Group (USA) Inc.

▶ Reflection Questions

1. Can you identify with any or all of the doctors? What is it about their lives and yours that make it possible or not possible to see similarities in their experiences and yours?

2. This reading describes stereotypes, poverty, crime, and death but also friends, studying, support, and dreams. It describes a thin line that "separates us—three twenty-nine-year-old doctors . . . —from these patients whose lives are filled with danger and desperation." At another point, the authors say: "The lives of most impressionable young people are defined by their friends, whether they are black, white, Hispanic, or Asian; whether they are rich, poor, or middle-class; whether they live in the city, the suburbs, or the country." Reflect on events and circumstances you or your friends have experienced that have left an impression on you. In what ways do these events and circumstances influence your perspective and beliefs?

3. The doctors shared that there were times when they wanted to give up and times when they made bad decisions. Think of times when you simply gave up or thought of giving up. When is it okay to give up and when is it not? Think of specific examples from your life. How have those times shaped your life?

Reading Two

This article describes the "flow state," or psychological high, that individuals feel when they accomplish a challenging task. Csikszentmihalyi, a noted professor of psychology, describes this flow state as something that comes from internal motivation, not from external goals or rewards. As you read this, think of going to and completing college as an internal or external reward.

Flow Learning—The Myth Buster

Ronald Gross

"This section will explore the alternatives to the fears and myths of learning. It starts by examining a distinctive state of mind and feeling in which learning is effortless and delightful. This state has been studied intensively by psychologists for the past fifteen years. They have interviewed and tested students, blue-collar workers, professionals, and the elderly. The findings all agree: when our brains are working in this distinctive state of mind, we can overcome our fears about learning.

This state is called *flow,* and it is vital to our personal happiness. The term was coined by the pioneer researcher in the field, Mihaly Csikszentmihalyi (pronounced Chick-SENT-me-hi, though he prefers to be called Mike), head of the Department of Behavioral Sciences at the University of Chicago and author of *Flow: The Psychology of Optimal Experiences.*

"What do we mean by being happy?" Professor Csikszentmihalyi asks. "Is it just pleasure and the absence of pain? These are rewarding conditions, indispensable to maintain psychic processes on an even keel. But happiness also depends on something else: the feeling that one is growing, improving. That process is, by definition, a process of learning, broadly defined. One might conclude that learning is necessary for happiness, that learning *is* the pursuit of happiness."

Flow is the state in which learning and happiness are most completely merged. An article in the *New York Times Magazine* described it as "a state of concentration that amounts to absolute absorption in an activity. In this state, action flows effortlessly from thought and you feel strong, alert and unselfconscious. Flow is that marvelous feeling that you are in command of the present and performing at the peak of your ability. . . . research suggests that flow may be a common aspect of human experience."

Flow happens in every activity. In sports, it's that moment of reaching the *zone* where your ability and performance excel. In music, it takes place when you know your instrument and the piece so well that you just *do* it, as if you have *become* the instrument and the music. In dancing, painting, surgery, and even writing, there's a sense of control, a profound focus on what you're doing that leaves no room to worry about what anyone will think of your work. There are a number of features that characterize the flow state:

Flow can occur when perceived challenges match perceived skills. Perhaps the most crucial feature is the delicate balance between what you *perceive* to be the challenges in the situation you face and how you *perceive* your own abilities to meet those challenges. Perception is important here, because, as has been seen, the mind *actively constructs* the situations it faces. *Any* activity can be turned into a flow experience if viewed in the right way.

The first step in recognizing the conditions for flow is to *have something to do,* an opportunity for action, a challenge. The next step is to recognize that you have some skills you can use to decide what to do next. The balance between these two will start the ball rolling for flow.

Let's try to make this issue of balance clearer by comparing it to experiences in which there is an *imbalance* between challenge and skills. Imagine you had to take a beginners' course in what you currently do for a living. Your skills and experience are already far beyond what is being taught. Sitting through endless explanations of things you already know would be agonizing torture, immensely boring. That sort of experience takes place in the Drone Zone.

Alternatively, suppose you attended a graduate seminar in something you know nothing about—quantum physics, for example. The speaker goes on and on, but you sit there, comprehending about one word in a hundred, hopelessly over your head. You are now in the Groan Zone.

Flow happens in the region between Groan and Drone. It happens when you need to use all you can bring to the situation—and to stretch yourself just a little bit more. *For flow to occur, the balance between what the situation demands and your skills must result in an advance, an increase in what you can do.* This gives us our first crucial characteristic for flow learning.

Flow states involve a sense of control in the situation. With that perceived balance comes another characteristic of the flow experience: a sense of control. Imagine sitting down to play a game of chess for the first time. You have some idea of how the pieces are supposed to move, but as the game develops, it may be hard to figure out what you should do next. Yet as you play more, and learn more, you start to recognize certain kinds of situations that repeat. You don't fall for the same traps again. You have a better idea of what to do, and so you have an increased sense of control instead of feeling as if you're helplessly floundering.

Flow happens in situations in which one has clearly defined goals and feedback. Games provide a good model for describing other features of the flow experience. According to Csikszentmihalyi, it is important in learning to have a clear sense of the goals in a situation and clear feedback about the results of your actions. This knowledge of what you're aiming for and what difference your actions make encourages you to concentrate on what is relevant to the situation, to become immersed in it.

In flow experiences, intense concentration on what is relevant develops the ability to merge unselfconscious action with awareness and to alter the experience of time. Think of kids who get involved in computer games, even the arcade shoot-'em-ups. What needs to be done to find the treasure or destroy the alien invaders is totally clear in each moment. And so it becomes easy to lose track of time, forget your hunger and even ignore pain until you stop playing.

Thus in a clearly defined situation in which challenge is balanced by skill and there is a sense of control, it becomes possible to focus concentration intensely on the relevant cues, to merge action and awareness in a way that drops any self-consciousness and may even change how the passage of time is experienced. This feature is our next essential in the flow experience.

Flow experiences arise from intrinsic motivation, not from concern with external rewards or goals. Csikszentmihalyi has found that this feature is as important as the balance of skills and challenge. It is also the most important part of flow for us as peak learners.

As we saw before in discussing learning fears and learning myths, feeding back information for the sake of a good grade can rob learning of its joy and make it torture. Sure, you can be pleased by a good grade, but it is not likely to make the process of cramming for exams any more pleasant.

On the other hand, if you're jamming on a guitar with friends or perfecting your jump shot on a basketball court, what makes those things fun, according to Csikszentmihalyi, is that you're doing them for their own sake. You may wind up with a good riff for a song or the ability to sink a basket from mid-court, but while you're getting there you are just having fun. That is, the experience of learning is enjoyable in itself, not for what you will eventually get out of it.

Csikszentmihalyi believes that people who use flow actually use *less* mental energy than those who are struggling to concentrate because they're bored or anxious. He sees the flow experience as something that's a built-in part of being human, of having a mind that processes information. In his view, new challenges are enjoyable because they prepare human beings to be involved with their environment and to succeed. For Csikszentmihalyi, the joys of learning are as natural as the pleasures of sex, and both serve evolutionary goals for the human species.

▶ Reflection Questions

1. In this reading, Gross cites an article in the *New York Times Magazine* that describes the flow state as "a state of concentration that amounts to absolute absorption in an activity . . . it is a marvelous feeling that you are in command of the present and performing at the peak of your ability." Can you think of a time in your life when you have experienced this? What factors led up to this point?

2. A student once described the feeling of the flow state when he was taking a test that he had studied for. Can you think of a time when this happened to you? Describe the feeling you had and what led up to it. What did this experience teach you about yourself?

Reading Three

Does going to college really pay off? Do college graduates really earn more money than those who do not attend? As you read this article, think about what else might be connected to individuals' earnings over a lifetime, other than the degree.

Job Outlook for College Graduates

Jill N. Lacey and Olivia Crosby

You've heard it again and again: Having a college degree leads to higher earnings and more career opportunities. But is it true?

For the most part, it is. When it comes to paychecks and prospects, conventional wisdom is right. On average, college graduates earn more money, experience less unemployment, and have a wider variety of career options than other workers do. A college degree also makes it easier to enter many of the fastest growing, highest paying occupations. In some occupations, in fact, having a degree is the only way to get your start.

According to statistics and projections from the U.S. Bureau of Labor Statistics (BLS), college graduates will continue to have bright prospects. Data consistently show that workers who have a bachelor's or graduate degree have higher earnings and lower unemployment than workers who have less education. And between 2002 and 2012, more than 14 million job openings are projected to be filled by workers who have a bachelor's or graduate degree and who are entering an occupation for the first time.

A college education can be costly, of course, in terms of both time and money. But the rewards can be bigger than the sacrifices if a degree helps you to qualify for occupations that interest you. . . .

In this article, a college graduate is defined as a person who has a bachelor's, master's, or doctoral (Ph.D.) degree or a professional degree, such as one in law or medicine. . . .

COLLEGE GRADUATES: IN DEMAND AND DOING WELL

More people are going to college now than ever before, in part because of the career advantages that a college degree confers. College-educated workers' higher earnings and lower unemployment are good reasons to go to college, and these benefits are also evidence of the demand for college graduates. Higher earnings show that employers are willing to pay more to have college graduates work for them. And lower unemployment means that college graduates are more likely to find a job when they want one.

More people going to college

The number of people who have a college degree has been increasing steadily. According to Current Population Survey data, the number of people aged 25 and older who have a college degree grew from 35 million to 52 million between 1992 and 2004, an increase of almost 50 percent. By mid-2004, nearly 28 percent of people aged 25 and older had a bachelor's or graduate degree. (See chart 1.)

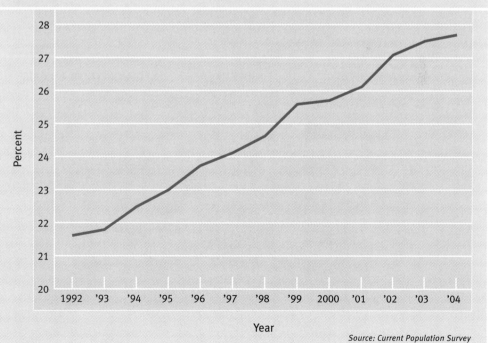

CHART 1
Percent of population aged 25 and older with a bachelor's or graduate degree, 1992–2004

Source: Current Population Survey

Higher earnings, lower unemployment

As a whole, college-educated workers earn more money than workers who have less education. In 2003, workers who had a bachelor's degree had median weekly earnings of $900, compared with $554 a week for high school graduates—that's a difference of $346 per week, or a 62 percent jump in median earnings. (Median earnings show that half of the workers in the educational category earned more than that amount, and half earned less.)

For workers who had a master's, doctoral, or professional degree, median earnings were even higher. In addition to earning more money, workers who had more education were also less likely to be unemployed. Chart 2 shows the median earnings and unemployment rates for workers at various levels of educational attainment.

Taken together, higher earnings and more regular employment amount to large differences in income over a lifetime. . . .

Higher earnings for workers who have a college degree are part of a long-term trend. Even when adjusted for inflation, the wages of college-educated workers have been rising over the past decade. (See chart 3.) Moreover, the earnings for college-educated workers have been increasing faster than the earnings for workers who do not have a bachelor's degree.

CHART 2
Unemployment and earnings for full-time workers aged 25 and over, by educational attainment, 2003

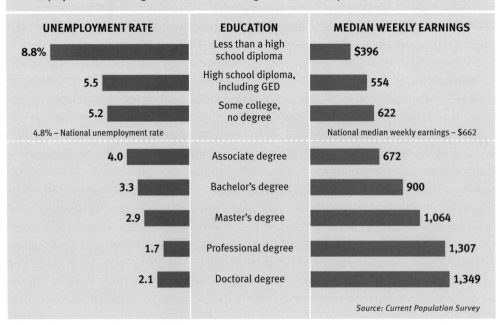

UNEMPLOYMENT RATE	EDUCATION	MEDIAN WEEKLY EARNINGS
8.8%	Less than a high school diploma	$396
5.5	High school diploma, including GED	554
5.2	Some college, no degree	622
4.8% – National unemployment rate		National median weekly earnings – $662
4.0	Associate degree	672
3.3	Bachelor's degree	900
2.9	Master's degree	1,064
1.7	Professional degree	1,307
2.1	Doctoral degree	1,349

Source: Current Population Survey

CHART 3
Real (inflation-adjusted) average annual earnings, by educational attainment, 1991–2001

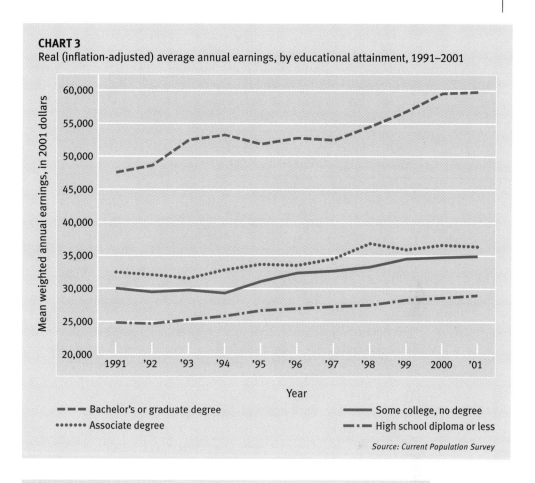

Source: Current Population Survey

The trouble with averages

Statistics about college graduates paint a rosy—and numerically accurate—picture of overall employment. But the data are based on college graduates as a whole. For every graduate who earns more than the median, another earns less. And while unemployment rates are low overall, many college graduates sometimes have trouble finding work, especially if they wait for the type of job they want.

The career prospects of individuals depend on many factors besides having a college degree. These factors include the local job market, the type of degree they have, their level of experience and skill, and the occupation they are trying to enter.

OPENINGS AND WHERE THEY WILL BE

Between 2002 and 2012, BLS projects 56 million job openings for workers who are entering an occupation for the first time. Of these, at least 14 million are expected to be filled by college-educated workers. More than half of these openings are expected to come from the need to fill newly created jobs.

The remaining openings for college-educated workers are projected to come from the need to replace workers who leave an occupation permanently. With many of today's college-educated workers poised to retire, replacement needs are expected to be great, especially in large occupations.

In some occupations, most workers have bachelor's or graduate degrees. In other occupations, education levels are more varied.

Many of the occupations that are expected to have the most openings for college graduates are in the business, computers and engineering, education, counseling, and healthcare fields.

"Pure college" occupations

For this analysis, it is assumed that each future job opening will be for a college-educated worker. In these "pure college" occupations, at least 60 percent of current workers aged 25–44 have a bachelor's or graduate degree, fewer than 20 percent have a high school diploma or less education, and fewer than 20 percent have some college courses but less education than a bachelor's degree. Even if some workers do not have a bachelor's or graduate degree, all openings are counted as being for college-educated workers because that most accurately reflects the job market new workers face. . . .

BLS projects that pure-college occupations will provide about 6.8 million openings over the 2002–12 decade for college graduates who are entering an occupation for the first time. Chart 4 shows the 20 pure-college occupations expected to provide the most openings during the projections decade. Like nearly all pure-college occupations, all but one of the occupations on the chart have earnings above $27,380, the 2002 median for all workers.

Despite high numbers of job openings, jobseekers can face strong competition when trying to enter some occupations, such as public relations specialists or management analysts. Because these occupations offer high earnings and prestige and because workers can qualify with many different college majors, the number of qualified workers who want these jobs could be greater than the number of openings. Analyses of job competition are possible for a few occupations, ones for which there is anecdotal evidence or for which other data exist. To qualify for many of the occupations shown on chart 4, workers need more than a bachelor's degree. In three of the occupations—lawyers, physicians and surgeons, and pharmacists—a professional degree is required. Similarly, physical therapists now train for their occupation only in a master's or doctoral degree program.

In other occupations, educational requirements are more flexible. About one-fourth of management analysts have a master's degree, for example, but many analysts do not have education beyond a bachelor's degree. School teachers, too, often have a graduate degree, but many teachers earn that degree after they begin their careers; while employed, they take graduate-level courses to gain skills, qualify for higher salaries, and maintain certification. In many occupations, employment and advancement opportunities improve with attainment of a graduate degree, even when one is not required for career entry.

CHART 4
"Pure college" occupations with the most job openings for college graduates entering the occupation for the first time, projected 2002–12

	OPENINGS (THOUSANDS)	MEDIAN ANNUAL EARNINGS, 2002
Postsecondary teachers	960	$49,090
Elementary school teachers, except special education	547	41,780
Secondary school teachers, except special and vocational education	458	43,950
Accountants and auditors	405	47,000
Management analysts	255	60,340
Special education teachers	233	43,450
Computer software engineers, applications	218	70,900
Lawyers	207	90,290
Physicians and surgeons	191	145,600+
Middle school teachers, except special and vocational education	182	41,820
Computer software engineers, systems software	156	74,040
Clergy	144	33,110
Pharmacists	114	77,050
Child, family, and school social workers	111	33,150
Education administrators, elementary and secondary school	99	71,490
Educational, vocational, and school counselors	86	44,100
Public relations specialists	75	41,710
Rehabilitation counselors	69	25,840
Mechanical engineers	69	62,880
Market research analysts	66	53,810

Education level often determines the type of work a person can do within an occupation. Psychologists, for example, usually need a doctoral degree to do independent, clinical work, but some school psychologists do not need this level of education. Social workers can get some jobs with a bachelor's degree, but to work in a clinical setting, they often need a graduate degree.

"Mixed education" occupations

Many college graduates work in occupations that employ workers who have a variety of education levels. Over the 2002–12 decade, about 23 million openings are projected to be in occupations in which the number of college-educated workers is significant—20 percent or more—but for which college is not the only level of education workers have. For example, of the 1.1 million job openings projected for registered nurses, over 650,000 are projected to be filled by bachelor's or graduate degree holders based on current educational attainment patterns. Overall, of the 23 million job openings in these "mixed education" occupations, BLS expects 7.5 million to be filled by college graduates.

Chart 5 shows the mixed-education occupations that are expected to provide the most openings over the projections decade for college graduates who are entering an occupation for the first time. In several of these occupations, such as registered nurses, police and sheriff's patrol officers, and wholesale and manufacturing sales representatives, the education levels of workers have been rising. When hiring workers, some employers prefer their new employees to be college graduates, even though many existing workers do not have a degree.

Sometimes, as is often the case for preschool teachers and social and human service assistants, having a degree benefits workers beyond helping them get the job. It may qualify workers to take on more complex tasks in the occupation, for example, or increase workers' opportunities for advancement and responsibility.

In other occupations—such as retail salespersons and customer service representatives—workers from every education level are represented even though most qualify after a few weeks or months of on-the-job training. A degree is not required, and many college graduates choose these occupations for reasons unrelated to education or training, such as plentiful opportunities or flexible hours.

Mixed-education occupations make it difficult to measure with certainty the demand for college graduates. Defining a college-level occupation is highly subjective. Some openings in an occupation might require a degree; for other openings, a degree might be useful; and for still other openings, a degree might not make much of a difference.

Occupations with increasing demand: Trends and themes

As a whole, occupations that employ mostly college graduates are expected to gain new jobs faster than other types of occupations. Between 2002 and 2012, pure-college occupations are projected to grow 22 percent overall, considerably faster than the 15-percent average growth projected for all occupations. Eighteen of the 20 pure-college occupations in chart 4 are projected to grow faster than the 15-percent average for all occupations.

Looking at job growth is important because occupations that are gaining jobs quickly are, in effect, showing rapidly increasing demand for workers. Some of the economic trends that are creating growth in pure-college and mixed-education occupations are described below by career field.

CHART 5
"Mixed education" occupations with the most job openings for college graduates entering the occupation for the first time, projected 2002–12

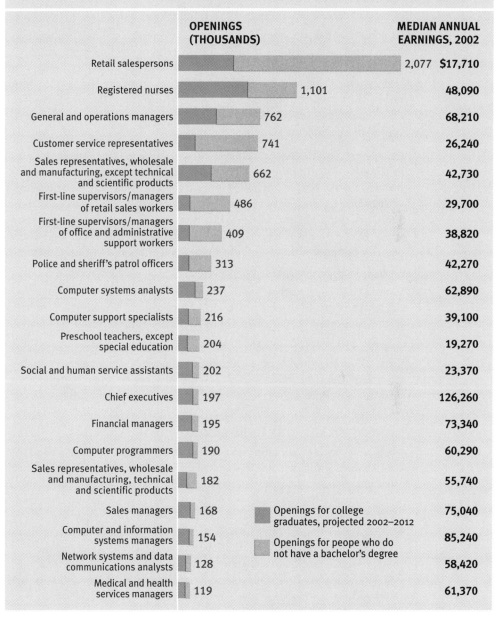

	OPENINGS (THOUSANDS)	MEDIAN ANNUAL EARNINGS, 2002
Retail salespersons	2,077	$17,710
Registered nurses	1,101	48,090
General and operations managers	762	68,210
Customer service representatives	741	26,240
Sales representatives, wholesale and manufacturing, except technical and scientific products	662	42,730
First-line supervisors/managers of retail sales workers	486	29,700
First-line supervisors/managers of office and administrative support workers	409	38,820
Police and sheriff's patrol officers	313	42,270
Computer systems analysts	237	62,890
Computer support specialists	216	39,100
Preschool teachers, except special education	204	19,270
Social and human service assistants	202	23,370
Chief executives	197	126,260
Financial managers	195	73,340
Computer programmers	190	60,290
Sales representatives, wholesale and manufacturing, technical and scientific products	182	55,740
Sales managers	168	75,040
Computer and information systems managers	154	85,240
Network systems and data communications analysts	128	58,420
Medical and health services managers	119	61,370

Openings for college graduates, projected 2002–2012

Openings for peope who do not have a bachelor's degree

Business, finance, and sales. The growing complexity of business is expected to increase the demand for college graduates in business and financial occupations. More workers will be needed to manage rising personal incomes, increased regulation of financial activity, and growing competition among businesses.

Sales occupations are expected to grow along with the overall economy. Although numerous workers in these occupations do not have a college degree, many others do. Having a degree is especially valued in occupations involving sales of complex scientific or technical products.

Computers and engineering. The demand for new products and new technology is expected to continue to drive growth in computer and engineering occupations. Occupations in emerging engineering specialties, including biotechnology and environmental engineering, are expected to gain jobs rapidly over the projections decade. However, these specialties are expected to remain small and provide fewer openings than larger engineering specialties, such as mechanical and computer engineering.

Counseling, social service, and psychology. Numerous social trends are projected to increase the number of counselors, social workers, and psychologists needed over the 2002–12 decade. More schools are hiring trained counselors. At the same time, more people are seeking counseling for family problems, substance abuse, and mental disorders. And to ease overcrowding at prisons, many offenders are being sent instead to rehabilitation facilities—where counselors, social workers, and psychologists are employed to assist them.

Education. Most opportunities in the field of education will come from the need to replace the many teachers and administrators who are expected to retire over the 2002–12 decade. But additional positions are projected because of efforts to reduce class sizes and because of increasing enrollments at colleges and universities.

Healthcare. As the population ages, the need for healthcare will increase, fueling the need for more healthcare practitioners. Moreover, improvements in medical technology will create more medical and rehabilitative treatments. Those treatments are prescribed and often administered by workers who have a college degree.

HOW THESE NUMBERS WERE DEVELOPED

There are many ways to measure job outlook by education, and each method has both strengths and limitations. This analysis focuses on future job openings because job openings show how many new workers will be able to enter an occupation.

Deciding which job openings will be filled by college graduates was more complicated. Counselors and jobseekers often ask which occupations are "college level." But answering that question is difficult because workers in most occupations come from many different educational backgrounds. This analysis used the education levels of current workers as an objective way to account for this variation.

Like any analysis based on projections and estimates, however, this one has limitations to its accuracy. Understanding these limitations will help readers to better use the results.

Methods used

To estimate the demand for college graduates between 2002 and 2012, BLS analysts got specific. First, they projected the number of job openings for workers entering each of more than 500 occupations over the decade. Next, analysts estimated how many of those openings would be filled by college graduates.

Measuring job openings. Job openings come from two sources: The need to fill newly created jobs and the need to replace workers who retire or leave an occupation permanently for other reasons.

To estimate the number of newly created jobs, analysts projected how much each occupation would grow or decline between 2002 and 2012. An occupation might gain jobs for many reasons. Sometimes, the demand for a specific good or service creates the need for additional workers in an occupation, such as when an increased use of computer software creates a greater need for software engineers. The way a good or service is provided can also lead to more jobs in an occupation. Rather than relying solely on teachers and administrators to guide and educate students, for example, more schools are hiring counselors and psychologists, creating more openings for those workers. In the same way, a decrease in the demand for a good or service or a change in production methods can reduce the number of jobs and openings in an occupation.

The second source of job openings is replacement needs. To estimate how many workers will need to be replaced during the projections decade, BLS analysts studied the ages of current workers and the length of time that workers in each occupation usually remain. In occupations that require high levels of training, workers tend to stay longer. In other occupations, especially those that have shorter training periods, workers tend to leave or retire more quickly.

Job openings for college graduates. After analysts projected the number of job openings for workers entering an occupation, they estimated how many of those openings would be for college graduates. Using information from 2000, 2001, and 2002 Current Population Survey data, analysts classified current workers' educational attainment into one of three categories: A high school diploma or less, some college but no bachelor's or graduate degree, or a bachelor's or graduate degree. If at least 20 percent of workers in an occupation belonged to a given educational category, that level was deemed significant. Expected openings were divided among each of these significant education categories, according to how common each category was.

For example, the occupation of administrative services managers includes workers in each educational category: About 23 percent have a high school diploma or less, 37 percent have some college coursework or an associate degree but no bachelor's degree, and 41 percent have a bachelor's or graduate degree. Projected openings were divided among the education categories using those percentages.

For some occupations, a bachelor's or graduate degree was the only education level common enough to be significant. At least 60 percent of workers in the occupation were college graduates. And fewer than 20 percent of workers belonged to the other two educational categories. In these 115 "pure college" occupations, every projected opening was considered to be for a college graduate.

In addition to using the three educational attainment categories, this article provides specific information about the types of degrees commonly required in some occupations. This type of information comes from the occupational analyses conducted for the *Occupational Outlook Handbook.*

Earnings data. This analysis uses earnings data from two surveys: The Current Population Survey and the Occupational Employment Statistics survey. Earnings data from the Current Population Survey, which includes information about workers' education levels, were used to compare earnings by education. Earnings data from the Occupational Employment Statistics survey, which is more comprehensive, provide median earnings for an occupation as a whole.

The two surveys are different. The Current Population Survey is a household survey that asks workers themselves to give earnings, occupational, and other types of information; it includes self-employed workers. The Occupational Employment Statistics survey, an establishment survey, asks employers to provide earnings and occupational information about their workers; it does not include the self-employed.

Limitations of the data

To measure job openings for college graduates, BLS analysts needed to make assumptions about the future. First, analysts assumed that the education levels in each occupation would remain roughly the same over the 2002–12 decade. In reality, the educational characteristics of some occupations change over time. Many occupations—such as registered nurses and police officers—have had a gradual increase in the number of workers who have a bachelor's degree.

Analysts also ignored education levels that were uncommon in an occupation; as stated previously, at least 20 percent of workers in an occupation had to have a given level of education for it to be considered significant. So, for example, even though almost 17 percent of engineering technicians have a college degree, none of that occupation's projected openings were counted as openings for college graduates.

Another limitation of this study is that it focuses on the number of job openings projected in an occupation. But job openings give only a partial view of the prospects that workers can expect. The number of people who will compete for those openings is also important. For most occupations, however, BLS analysts do not have enough information to analyze the competition for jobs.

Finally, the accuracy of this study is limited by its use of survey data. Surveys are always subject to some error because not every worker is counted and because the information gathered is sometimes incorrect. In addition, the education levels of many occupations could not be determined with statistical accuracy because the number of workers surveyed was too small. In those cases, analysts substituted the education levels of similar occupations or groups of occupations that had larger numbers of workers.

Even with its assumptions and limitations, however, there is evidence that estimating future job openings using the analysis described here produces accurate results. When existing jobs are separated into educational categories in such a way, the results closely match current numbers.

Source: "Job Outlook for College Graduates" by Jill N. Lacey and Olivia Crosby, *Occupational Outlook Quarterly,* Winter 2004-05.

▶ Reflection Questions

1. In this reading the average earnings of individuals with a college education are compared with those of individuals who did not go to college. It also points out that college graduates have less unemployment. Did this surprise you? Why or why not?

2. Can you think of an instance when it would not be "valuable" to attend college?

3. What do the authors mean by "pure college" occupations? In the past, these same jobs may have been held by individuals without a college degree. Why do you think this has changed? Do you agree that now these jobs should require a degree?

4. Other than monetary, what other benefits might one realize from going to college?

5. In the future, the jobs that are now in demand might change. What might account for this change?

 ## Writing Assignment

audience: A significant person in your life

purpose: To share (describe, predict, self-assess) what you think college will be like

length: Minimum of three typed pages, double-spaced

Your first assignment begins with writing a letter to a significant person in your life (a parent, teacher, or mentor, for example) describing what you think your first semester in college will be like and what you want. Describe why you are in college and what you hope to achieve. How long do you think getting a college education will take? What obstacles might you encounter along the way? Be very specific when it comes to obstacles.

How will you spend your days? How much time do you think you will study? Where will you study and with whom, or will you study alone? Do you think you will ever give up? What kinds of things do you think you will give up on? Can you think of anything you will do to help yourself stay on track?

Are you concerned about doing well? Do you think you will need help? If so, in what subjects? What is it that you want to accomplish at the end of the semester or your time in college? Is it really worth it to you to go to college? Will you get support or go it alone? Are you worried about any part of going to college? Are you concerned about relationships? Roommates? Finances?

Include in this letter, specific examples of what you learned from the three readings. Can you think of a situation that you have experienced similar to that of the doctors? Was there ever a time when you really wanted something, worked hard for it, and achieved it? Did you ever experience the flow state? What things did you learn from these readings and how can you apply them to your life? Apply the Power Process. *Did you discover what you want?*

Think of one challenge for yourself this week. What will you work hard at? Describe how you might feel when you achieve it. Have you discovered what you want as a result of the readings?

When you are done with the letter, seal it and give it to your instructor who will hold it, unopened, and return it to you at the end of the semester. Your final assignments will be to look at this letter and reflect about what happened during your first semester from the time you wrote it.

 Journal Entries: DISCOVERY AND INTENTION STATEMENTS

Write about what you were thinking when you were writing your letter. Were you thinking about what you should do, as opposed to what you think you will do? Were you completely honest with yourself? Are you nervous about living up to what you think your parents want you to do? Write down and describe any thoughts you had writing this letter. In addition, write one or two sentences about what you have learned and what you intend to do as a result of having read these readings, what you will do to make it work, and what you risk if you do not do what you intend to do.

Mastering Vocabulary

List five words that were new or relatively new to you. For each, include which reading you found the word in, the definition, and where you got the definition from, as well as a time or place you might use the word again. For example:

Intrinsic motivation in the reading "The Flow State" by Ronald Gross. The desire to satisfy natural needs and interests, which includes a desire to understand and make sense of the world. *Glossary of Gifted Education.*

I could use this when I am describing the reasons I should do well on a test. I want to do well on a test because it will make me feel good. It is not to please others. My intrinsic motivation will drive my success.

1.

2.

3.

4.

5.

 ## Additional Activities

Pair up with a classmate and share an event in your life where you experienced the flow state. Share with each other what you plan to achieve this week. Consider being support persons for each other as you both consider trying something new. Support persons can email each other and see how the other is doing in what he or she wants to accomplish. They can plan to meet once during the week. They can ask each other what will provide support for the other.

Online Study Center **Improve Your Grade**
Visit the Online Study Center for resources and exercises to accompany this text
http://college.hmco.com/pic/msreader1e

CHAPTER ONE

Ideas Are Tools

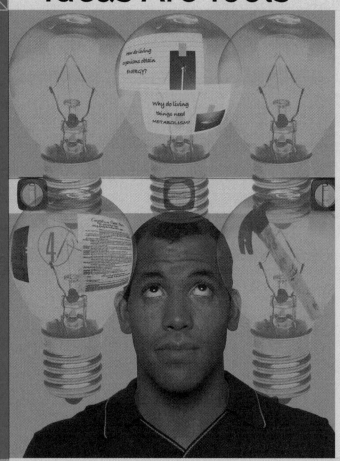

In this chapter we examine the concept that there is more than one way to accomplish something. What works for one person may not work for another. What works for someone in a particular situation may not work for the same person in another situation. As you learn more about yourself, you also have to learn that there is more than one way for you to accomplish something.

Regardless of what we know about ourselves and the way we learn, we must explore what it is that motivates us to succeed—or not. Perhaps we are motivated by the fact that college graduates earn more than those who do not have a degree. Perhaps it is the fact that we want to better our lives. The motivation to go to college may vary by individual, but regardless, the desire to learn is central for all.

The Power Process: I Create It All

There are many ideas in this book. When you first encounter them, don't believe any of them. Instead, think of them as tools.

For example, you use a hammer for a purpose—to drive a nail. When you use a new hammer, you might notice its shape, its weight, and its balance. You don't try to figure out whether the hammer is "right." You just use it. If it works, you use it again. If it doesn't work, you get a different hammer.

This is not the attitude most people adopt when they encounter new ideas. The first thing most people do with new ideas is to measure them against old ones. If a new idea conflicts with an old one, the new one is likely to be rejected.

People have plenty of room in their lives for different kinds of hammers, but they tend to limit their capacity for different kinds of ideas. A new idea, at some level, is a threat to their very being—unlike a new hammer, which is simply a new hammer.

Most of us have a built-in desire to be right. Our ideas, we often think, represent ourselves. And when we identify with our ideas, they assume new importance in our lives. We put them on our mantels. We hang them on our walls. We wear them on our T-shirts and display them on our bumpers. We join associations of people who share our most beloved ideas. We make up rituals about them, compose songs about them, and write stories about them. We declare ourselves dedicated to these ideas.

Some ideas are worth dying for. But please note: This book does not contain any of those ideas. The ideas on these pages are strictly "hammers."

Imagine someone defending a hammer. Picture this person holding up a hammer and declaring, "I hold this hammer to be self-evident. Give me this hammer or give me death. Those other hammers are flawed. There are only two kinds of people in this world: people who believe in this hammer and people who don't."

That ridiculous picture makes a point. This book is not a manifesto. It's a toolbox, and tools are meant to be used. This viewpoint is much like one advocated by psychologist and philosopher William James. His approach to philosophy, which he called pragmatism, emphasized the usefulness of ideas as a criterion of truth.[1] James liked to talk about the "cash value" of an idea—whether it leads to new actions and new results.

If you read about a tool in this book that doesn't sound "right" or one that sounds a little goofy, remember that the ideas here are for using, not necessarily for believing. Suspend your judgment. Test the idea for yourself.

If it works, use it. If it doesn't, don't.

Ask: What if it's true?

When presented with a new idea, some of us take pride in being critical thinkers. We look for problems. We probe for weaknesses. We continue to doubt the idea until there's clear proof. Our main question seems to be "What's wrong with this idea?"

This approach can be useful when it is vital to expose flaws in ideas or reasoning. On the other hand, when we constantly look for what's wrong with new ideas, we might not recognize their value. A different and potentially more powerful approach is to ask yourself "What if that idea is true?" This opens up all sorts of new possibilities and variations. Rather than looking for what's wrong, we can look for what's potentially valuable. Faced with a new idea, we can stay in the inquiry, look deeper, and go further.

Keep looking for answers

The light bulb, the airplane, the computer chip, the notion of the unconscious—these and many other tools became possible when their inventors practiced the art of continually looking for additional answers.

Another way to expand your toolbox is to keep on looking for answers. Much of your education will be about finding answers to questions. Every subject you study—from algebra to history to philosophy—poses a unique set of questions. Some of the most interesting questions are those that admit many answers: How can we create a just society? How can we transmit our values to the next generation? What are the purposes of higher education? How can we prevent an environmental crisis?

Other questions are more personal: What career shall I choose? Shall I get married? Where shall I live and how shall I spend my leisure time? What shall I have, do, and be during my time on Earth?

---

[1] William James, *Pragmatism and Other Essays* (New York: Washington Square, 1963).

Perhaps you already have answers to these questions. Answers are wonderful, especially when they relate to our most persistent and deeply felt questions. Answers can also get in the way. Once we're convinced that we have the "right" answer, it's easy to stop looking for more answers. We then stop learning. Our range of possible actions becomes limited.

Instead of latching onto one answer, we can look for more. Instead of being content with the first or easiest options that come to mind, we can keep searching. Even when we're convinced that we've finally handled a problem, we can brainstorm until we find five more solutions.

When we keep looking for answers, we uncover fresh possibilities for thinking, feeling, and behaving. Like children learning to walk, we experience the joy of discovery.

A caution

A word of caution: Any tool—whether it's a hammer, a computer program, or a study technique—is designed to do a specific job. A master mechanic carries a variety of tools because no single tool works for all jobs. If you throw a tool away because it doesn't work in one situation, you won't be able to pull it out later when it's just what you need. So if an idea doesn't work for you and you are satisfied that you gave it a fair chance, don't throw it away. File it away instead. The idea might come in handy sooner than you think.

And remember, this book is not about figuring out the "right" way. Even the "ideas are tools" approach is not "right."

It's a hammer . . . (or maybe a saw).

Readings

The readings in this chapter are about the kinds of skills that are needed to succeed now and in the future. They are chosen to encourage you to take a critical look at yourself and identify your strengths and challenges. They are chosen to explicitly be concerned with the idea of thinking critically and the stages of development. Finally, a reading is chosen that presents the life stories of successful individuals, the "moments of truth" in their lives, and the lessons they share.

Reading One

Before you read the following, consider the skills that people will need for the twenty-first century and beyond. What are the skills that you want to develop? What tools will you use to help you do so? Finally, think of some characteristics of highly successful people. This article discusses the fact that the skills individuals need for the twenty-first century and beyond are those provided by a liberal arts education and encompass both educational and human development.

Liberal Education, Work, and Human Development

Arthur W. Chickering

Since Cambridge University began 600 years ago, colleges and universities have assumed that liberal education and preparation for work go hand in hand. A college education should lead to a better job as well as a better life. You probably want your education to lead to a good job and a good life also. But can you pursue a rich liberal education and also come out prepared for a successful career? Or do our current social conditions and work requirements mean they must be addressed separately?

LIBERAL EDUCATION

One of the first, and best, definitions of liberal education comes from Cardinal Newman's *The Idea of a University* (1852):

> *A University training . . . aims at raising the intellectual tone of society, at cultivating the public mind, at purifying the national taste, at supplying true principles to popular enthusiasm, and fixed aims to popular aspiration in facilitating the exercise of political power and refining the intercourse of private life. It gives one a clear conscious view of one's own opinions and judgments, a truth in developing them, an eloquence in expressing them, and a force in urging them. It teaches one to see things as they are, to go right to the point, to disentangle a skein of thought, to detect what is sophisticated, and to discard what is irrelevant. It prepares one to fill any post with credit and to master any subject with facility. It shows one how to accommodate oneself to others, how to influence them, how to come to an understanding with them, how to bear with them. One is at home in any society, one has common ground with every class, one knows when to speak and when to be silent, one is able to converse, one is able to listen, one can ask a question pertinently and gain a lesson seasonably when one has nothing to impart oneself. . . . One is a pleasant companion and a comrade you can depend on. . . . One has a repose of mind which lives in itself, while it lives in the world, and which has resources for its happiness at home when it cannot go abroad.*

Take that paragraph apart and you have the key objectives for liberal education:

- Communication skills—"an eloquence in expressing them and a force in urging them."
- Critical thinking skills—"to see things as they are, to go right to the point, to disentangle a skein of thought, to detect what is sophisticated, and to discard what is irrelevant."
- Interpersonal competence, respect for others, empathy—"how to accommodate oneself to others, how to influence them, how to come to an understanding with them, how to bear with them."

- Preparation for work and learning how to learn—"to fill any post with credit and to master any subject with facility."
- Cultural sophistication and cross-cultural understanding—"one is at home in any society, one has a common ground with every class."
- Capacity for intimacy—"a pleasant companion and comrade you can depend on."
- Clarity of values and integrity—"a clear conscious view of one's own opinions and judgments, a truth in developing them."
- A basic sense of identity—"a repose of mind which lives in itself, while it lives in the world."

That's a good list. You probably would like to achieve many of those outcomes yourself. There may be others you might want to add, like computer literacy, computational skills, developing artistic talents. But perhaps this list will serve as we turn to preparation for work.

PREPARATION FOR WORK

The Bible says that work became necessary because of a divine curse. When Adam ate the apple, he threw away Paradise without toil and turned the world into a workhouse. Today we view work not as a curse but a blessing. Useful work is an antidote to stagnation. Complex, challenging work is a major stimulus for personal development. Achievement, contribution, and productivity are the cornerstones for self-respect.

Our changing orientation toward work grows out of the changing nature of *work*, away from repetitive, mindless, physically demanding drudgery, toward "service workers" and "knowledge workers." The key to effective service is *quality*, not *quantity*. Achieving high-quality service is more complicated than producing high-quality goods. A television set is a complex instrument, but producing high-quality sets in large numbers is much easier than producing high-quality programming. Designing high-powered automobiles and supersonic airplanes requires high-level technological skills but we are far from designing environments and transportation systems that effectively serve human needs. To work in this kind of "post-industrial" and "post-technological" knowledge and service society, with rapidly changing job structures and a global economy, you need broad-based competence and adaptablity.

There is a growing body of research that identifies the skills, abilities, and personal characteristics required for effective careers. One of the early studies by George Klemp [an expert in competency based assessment of job skills] and his colleagues examined a variety of career areas including human services, military services, small businesses, police work, sales, civil service, and industry management among others. What did they find?

Our most consistent—though unexpected—finding is that the amount of knowledge one acquires of a content area is generally unrelated to superior performance in an occupation and is often unrelated even to marginally acceptable performance. Certainly many occupations require a minimum level of knowledge on the part of the individual for the satisfactory discharge of work-related duties, but even more occupations require only that the individual be willing and able to learn new things. . . . In fact, it is neither the acquisition of knowledge nor the use of knowledge that distinguishes the outstanding performer, but rather the *cognitive skills* that are developed and exercised in the process of acquiring and using knowledge. These *cognitive* skills constitute the first factor of occupational success.

What cognitive skills are most important to success at work?

1. Information processing skills related to learning, recall, and forgetting.
2. Conceptualizing skills [which] enable individuals to bring order to the informational chaos that consistently surrounds them. . . . such skills go beyond an ability to analyze. . . . They involve an ability to synthesize information from a prior analysis.
3. The ability to understand many sides of a controversial issue. Persons with this skill can resolve informational conflicts better than persons who can't conceptualize in this way. Persons without such skills typically resolve conflicts by denying the validity of other points of view and are equipped to mediate disputes or to understand what their positions have in common with the positions of others.
4. The ability to learn from experience . . . , the ability to translate observations from work experience into a theory that can be used to generate behavioral alternatives.

The second major factor linked with success in the world of work involves *interpersonal* skills:

1. Non-verbal Communication—"Fluency and precision in speaking and writing is important of course, but often it is the nonverbal component of communication, both in sending and receiving information, that has the greater impact."
2. "Accurate empathy"—the ability to *diagnose* a human concern and to respond appropriately to the needs of the other. There are three aspects to this skill: (a) positive regard for others, (b) giving another person assistance, whether asked for or not, that enables that other person to be effective, and (c) controlling hostility or anger that, when unleashed on another, make that person feel powerless and ineffective.

But these cognitive and interpersonal skills by themselves do not guarantee superior performance. The third critical factor is *motivation.*

Motivation is, a need state . . . and for a variety of reasons people are often unable to translate their dispositions into effective action. . . . This variable describes a person who habitually thinks in terms of cause and outcomes as opposed to one who sees the self as an ineffective victim of events that have an unknown cause. . . . Our own analysis of complex management jobs . . . has shown that a person who takes a proactive stance, who initiates action and works to dissolve blocks to progress, will, with few exceptions, have the advantage over a person who is reactive, who does not seek new opportunities, but sees the world as a series of insurmountable obstacles.

So effective performance in the world of work involves a clear set of cognitive skills, interpersonal skills, and motivational characteristics. You probably have some of these skills already well-developed. But you can use courses and classes as well as activities outside of the academic program to improve them and work on others which need strengthening. The chart below compares Newman and Klemp. There seems to be a striking agreement. This agreement supports higher education's traditional assumptions about the congruence of a liberal education and preparation for work.

HUMAN DEVELOPMENT

How do our desired outcomes for liberal education, and the skills and personal characteristics required for effective careers, correspond with what we know about major dimensions of human development? Jane Loevinger's research and theory concerning ego development provide one of the most comprehensive formulations currently available. "Ego development" is a good way to approach the issue because it is a "master trait" whose different structures heavily influence our perceptions, our thinking, and our behavior. Loevinger posits four structures or areas of ego development, namely, (a) *impulse control* and *character development*, (b) *interpersonal style*, (c) *conscious preoccupations*, and (d) *cognitive style*. There is a sequence of developmental stages in these four structures beginning with the "Pre-social" and "Symbiotic" stages associated with infancy and childhood. The six major stages associated with adolescence and adulthood range from "Impulsive," "Self-protective," "Conformist," "Conscientious," "Autonomous," and "Integrated." The higher stages are conceptually complex and have high tolerance for ambiguity. For example, integrated

Liberal Education and Preparation for Work

NEWMAN: LIBERAL EDUCATION OBJECTIVES	KLEMP: COMPETENCE AND CHARACTERISTICS FOR WORK
Clarity of values, integrity	
Communication skills	Communication skills
Critical thinking skills	Information processing skills, conceptualizing skills
Preparation for work	
Learning how to learn	Ability to learn from experience
Cross-cultural understanding	Ability to understand many sides of a complex issue
Empathy, understanding, respect for others	Accurate empathy, positive regard for others
Loyalty and intimacy	Giving assistance, controlling impulsive feelings
Sense of self in social and historical context	Define oneself as actor, cognitive initiative, proactive stance

persons have reconciled their inner conflicts, renounced the unattainable, and cherish individuality.

The higher stages of the four structures integrate areas of development that include the major kinds of competence and personal characteristics addressed by Newman and found by Klemp, which are associated with liberal education and preparation for work. For example, the structures labeled *conscious preoccupations* and *cognitive style* describe the kinds of changes necessary to achieve high level communication skills, critical thinking ability, information processing and conceptualizing skills, and the ability to understand many sides of a complex issue. The structures labeled impulse control, character development, and interpersonal style describe the changes necessary for cross-cultural understanding; respect, empathy, and positive regard for others; giving assistance; and controlling impulsive feelings.

Ego development theory shows that when you pursue a liberal education and the skills and characteristics required for successful work you are tackling the bedrock task of taking charge of your own development. Can you pursue a liberal education and prepare for successful work at the same time? Certainly. In fact, if you short-change yourself in achieving some of these key outcomes for liberal education, you will lack some of the key characteristics required for a successful career and, more importantly, you will fall short of achieving your own developmental potential for a rich, complex, challenging life.

From "Liberal Education, Work and Human Development," by Arthur W. Chickering, *American Association for Higher Education Bulletin*, Vol. 33, No. 7, March 1981, pp. 1, 11-13, 16. Reprinted by permission of the author.

▶ Reflection Questions

1. On the basis of the work from Cardinal Newman's *The Idea of a University* (1852), Chickering suggests eight objectives for a liberal education. While he supports the idea that *all* are important, rank these objectives from most important to least important. Defend your ranking.

2. On the basis of the work of George Klemp, Chickering lists a number of cognitive skills that are important to success on the job. How might "the ability to understand many sides of a controversial issue" be important as the demographics of the work force change in the twenty-first century and beyond?

3. What is the relationship between ego development and "taking charge of your own development" as suggested by this article? How can you apply "taking charge of your own development" to your time in college?

Reading Two

This reading describes the steps from simple to complex in how we learn to think critically. Of interest are the stages of development that first-year students may be at. First-year students are often at a level of dualistic thinking, a black-or-white, right-or-wrong way of looking at information and situations.

Developmental Foundations of Critical Thinking

Joanne Gainen Kurfiss

Discrepancies between students' and professors' assumptions about knowledge probably account for a major share of the frustration both groups experience when critical thinking is required in a course. Models of college students' intellectual development provide a framework for understanding how students come to terms with this discrepancy.

BACKGROUND OF THE RESEARCH

The first studies of intellectual and ethical development in college were conducted at Harvard by William Perry and his associates. They interviewed over 100 students, nearly all male, in two separate four-year studies at Harvard and Radcliffe in the late 1950s and early 1960s.

Research on women's intellectual and ethical development by Belenky and associates has shown that while the broad categories of the scheme are similar to those identified by Perry, contemporary women frequently differ from the men and women interviewed by Perry in their view of authority, truth, and knowledge.

"STAGES" OF INTELLECTUAL DEVELOPMENT

The following summary of intellectual development in college integrates Belenky and associates' extensive research on women's perspectives with the earlier findings reported by Perry. The summary is organized into four major categories or levels and suggests how students at each developmental level will respond to tasks that require critical thinking.

Level 1: Dualism or Received Knowledge. Many students believe that knowledge is a collection of discrete facts; therefore, learning is simply a matter of acquiring information delivered by the professor in concert with the text. Information is either correct or it is not; hence, Perry's label for this belief system is "dualism." Dualistic thinkers do not realize the degree to which the information presented in a course or textbook is selected, interpreted, and systematized. They view the professor as the authority, presenting factual knowledge known to all experts in the discipline. Their dependence on authority as the source of all knowledge led Belenky and her associates to refer to this belief system as "received knowledge." Professors are always more or less right in this view, because, as one student says, "They have books to look at. Things that you look up in a book, you normally get the right answer."

For these students, the concept of interpretation, essential to critical thinking, is puzzling. Doesn't the text mean what it says? Why can't the author just say what he or she means? They may become confused or indignant when professors ask them to reason independently. Here is one student's response to a general education course that emphasizes thinking:

> It's supposed to reach you to—ah, reason better. That seems to be the, the excuse that natural science people give for these courses—they're supposed to teach you to arrive to more logical conclusions and look at things in a more scientific manner. Actually, what you get out of that course is you, you get an idea that science is a terrifically confused thing in which nobody knows what's coming off anyway.

In the face of "so many conflicting doctrines and opinions," many students in this first level opt "just to keep quiet until [they] really know just what the answer is." Rather than reflecting a personality characteristic like "passivity" or "vocationalism," their resistance to critical thinking reflects a legitimate developmental quandary as they encounter a world far more complex than they have realized.

Level 2: Multiplicity or Subjective Knowledge. Before students can accept the challenges and responsibilities of independent thinking, they must recognize that "conflicting doctrines and opinions" are an inevitable and legitimate feature of knowledge. And they must begin to develop trust in their "inner voices" as a source of knowledge. This is the work of the second level of intellectual development as described by Perry and by Belenky and associates.

In some courses, particularly those in the humanities and social sciences, students encounter numerous conflicts of interpretation and theory. Most students gradually acknowledge the existence of unknowns, doubts, and uncertainties, at least in some areas of knowledge. When the facts are not known, knowledge is a matter of "mere opinion." When no absolute truth exists, one "opinion" is as good as another, and teachers "have no right to call [the student] wrong" on matters of opinion. Many conflicts over grades probably arise from students' failure to understand, or professors' failure to communicate, the criteria used to judge "opinion" papers.

Perry's term "multiplicity" emphasizes his position's departure from dichotomous thinking. Belenky and associates' term "subjective knowledge" highlights women's tendency to turn inward, away from external authorities as their primary source of knowledge. The majority of college students subscribe to this category of epistemological beliefs.

Multiplicity/subjective knowledge is a crucial turning point in the development of critical thinking. Students at this level recognize complexity but have not yet learned how to navigate its waters. They perceive no basis other than intuition, feeling, or "common sense" on which to judge the merits of the opinions they now accept as reflections of legitimate differences.

Level 3: Relativism or Procedural Knowledge. Insistent pressure from peers (for example, in arguments in the residence hall or coffee shop) and from faculty (to give reasons for opinions offered in class discussion, on examinations, or in term papers) leads some students to realize that "opinions" differ in quality. Good opinions are supported with *reasons*. Students learn that they must examine an issue "in complex terms, weighing more than one factor in trying to develop your own opinion." In the arts, students learn that they must substitute analysis using "objective" criteria based on factors in the work for personal responses to its mood and character. Belenky and associates' term "procedural knowledge" captures this emphasis on using disciplinary methods of reasoning. Perry labels this belief system "relativism," because it assumes that what counts as true depends on (is relative to) the frame of reference used to evaluate the phenomenon in question. Many writers use the term "contextualism" or "contextual relativism" to describe this way of thinking.

Level 3 beliefs reflect the traditional academic view of reasoning as objective analysis and argument. Belenky and associates noticed, however, that some women employed an alternative procedure for developing opinions, which they called "connected knowledge." Connected knowledge attempts to understand the reasons for another's way of thinking. The student undertakes a "deliberate, imaginative extension of one's understanding into positions that initially feel wrong or remote." Connected knowledge differs from the objective analytical model of thinking, which they called "separate knowledge." Confronting a poem, separate knowers ask, "What techniques can I use to analyze it?" In contrast, connected knowers ask, "What is this poet trying to say to me?" Connected knowledge does not preclude analysis or criticism; it does, however, begin with a more empathic treatment of divergent views.

In Perry's study, most students came to realize that the "academic" method of deciding issues is generally applicable, because knowledge is inherently indeterminate. Subsequent studies have found fewer than half of college seniors subscribing to this perspective.

Level 4: Commitment in Relativism or Constructed Knowledge. The reasoning procedures of level 3 illuminate a situation, but they do not provide definitive answers. Ultimately, individuals must take a position and make commitments, even though they can have no external assurances of the "correctness" of what they choose to do or believe. Hence, Perry labels this perspective "commitment in relativism."

"Constructed knowledge," as described by Belenky and associates, integrates knowledge learned from others with the "inner truth" of experience and personal reflection. At this level, students understand that knower and known are intimately intertwined and exist in a particular historical and cultural context. Even in the sciences, this realization is possible, as one senior honors student observes:

> In science you don't really want to say that something's true. You realize that you're dealing with a model. Our models are always simpler than the real world. The real world is more complex than anything we can create. We're simplifying everything so that we can work with it, but the thing is really more complex. When you try to describe things, you're leaving the truth because you're oversimplifying.

Constructed knowledge as described in [Belenky's] *Women's Ways of Knowing* captures the interplay of rationality, caring, and commitment that is the ultimate goal of education. Constructed knowers are able to take "a position outside a particular context or frame of reference and look back on 'who' is asking the question, 'why' the question is asked at all, and 'how' answers are arrived at." They include the *self* in their knowing process, no longer executing a procedure but now becoming passionately engaged in the search for understanding. They are committed to nurturing rather than criticizing ideas; they may withdraw into silence if they believe the other person is not really listening, be it spouse, acquaintance, professor, or colleague. They seek integrated, authentic lives that contribute to "empowerment and improvement in the quality of life of others."

From Joanne Gainen Kurfiss, "Critical Thinking: Theory, Research, Practice, and Possibilities", ASHE-ERIC Higher Education Report No. 2, 1988, pp. 51-56. Copyright c 1988. Reprinted with permission of John Wiley & Sons, Inc.

▶ Reflection Questions

1. Kurfiss begins this reading with the suggestion that there are discrepancies between what professors and students assume about knowledge. Have you ever encountered this? Has there been a time when a professor or teacher asked you to respond to something and you thought you understood what she wanted, only to find out you didn't answer the question the way she wanted? Describe the experience.

2. In this reading, work by Perry and later work by Belenky have identified stages of intellectual development. Describe a situation where a first-year college student may be operating at level 1 (dualism or received knowledge). Next, think of a situation that may help the student move on to level 2 (multiplicity or subjective knowledge).

3. Perry describes level 4 as "commitment in relativism" and Belenky describes it as "constructed knowledge." What is meant by these definitions? Are their ideas in conflict? How do you explain the fact that these labels can coexist?

Reading Three

Six highly successful women and men share meaningful moments they experienced that helped to motivate them and shape their lives. These moments may be trivial and may go unnoticed at the time, or they may come in the form of a crisis or great challenge. In the end we are profoundly impacted and changed by these experiences.

My Moment of Truth

Caroline V. Clarke and Sonja D. Brown

We all have them. Those moments that fundamentally change us. We may not always recognize them as they're happening, but we look back and they are crystal clear—the turning points that shape our lives, alter our direction, offer us a deeper understanding of who we are or want to become. Moments of truth often come in the guise of a challenge or even a crisis; an experience that threatens to topple us rather than teach us. Sometimes no great strife is involved at all. Revelation comes in all forms. But the result is always the same: We are molded by specific events and experiences. Their duration can be brief but their impact is everlasting. The lessons they teach help and heal us. They provide answers to questions we may not have even known we had. They liberate us.

Sharing these lessons, and our memories of the events that produced them, reminds us that we all ultimately face the same basic truths—that life is short and we each have our own path to travel; that success is relative and commitment to something other than yourself and your bank account is imperative; that your journey is not defined by your talents or gifts, but by your choices; and that at the end of the day, you alone will have to live with those choices— good and bad.

Black Enterprise asked six highly successful women and men to share their most meaningful moments of truth. Perhaps their responses will speak to some of the yearnings in your heart. In reading their stories, you may experience a moment of truth all your own.

The Summer I Discovered Coltrane

Wynton Marsalis, *Jazz Musician*
Artistic Director at Jazz at Lincoln Center

The segregated south is not a very creative atmosphere for a young, black boy, but Wynton Marsalis became an artist nonetheless. One of six, he grew up in New Orleans and has been around music all his life. His father is a musician, some of his siblings are musicians, and he has played music, the trumpet, for some 30 of his 41 years.

He is currently the artistic director of Jazz at Lincoln Center (J@LC), the 12-year old, nonprofit arts organization dedicated to the creation, centralization, and distribution of the only original style of music to come out of this country and go international. And you can tell from the passion in his slightly husky, slightly Cajun-accented voice that there's nothing else he'd rather be doing: "To transform American cultural mythology through the integration of ideas—that's what this is all about. We want Jazz at Lincoln Center to be a place for the innovation of the arts through the focus of jazz, because jazz music is always collaborating with the other arts—film, dance, you name one."

Listening to him play and lecture and talk about his music, his work, and the places jazz has taken him, one would think this Juilliard-trained, nine-time Grammy award-winning jazz and classical musician has loved jazz and classical music from the time he was able to hold a trumpet. Not so. "Mama took us to see classical orchestras play a few times, but I didn't know anything about classical music. I couldn't get into it. Daddy always played jazz, but I didn't like that either. I liked them [the musicians his father played with] but I didn't like the music. And I didn't understand his dedication to it. The funk bands I knew used to pack the house; I played in a funk band when I was a teenager. But whenever daddy played, there would only be 10 or 15 people around.

"Jazz musicians were strange to me. I liked Earth Wind and Fire, and Parliament; I was used to people in shiny suits and costumes and stuff. The people on the covers of my daddy's jazz albums looked funny to me. They were dressed normal and looked all serious."

Then one day when Marsalis was 12 years old, he came home from his summer job and decided to try something. "I came home from work one day and put on one of my daddy's John Coltrane records. I didn't like it." And for most of us, that would have been the end of it. Went there, tried that, didn't like it. But something was happening that Marsalis didn't quite understand. "I played it again. I still didn't like it, but I kept playing it. There was something about it, something about the sound that I couldn't get away from, something that compelled me to keep playing it and playing it and playing it. And then I started listening to other people. That's when I started to realize I wanted to be a jazz musician. I had always played, but now I wanted to be good. I wanted to play like 'trane, like Miles [Davis], and everybody else I was listening to.

"[Jazz] helped me understand life and my place in it. Music is like that, it's spiritual. It goes beyond emotion; music can take you to a whole different consciousness. My whole approach to *everything* changed, not just playing. I remember playing a Hayden concerto when I was about 14. I began to appreciate all different kinds of music. Jazz taught me how to listen. I didn't just have to hear the same beat over and over again. I could listen to five, ten minutes of music and appreciate it, it didn't just have to be a [popular] hook."

Now, almost 30 years and one Pulitzer Prize in Music later, Marsalis *is* jazz. He plays it, composes it, teaches it, and it's always in his head—at any moment he's liable to surprise you with a riff on his trumpet, which is never far from him, or break out into spontaneous scatting, tapping his foot to a mental rhythm. "I just want people to be aware of jazz, to make the music available through recordings and broadcasts, and to produce more jazz musicians who can play," he says. "There's not any one thing I want people to think about this music, I just want them to be aware of it and check it out. And to come check us [J@LC] out. 'Cause we swing!"

Losing—and Finding—the Source of My Strength

LISA PRICE, *President, Carol's Daughter Inc.*

The names of Lisa Price's homemade body and spirit care products are as irresistible as their beautiful scents and rich textures. There's Mango Body Butter, Honey Pudding, and Shea Butter Skin Smoothie, many of which have found their way into the homes of celebrities including Jada Pinkett-Smith, Halle Berry, and Chaka Khan. But each of Price's personal care creations also bears the name Carol's Daughter, which has an appeal all its own. "Ten years ago, when I was starting my business and looking for a name, I made two lists," Price remembers. "One had all the things I was, and the other had all the things I wanted to be. One of the things I was was Carol's daughter. When I read it out loud I got goose bumps. It just seemed right, and it stuck."

Price started mixing creams and potions in the kitchen of her Brooklyn, New York, brownstone in 1990. Encouraged by the reactions of family and friends—including, of course, her mom, Carol Hutson—she officially started her business in 1993. Once Carol's Daughter was up and running, the list of reasons the company name was such a perfect fit kept growing. "I have two young sons and my mother helped me with them whenever she could," says Price. "She helped me hire staff when I first started to grow. Some teenagers on her block were looking for work and she sent them to me. One of them worked here for six years, another one still works here.

"Whenever I got riled up and couldn't figure out how I was going to juggle this and that, she would give me the strategy to get through it. She never let me get down on myself. She always believed in me.

"I'll never forget the day I did the *Oprah Winfrey Show*. You know how the universe conspires to mess you up on the days you most need everything to be okay? Well, that was going on. Nothing was falling into place. I was supposed to catch a plane to Chicago and I didn't know how I was going to make it. I called her, and my mom—who was never a person who used foul language—said: 'Listen to me. I'm talking to you now as your mother. This is your dream and it is coming true. If anybody tries to get in your way today with any bull, forget them. You pack your bags and get on that plane!' I just nodded and did exactly what she said."

Hutson was such a strong, proud, and positive person that, although she used a walker to move around, few people knew she had been battling a neuromuscular disease throughout her entire adult life. The battle required her to take drugs that suppressed her immune system, which weakened her and made her susceptible to illness. This past Valentine's Day, Hutson died. She was 60.

Price, the oldest of eight children ranging in age from her youngest sister's 8 to her own 41 years, handled the funeral and memorial plans with grace. But when it was all over, the depth of her loss began to set in. "Mommy was always there. We were so close. To not have that has really thrown me. I reach for the phone and realize she's not there, and it hits me all over again." But a deeper realization took hold of Price soon after her mother's death, and it made her question the essence of who she was. "People always tell me I'm strong. They'll say, 'How do you keep it all together?' I always felt like I was strong, like I was that person other people saw, but suddenly I felt like a fraud. I thought, 'It's not me, it's her. It's Mommy.'

"It's not that I took her for granted while she was here, I just never realized how much she did to hold me up and get me through. I just keep reminding myself what she would say, what she would do, what she would want. And I've been praying a lot. She'd always remind me to pray and reassure me that God would not give me more than I could handle. That keeps me going.

"Somebody told me at the funeral that I should never feel sad thinking that my mother didn't know how much I loved her because I showed her while she was alive. I honored her by naming something for her while she was here. I'll never forget how I felt the first time I read the words Carol's Daughter. It's who I'll always be; and those two words define me much more than I knew."

My Hall of Fame Wake-Up Call

MICHAEL HAYNES, *Vice President of Player Development, the National Football League*

Mike Haynes will never forget the moment that changed his life forever. In fact, he talks about it regularly, especially to the pro football players whose lives he seeks to change forever. It was 1976 and he was the New England Patriots' number one draft choice out of Arizona State (ASU). His college team was undefeated in his senior year and had played in three Fiesta Bowls, and his stellar performance earned him a place in the College Football Hall of Fame. He dropped out of college in his senior year after the NFL made him that fabled offer he couldn't refuse. "Once I got drafted, that was it," says Haynes, a cornerback who was the first in his family to attend college. "I figured people went to college to get a good job and I had a great job."

His pride only grew when he walked into the locker room his rookie year with the Patriots to find his locker next to George Webster's. "I didn't know much about Webster, but I knew my college coach had a plaque of him on his wall, which said Greatest College Player of All Time. I couldn't believe my locker was right next to his." But Webster was already ten years into his pro career, and one day, late in the season, Haynes came in to find Webster's locker empty. The greatest college player of all time had been cut from the team. "I thought there'd be a big press conference," says Haynes, his voice still laced with disbelief. "I thought the coaches and players would make a big deal over it. But there was just a brief mention of it at the bottom of somebody's column in the paper. No press conference, no big announcement—nobody said or did anything. I thought, 'Wow. That's the way the greatest college player of all time goes out?' I knew then I had to go back to school; I had to have something that no one could take away from me."

Haynes went back to ASU to pursue his degree in finance, but not before getting another rude awakening—finding out how long it would take to get it. "I went to talk to this guidance counselor, and when he told me how many credits I still needed, my eyes just welled up. As a college freshman, I had made the dean's list. But as my commitments to football and track grew, I took lighter loads until I was taking the minimum number of credits I needed to remain eligible to participate in college athletics. I couldn't believe I had been so naive [about my studies] but I still wanted [my degree]. So I started taking courses in the off-season, some even during the season. And I did a few internships in finance, which I really enjoyed. I even started thinking about going to Harvard Business School. I went back [for my bachelor's] in '77 and didn't get my degree until '82. When I got it, I thought, 'No one can take this away from me. I deserved it, I worked hard for it, and I'll always have it.' It didn't just improve my prospects for life after football, it improved my self-image."

In a profession where the average career lasts only three and a half years, Haynes went on to have a long and impressive one, ultimately joining the Los Angeles Raiders, and winning the 1983 Super Bowl before retiring at age 37 in 1991. He was inducted into the Pro Football Hall of Fame in 1997. When he retired, despite his early wake-up call with Webster, he did so grudgingly and without the assistance he offers pro football players today as head of a program designed to help them through such transitions.

Haynes began doing sports broadcasting and helped launch a golf tour for pro athletes. The latter led to a job as global licensing manager, and then vice president of recreational golf development, for the Callaway Golf company. The NFL job came along at a time when he was needing a change. "I wanted to do something I was passionate about," says Haynes, now 49. "This is it. I see myself as a change agent. I have a great opportunity to make some positive changes in people's lives. A lot of guys go to college just to get to the pros or to play college sports. If we could get those guys to value education, they could have a different life. There's a perception that athletes make so much money, they don't need to finish their degree. I played for a long time, I made more money than the average person ever will, and I know how wrong that perception is."

The Day I Downsized Myself

PAMELA NEFERKARA, *U.S. Retail Presentation Director, Nike Inc.*

In 1997, Pamela Neferkara was the quintessential high achieving corporate professional, making good on all of the promise highlighted ten years earlier when she was featured as one of "Ten Young Achievers" in Ebony magazine. As a category director of personal care products for Bristol-Myers Squibb Products in New York City, Neferkara managed the day-to-day operations of a $170 million brand portfolio. She led a marketing group of six and a cross-functional senior management team of 25. The next logical step for the alumnus of Old Dominion University in Norfolk, Virginia, and of Syracuse University in upstate New York, was vice president and she knew it. She'd been working toward it for a decade. Then something changed. In fact, in rapid succession, several things changed.

"The decision was made to divest one of the brands I was responsible for, and my boss asked me to think about how I would reorganize the marketing group," says Neferkara. "Everything came together in that moment. I thought about it and recommended that they eliminate my position. Why? It was the right thing to do. If anyone else had looked at it, they would have come to the same conclusion. I probably would not have seen the possibility of my leaving had I not been, in the back of my mind, thinking I needed a change. As category director, I had a lot more exposure to VPs and upper management than I had [earlier at Nike. Becoming a VP] was the next step for me and, from a skill set and capability standpoint, there's no question I could have done it, but I started to question whether that was the lifestyle I really wanted." She realized that the answer was no.

Neferkara was asked to stay and manage the divestiture program, and was given a lucrative severance package that enabled her to take a year off from working. "That year was a critical one in my life," she says. "That year gave me perspective. I was so focused on my corporate life that I didn't really understand the rest of my life. People talk about work/life balance and I really had very little sense of what any of that meant." As a result, Neferkara found that just having time to be in her Montclair, New Jersey, neighborhood was a huge source of joy. "Until I took that year off, I had no idea what went on in my neighborhood," she says. "I didn't even know what went on in my house." She took advantage of the time by working with her husband, renovating their 1928 Tudor-style home.

She had started a consulting business from her home when, in 1999, she got a call from a headhunter who had tracked her down through a former secretary. "Nike was looking for marketing executives." As fate would have it, Nike was just developing its Jordan brand. "The job was in Beaverton, Oregon, just outside Portland. I grew up in D.C. I had flown over Oregon, but never stepped foot in it. I went out for the interview, thinking there was no way I would ever move, but I figured I should keep those interviewing skills in practice. What I found is that it's beautiful out here. There were so many great quality of life aspects, and the job, which I didn't think I would have the applicable experience for, turned out to be a great fit." Neferkara joined Nike Inc. as director of marketing for the Jordan brand.

Four years later, Neferkara's family, which now includes a 16-month-old son, is happily settled in Portland. In her current job she oversees the retail marketing, field services, and store displays of billions of dollars worth of Nike products throughout the U.S., heading up a team of 110 people. Just as important to her, she lives just three miles from her office, which is located on a lovely campus where hitting the gym is not necessarily viewed as goofing off. "Rather than being disconcerting, stepping away from the goals I'd been targeting for so long was liberating," says Neferkara, 40. "My viewfinder went from being very laser-like to being as broad as it could be. Suddenly, I was open to anything, and once that happened, the Nike opportunity—something I would never have pursued—came and found me. This whole experience has underscored for me the idea of keeping an open mind toward life and not limiting myself. Sure, I gave up something, but I gained something else. Life is full of those opportunities if you're open to them."

Meeting a Woman Who Lives Her Faith

DR. CHRISTOPHER LEGGETT, *Interventional Cardiologist,*
Medical Associates of North Georgia

Dr. Christopher Leggett is the tenth of 11 children raised in a family that strongly values two things: God and education. His father was a Baptist minister and Leggett was a typical minister's son in many ways. He was respectful and achievement-oriented, attending prep school at Andover before going to college at Princeton University. But, by his own admission, he was also a bit wild. "When you grow up the way I do, you think you have a good sense of right and wrong. But in high school and college, I was out of control," Leggett says. Then he met a girl.

"I met my wife, Denise, in 1980. Until I met her, I never knew anybody for whom God was their best friend. I knew plenty of people who went to church, but we were all partying until 5 A.M. on Saturday then singing in the choir on Sunday. Denise, even at that young age, talked to God all the time. Her father was an evangelist and she observed a Saturday Sabbath.

"Denise dreamed of being a lawyer her whole life. But junior year, when it came time for her to take the [law school entrance exam], she found out they only gave it on Saturdays. My advice was: Take the test on Saturday and ask the Lord to forgive you on Sunday. But she had concluded that if the Lord didn't work this out for her, He had something better in mind for her to do. I'm sitting on the sidelines saying, 'Baby, I love the Lord too, but I'd be sitting in there taking that test.' She wouldn't do it but she kept studying hard. I'm watching her study, knowing there's no Sunday test date, thinking, 'What are you doing? Why are you studying?' She'd just say, 'I have faith that the Lord is going to work this out for me.'

"As it turned out, that year they offered the test on Sunday in about five cities throughout the U.S. One was Cleveland and she was living in Columbus, just a drive away. They didn't announce the Sunday option until the week before the test, but she was ready because she'd kept studying, even when she knew it might not happen for her. I was amazed. I decided right then that I needed to get serious about my relationship with the Lord. I watched her just continue to study and apply herself that summer, and I learned how to live what you believe. Seeing the depth of her faith changed my life."

When Leggett returned to Princeton the next year, he had stopped partying on Saturday nights and would spend most of Sunday in church. He also began hitting the books with a new resolve. "Once I embraced the whole concept of true discipline and mental strength, I went from being a decent student to being off the charts. I wasn't any smarter, I was just in a different place, mentally and spiritually. You can be highly educated and have great talents, but if you have no self-control, you'll never reach your potential. Your state of mind is the greatest predictor of your future."

Leggett went on to attend Case Western Reserve School of Medicine in Ohio, marrying Denise while he was still a student. He received his cardiology training at some of the best facilities in the world—Johns Hopkins Hospital in Baltimore and Emory University Hospital in Atlanta, among others. He attributes all of these opportunities to God's work in his life. Today, at age 42, he is one of the most renowned interventional cardiologists in the country, named on BE's most recent list of America's leading black doctors (August 2001).

"I never feel like I have to be totally dependent on myself to ensure my success," he says. "It's so liberating not to depend on man or anyone in your immediate environment to sanction your steps. I totally depend on God to create my pathway. That makes me feel somewhat impenetrable, even in today's world."

Leggett's faith also gets him through the do-or-die moments he faces in his work almost daily. "People try every day to hurt you. They try every day to limit your success or destroy you. But they can't. You have angels watching over you and they can't. I'm not trying to be all existentialist, that's just where I am. And I will always have my wife and that summer to thank for that."

When I Finally Asked, "What Do I Want?"

Dominique Dawes, *Olympic Gold Medalist Motivational Speaker*

Dominique Dawes' young life has been a series of dazzling, dramatic highlights. She began taking gymnastics at age 6 and was competing by age 10. Just five years later, she burst onto the international scene in 1992, becoming the first African American gymnast to ever qualify and compete in the Olympic Games in Barcelona.

By the time she retired, following the 2000 Olympic Games in Sydney, Australia (Dawes retired twice—once in 1998 and finally in 2000), she had won more national championship medals than any other athlete—male or female—

as well as four world championship medals, two Olympic bronze medals and one gold. Perhaps because Dawes was saturated by the spotlight for so many years, her moment of truth came at a quiet time, devoid of drama, cameras, coaches, or fans. "I was sitting at home just thinking, brain-storming about my life," she recalls. "There was no real single experience that brought me to that moment. I had retired (for the first time), I was working on my degree in communications from the University of Maryland, and I was doing a lot of [public] speaking, some gymnastics commentary, and some acting. (Dawes played cheerleader Patty Simcox in the 1997 Broadway production of *Grease.*) I had been doing all of the things everyone around me kept telling me I'd be good at. But I was somewhat on autopilot. I was doing things to please other people, not because I really had a passion for them. I was almost a robot. Whatever people said was good for me, I'd just say, 'Okay. Fine. I'll do it.'"

But one night, at home alone in Maryland, Dawes confronted a critical question for the first time. "I asked myself what I really wanted to do. I felt almost like I was dreaming, I had never asked myself that. From the time I was young, I was guided in a very structured way. That was good for my gymnastics career, I needed it then. But when I retired, I kept waiting for someone to tell me what to do—like they always had. And they did. But a wonderful friend sat me down one day and made me realize that I wasn't happy doing those things. At home alone that night, I finally realized, this is my life and I need to pave my own path. I also came to the realization that the key to failure is trying to please everyone. I needed to figure out for myself what Dominique loves to do, wants to do, and is really good at. That was the beginning of my changing the way I thought about my life."

It also sparked a change in her approach to opportunity. "Something would come up and I'd force myself to stop and ask myself, 'What is this going to do for me? What are the pros and cons of it for me, not for other people?' I did a great deal of praying, soul searching, and writing. And it took about two years to really change the way I thought and accept that I do have likes and dislikes, and dreams and goals that don't match up with other people's."

Now 26, Dawes does a lot of motivational speaking targeting youth. She would like to do more local and international broadcasting, sports commentary in particular. She'd also like to be a spokesperson for self-esteem and health-related issues for kids. Dawes has recently begun coaching gymnastics privately at Hill's Gymnastics in Gaithersburg, Maryland, the gym in which she grew up training, owned by Kelli Hill, the man who coached her from the time she was 6. "When I finally retired (in 2000)—from gymnastics and from living for other people—I felt like I had a 1,000 pound weight lifted off me," she says. "That's how I feel now—like I have been totally freed! I'm free to do what I like, and what I want. This is the life that I want."

"My Moment of Truth," by Caroline V. Clarke and Sonja Brown, *Black Enterprise,* July 2003. Reprinted by permission.

▶ Reflection Questions

1. Wynton Marsalis said, "jazz (music) helped me understand my life and my place in it." How does this sentiment relate to his practice of listening to a record over and over again, even when he didn't like it? Is there an activity in your life that you identify with in this way?

2. Michael Haynes dropped out of college in his senior year. Why, and what made him go back to college? Was it worth it? Why does he consider himself a change agent?

3. Of these six individuals, which one inspired you the most? Why?

Writing Assignment

audience: A sibling, relative, or friend who is in middle school or high school

purpose: To persuade him, or her, to think about how he might make the most of his time in school in preparation for college and life after college

length: Minimum of three typed pages, double-spaced

Write a letter to one of the individuals suggested above, first describing what you have learned about the importance of critical thinking. Then describe how many first-year college students think and what the ultimate goal of critical thinking is. Connect this to what Chickering suggests are some of the important objectives of college. Include why they are important. Give some examples from the "My Moment of Truth" reading that connect to these objectives. Remember your goal is to help a young adult think about what he might be doing now in preparation for the future. Conclude by telling him that this is advice you either did follow or wish you had followed. Give specific suggestions about what he might do.

▶ Journal Entries: DISCOVERY AND INTENTION STATEMENTS

Had you ever thought about the way you think? What are your goals for a college education? Have you considered what strengths you have and how they might connect with the skills needed to be a successful individual in the work world? What are the things you might need to work on and why? One night when she was home alone, the Olympic gold medalist Dominique Dawes asked herself the ultimate question: "What do I really want to do?" Ask yourself that question now, and write down your answer. Write down and describe any thoughts you have while thinking this through.

How do these readings relate to the Power Process? What are some of the tools that you will need to have to succeed in college based on the readings? Can you think of some specific examples of situations where you might use these tools? Write a few sentences about what you have learned, what you intend to do as a result of these readings, what you will do to make it work, and what you risk if you do not do what you intend to do.

Mastering Vocabulary

List five words that were new to you (more or less if necessary). For each, include which reading you found the word in, the definition, and where you got the definition from, as well as a time or place you might use the word again.

1. _____

2. _____

3. _____

4. _____

5. _____

 ## Additional Activities _____

1. Pair up with a classmate and share an event in your life when you felt you did not see another person's point of view. Plan to observe your own behavior and others' this week and make note of at least two situations when you or a person you are observing do not agree with another. Note how you or the person you are observing feels (probably frustrated) when there is no agreement. Also, observe both nonverbal and verbal behavior. That is, if you notice that two individuals disagree, observe how they respond. Can you tell from their body language that they are upset? Do they use language that puts the other person down? Or do they validate the opposing viewpoint, but still maintain their own position?

2. If you cannot observe behavior during the week, plan a simple role play with your partner for next week's class. The role play should include examples of dualistic thinking, a demonstration of at least two skills suggested by Chickering that are important in a college education, and a "moment of truth."

3. An additional activity might include a short article for the college newspaper about the different kinds of thinking first-year college students have as opposed to those of their professors. Conclude the article with some suggestions on how to develop the skills that professors want students to have.

4. Develop a PowerPoint presentation on one of the following:

   - The Role of Liberal Arts in Preparing Individuals for the Twenty-first Century

   - Stages of Intellectual Development as Defined by Kurfiss

   - Characteristics of Highly Successful Individuals

Online Study Center   **Improve Your Grade**
Visit the Online Study Center for resources and exercises to accompany this text
http://college.hmco.com/pic/msreader1e

CHAPTER TWO

Be Here Now

In this chapter you are encouraged to step back, take a hard look at yourself, and think about why you do what you do and feel the way you feel. In the previous chapter you were asked to answer the question posed by the Olympic champion Dominique Dawes: "What do I really want to do?" Do I want to just slide through college and put in minimum effort? Do I have ambition for some things and not others? Do I want to get everything I can out of college including academics and balance in my social life? Am I clear about what really is important to me? Is what is important to me compatible with going to college? If you are in college for the wrong reasons (i.e., because you don't want to go to work, because you don't know what else to do, because your parents told you that you have to go to college), your chances of finishing are not as good as those of students who go to college for the right reasons. Students who are not committed to their education often have difficulty putting forth all of the effort and focus that is needed to succeed. Students may have high goals and know their major, but they are so preoccupied with thinking about something else (maybe due to stress or uncertainty) they cannot focus. The most successful students know themselves, are thinking about what they are doing now, doing it well, and planning for the future.

The Power Process: Be Here Now

Being right here, right now is such a simple idea. It seems obvious. Where else can you be but where you are? When else can you be there but when you are there?

The answer is that you can be somewhere else at any time—in your head. It's common for our thoughts to distract us from where we've chosen to be. When we let this happen, we lose the benefits of focusing our attention on what's important to us in the present moment.

To "be here now" means to do what you're doing when you're doing it and to be where you are when you're there. Students consistently report that focusing attention on the here and now is one of the most powerful tools in this book.

Leaving the here and now

We all have a voice in our head that hardly ever shuts up. If you don't believe it, conduct this experiment: Close your eyes for 10 seconds and pay attention to what is going on in your head. Please do this right now.

Notice something? Perhaps your voice was saying, "Forget it. I'm in a hurry." Another might have said, "I wonder when 10 seconds is up." Another could have been saying, "What little voice? I don't hear any little voice." That's the voice.

This voice can take you anywhere at any time— especially when you are studying. When the voice takes you away, you might appear to be studying but your brain is at the beach.

All of us have experienced this voice, as well as the absence of it. When our inner voices are silent, time no longer seems to exist. We forget worries, aches, pains, reasons, excuses, and justifications. We fully experience the here and now. Life is magic. There are many benefits of such a state of consciousness. It is easier to discover the world around us when we are not chattering away to ourselves about how we think it ought to be, has been, or will be. Letting go of inner voices and pictures—being totally in the moment—is a powerful tool. Do not expect to be rid of daydreams entirely. That is neither possible nor desirable. Inner voices serve a purpose. They enable us to analyze, predict, classify, and understand events out there in the "real" world.

Your stream of consciousness serves a purpose. When you are working on a term paper, your inner voices might suggest ideas. When you are listening to your sociology instructor, your inner voices can alert you to possible test questions. When you're about to jump out of an airplane, they could remind you to take a parachute. The trick is to consciously choose when to be with your inner voices and when to let them go.

Returning to the here and now

A powerful step toward returning to the here and now is to notice when we leave it. Our mind has a mind of its own, and it seems to fight back when we try to control it too much. If you doubt this, for the next 10 seconds do not, under any circumstances, think of a pink elephant. Please begin not thinking about one now.

Persistent image, isn't it? Most ideas are this insistent when we try to deny them or force them out of our consciousness.

For example, during class you might notice yourself thinking about a test you took the previous day or a party planned for the weekend or the DVD player you'd like to have.

Instead of trying to force a stray thought out of your head—a futile enterprise—simply notice it. Accept it. Tell yourself "There's that thought again." Then gently return your attention to the task at hand. That thought, or another, will come back. Your mind will drift. Simply notice again where your thoughts take you and gently bring yourself back to the here and now.

Another way to return to the here and now is to notice your physical sensations. Notice the way the room looks or smells. Notice the temperature and how the chair feels. Once you've regained control of your attention by becoming aware of your physical surroundings, you can more easily take the next step and bring your full attention back to your present task.

We can often immediately improve our effectiveness—and our enjoyment—by fully entering into each of our activities, doing one thing at a time.

For example, take something as simple as peeling and eating an orange. Carefully notice the color, shape, and texture of the orange. Hold it close to your nose and savor the pungent, sweet smell. Then slowly peel the orange and see if you can hear every subtle sound that results. Next take one piece of the orange and place it in your mouth. Notice the feel of the fruit on your tongue. Chew the piece slowly, letting the delicious juice bathe your taste buds. Take note of each individual sensation of pleasure that ripples through your body as you sample this delicious treat.

"Be here now" can turn the act of eating an orange into a rich experience. Imagine what can happen when you bring this quality of attention to almost everything that you do.

Choose when to be here now

Remember that no suggestion is absolute—including the suggestion to do one thing at a time with full, focused attention. Sometimes choosing to do two or more things at once is useful, even necessary. For example, you might study while doing laundry. You might ask your children to quiz you with flash cards while you fix dinner.

The key to this Power Process is to *choose*. When you choose, you overcome distractions and stay in charge of your attention.

Experiment with noticing your inner voices. Let go of the ones that prevent you from focusing on learning. Practice the process. Be here now, moment by moment.

The here and now in your future

You also can use this Power Process to keep yourself pointed toward your goals. In fact, one of the best ways to get what you want in the future is to realize that you do not have a future. The only time you have is right now.

The problem with this idea is that some students might think "No future, huh? Terrific! Party time!" Being in the here and now, however, is not the same as living for today and forgetting about tomorrow.

Nor is the "be here now" idea a call to abandon goals. Goals are merely tools we create to direct our actions right now. They are useful only in the present. Goals, like our ideas of the past and future, are creations of our minds. The only time they are real is in the here and now.

The power of this idea lies in a simple but frequently overlooked fact: The only time to do anything is now. You can think about doing something next Wednesday. You can write about doing something next Wednesday. You can daydream, discuss, ruminate, speculate, and fantasize about what you will do next Wednesday.

But you can't do anything on Wednesday until it is Wednesday.

Sometimes students think of goals as things that exist in the misty future. And it's easy to postpone action on things in the misty future, especially when everyone else is going to a not-so-misty party.

However, the word *goal* comes from the Anglo-Saxon *gaelan*, which means "to hinder or impede," as in the case of a boundary. That's what a goal does. It restricts, in a positive way, our activity in the here and now. It channels our energy into actions that are more likely to get us what we really want. That's what goals are for. And they are useful only when they are directing action in the here and now.

The idea behind this Power Process is simple. When you plan for the future, plan for the future. When you listen to a lecture, listen to a lecture. When you read this book, read this book. And when you choose to daydream, daydream. Do what you're doing when you're doing it.

Be where you are when you're there. Be here now ... and now ... and now.

Readings

The readings in this section are about being in the moment. They are articles about enjoying life and planning a life that makes the most of everything. They are chosen to encourage you, to help you identify the qualities of successful people, and to find balance and set goals. They discuss ambition and how it is connected to purpose. How do you want to spend your days, your life? Do you want to rush from moment to moment? Do you want to feel pressured and unprepared, or do you want to feel organized and in control? Do you want to have time to "smell the roses" and feel you have lived a life that has made a difference?

Reading One

This reading is about what it takes to be successful. Eisenberg suggests that we are born with the will to be successful. For example, almost all babies want to walk and will continue to keep trying even if they fall. In addition, Eisenberg suggests that by "instilling confidence, encouraging some risk taking, being accepting of failure and expanding in the areas in which children may be successful, both parents and teachers can reignite that innate desire to achieve" if it is lost. Reading this selection, think about ways you might help yourself reignite, maintain, or ignite your desire to achieve. If you are igniting or reigniting, think about why this happened.

How to Help Them Succeed
Daniel Eisenberg

Anyone who doubts that children are born with a healthy amount of ambition need spend only a few minutes with a baby eagerly learning to walk or a headstrong toddler starting to talk. No matter how many times the little ones stumble in their initial efforts, most keep on trying, determined to master their amazing new skill. It is only several years later, around the start of middle or junior high school, many psychologists and teachers agree, that a good number of kids seem to lose their natural drive to succeed and end up joining the ranks of underachievers. For the parents of such kids, whose own ambition is often inextricably tied to their children's success, it can be a bewildering, painful experience. So it's no wonder some parents find themselves hoping that, just maybe, ambition can be taught like any other subject at school.

It's not quite that simple. "Kids can be given the opportunities [to become passionate about a subject or activity], but they can't be forced," says Jacquelynne Eccles, a psychology professor at the University of Michigan, who led a landmark, 25-year study examining what motivated first- and seventh-graders in three school districts. Even so, a growing number of educators and psychologists do believe it is possible to unearth ambition in students who don't seem to have much. They say that by instilling confidence, encouraging some risk taking, being accepting of failure and expanding the areas in which children may be successful, both parents and teachers can reignite that innate desire to achieve.

Figuring out why the fire went out is the first step. Assuming that a kid doesn't suffer from an emotional or learning disability, or isn't involved in some family crisis at home, many educators attribute a sudden lack of motivation to a fear of failure or peer pressure that conveys the message that doing well academically somehow isn't cool. "Kids get so caught up in the moment-to-moment issue of will they look smart or dumb, and it blocks them from thinking about the long term," says Carol Dweck, a psychology professor at Stanford. "[You have to teach them that] they are in charge of their intellectual growth." Over the past couple of years, Dweck has helped run an experimental workshop with New York City public school seventh-graders to do just that. Dubbed Brainology, the unorthodox approach uses basic neuroscience to teach kids how the brain works and how it can continue to develop throughout life. "The message is that everything is within the kids' control, that their intelligence is malleable," says Lisa Blackwell, a research scientist at Columbia University who has worked with Dweck to develop and run the program, which has helped increase the students' interest in school and turned around their declining math grades. More than any teacher or workshop, Blackwell says, "parents can play a critical role in conveying this message to their children by praising their effort, strategy and progress rather than emphasizing their 'smartness' or praising high performance alone. Most of all, parents should let their kids know that mistakes are a part of learning."

Some experts say our education system, with its strong emphasis on testing and rigid separation of students into different levels of ability, also bears blame for the disappearance of drive in some kids. "These programs shut down the motivation of all kids who aren't considered gifted and talented. [They] destroy their confidence," says Jeff Howard, a social psychologist and president of the Efficacy Institute, a Boston-area organization that works with teachers and parents in school districts around the country to help improve children's academic performance. Howard and other educators say it's important to expose kids to a world beyond homework and tests, through volunteer work, sports, hobbies and other extracurricular activities. "The crux of the issue is that many students experience education as irrelevant to their life goals and ambitions," says Michael Nakkula, a Harvard education professor who runs a Boston-area mentoring program called Project IF (Inventing the Future), which works to get low-income underachievers in touch with their aspirations. The key to getting kids to aim higher at school is to disabuse them of the notion that classwork is irrelevant, to show them how doing well at school can actually help them fulfill their dreams beyond it. Like any ambitious toddler, they need to understand that you have to learn to walk before you can run.

"How To Help Them Succeed" by Daniel Eisenberg, *Time,* November 6, 2005. © 2005 TIME Inc. reprinted by permission.

▶Reflection Questions

1. If you were given the job to unearth ambition in a group of college students, what would you tell them to do? Use yourself as an example. When did your "fire" start or when did it go out, and why?

2. In this reading Eisenberg suggests that the reason some students lose their ambition is related to a tracking system. For example, some students are placed in gifted and talented programs while others are not. Do you agree with this system? Why or why not? What could be done to make this system work?

3. Michael Makkula suggests that the "key to getting kids to aim higher at school is to disabuse them of the notion that class work is irrelevant, to show them how doing well at school can actually help them to fulfill their dreams and beyond." How does this assessment compare with your own feelings toward your course work? Think of a class that you don't think is relevant to your life goals and ambition. Why do you think this? What are some ways that you could change this perception?

Reading Two

In this second reading about ambition, Kluger discusses some of the advantages and disadvantages of being highly ambitious. For example, heart attacks, ulcers, and other stress-related ills are more common among high achievers. Also, some high achievers can become arrogant and conceited and cannot live without power. Yet, high achievers often reap rewards that an average person could never attain. What do you want out of your life? Are you clearly on the path to getting it?

Ambition: Why Some People Are Most Likely to Succeed

Jeffrey Kluger

You don't get as successful as Gregg and Drew Shipp by accident. Shake hands with the 36-year-old fraternal twins who co-own the sprawling Hi Fi Personal Fitness club in Chicago, and it's clear you're in the presence of people who thrive on their drive. But that wasn't always the case. The twins' father founded the Jovan perfume company, a glamorous business that spun off the kinds of glamorous profits that made it possible for the Shipps to amble through high school, coast into college and never much worry about getting the rent paid or keeping the fridge filled. But before they graduated, their sense of drift began to trouble them. At about the same time, their father sold off the company, and with it went the cozy billets in adult life that had always served as an emotional backstop for the boys.

> *A fire in the belly doesn't light itself. Does the spark of ambition lie in genes, family, culture—or even in your own hands? Science has answers*
>
> **—Jeffrey Kluger**

That did it. By the time they got out of school, both Shipps had entirely transformed themselves, changing from boys who might have grown up to live off the family's wealth to men consumed with going out and creating their own. "At this point," says Gregg, "I consider myself to be almost maniacally ambitious."

It shows. In 1998 the brothers went into the gym trade. They spotted a modest health club doing a modest business, bought out the owner and transformed the place into a luxury facility where private trainers could reserve space for top-dollar clients. In the years since, the company has outgrown one building, then another, and the brothers are about to move a third time. Gregg, a communications major at college, manages the club's clients, while Drew, a business major, oversees the more hardheaded chore of finance and expansion. "We're not sitting still," Drew says. "Even now that we're doing twice the business we did at our old place, there's a thirst that needs to be quenched."

Why is that? Why are some people born with a fire in the belly, while others—like the Shipps—need something to get their pilot light lit? And why do others never get the flame of ambition going? Is there a family anywhere that doesn't have its overachievers and underachievers—its Jimmy Carters and Billy Carters, its Jeb Bushes and Neil Bushes—and find itself wondering how they all could have come splashing out of exactly the same gene pool?

Of all the impulses in humanity's behavioral portfolio, ambition—that need to grab an ever bigger piece of the resource pie before someone else gets it—ought to be one of the most democratically distributed. Nature is a zero-sum game, after all. Every buffalo you kill for your family is one less for somebody else's; every acre of land you occupy elbows out somebody else. Given that, the need to get ahead ought to be hard-wired into all of us equally.

And yet it's not. For every person consumed with the need to achieve, there's someone content to accept whatever life brings. For everyone who chooses the 80-hour workweek, there's someone punching out at 5. Men and women—so it's said—express ambition differently; so do Americans and Europeans, baby boomers and Gen Xers, the middle class and the well-to-do. Even among the manifestly motivated, there are degrees of ambition. Steve Wozniak co-founded Apple Computer and then left the company in 1985 as a 34-year-old multimillionaire. His partner, Steve Jobs, is still innovating at Apple and moonlighting at his second blockbuster company, Pixar Animation Studios.

Not only do we struggle to understand why some people seem to have more ambition than others, but we can't even agree on just what ambition is. "Ambition is an evolutionary product," says anthropologist Edward Lowe at Soka University of America, in Aliso Viejo, Calif. "No matter how social status is defined, there are certain people in every community who aggressively pursue it and others who aren't so aggressive."

Dean Simonton, a psychologist at the University of California, Davis, who studies genius, creativity and eccentricity, believes it's more complicated than that. "Ambition is energy and determination," he says. "But it calls for goals too. People with goals but no energy are the ones who wind up sitting on the couch saying 'One day I'm going to build a better mousetrap.' People with energy but no clear goals just dissipate themselves in one desultory project after the next."

Assuming you've got drive, dreams and skill, is all ambition equal? Is the overworked lawyer on the partner track any more ambitious than the overworked parent on the mommy track? Is the successful musician to whom melody comes naturally more driven than the unsuccessful one who sweats out every note? We may listen to Mozart, but should we applaud Salieri?

Most troubling of all, what about when enough ambition becomes way too much? Grand dreams unmoored from morals are the stuff of tyrants—or at least of Enron. The 16-hour workday filled with high stress and at-the-desk meals is the stuff of burnout and heart attacks. Even among kids, too much ambition quickly starts to do real harm. In a just completed study, anthropologist Peter Demerath of Ohio State University surveyed 600 students at a high-achieving high school where most of the kids are triple-booked with advanced-placement courses, sports and after-school jobs. About 70% of them reported that they were starting to feel stress some or all of the time. "I asked one boy how his parents react to his workload, and he answered, 'I don't really get home that often,'" says Demerath. "Then he handed me his business card from the video store where he works."

Anthropologists, psychologists and others have begun looking more closely at these issues, seeking the roots of ambition in family, culture, gender, genes and more. They have by no means thrown the curtain all the way back, but they have begun to part it. "It's fundamentally human to be prestige conscious," says Soka's Lowe. "It's not enough just to be fed and housed. People want more."

If humans are an ambitious species, it's clear we're not the only one. Many animals are known to signal their ambitious tendencies almost from birth. Even before wolf pups are weaned, they begin sorting themselves out into alphas and all the others. The alphas are quicker, more curious, greedier for space, milk, Mom—and they stay that way for life. Alpha wolves wander widely, breed annually and may live to a geriatric 10 or 11 years old. Lower-ranking wolves enjoy none of these benefits—staying close to home, breeding rarely and usually dying before they're 4.

Humans often report the same kind of temperamental determinism. Families are full of stories of the inexhaustible infant who grew up to be an entrepreneur, the phlegmatic child who never really showed much go. But if it's genes that run the show, what accounts for the Shipps, who didn't bestir themselves until the cusp of adulthood? And what, more tellingly, explains identical twins—precise genetic templates of each other who ought to be temperamentally identical but often exhibit profound differences in the octane of their ambition?

Ongoing studies of identical twins have measured achievement motivation—lab language for ambition—in identical siblings separated at birth, and found that each twin's profile overlaps 30% to 50% of the other's. In genetic terms, that's an awful lot—"a benchmark for heritability," says geneticist Dean Hamer of the National Cancer Institute. But that still leaves a great deal that can be determined by experiences in infancy, subsequent upbringing and countless other imponderables.

Some of those variables may be found by studying the function of the brain. At Washington University, researchers have been conducting brain imaging to investigate a trait they call persistence—the ability to stay focused on a task until it's completed just so—which they consider one of the critical engines driving ambition.

The researchers recruited a sample group of students and gave each a questionnaire designed to measure persistence level. Then they presented the students with a task—identifying sets of pictures as either pleasant or unpleasant and taken either indoors or outdoors—while conducting magnetic resonance imaging of their brains. The nature of the task was unimportant, but how strongly the subjects felt about performing it well—and where in the brain that feeling was processed—could say a lot. In general, the researchers found that students who scored highest in persistence had the greatest activity in the limbic region, the area of the brain related to emotions and habits. "The correlation was .8 [or 80%]," says professor of psychiatry Robert Cloninger, one of the investigators. "That's as good as you can get."

It's impossible to say whether innate differences in the brain were driving the ambitious behavior or whether learned behavior was causing the limbic to light up. But a number of researchers believe it's possible for the nonambitious to jump-start their drive, provided the right jolt comes along. "Energy level may be genetic," says psychologist Simonton, "but a lot of times it's just finding the right thing to be ambitious about." Simonton and others often cite the case of Franklin D. Roosevelt, who might not have been the same President he became—or even become President at all—had his disabling polio not taught him valuable lessons about patience and tenacity.

Is such an epiphany possible for all of us, or are some people immune to this kind of lightning? Are there individuals or whole groups for whom the amplitude of ambition is simply lower than it is for others? It's a question—sometimes a charge—that hangs at the edges of all discussions about gender and work, about whether women really have the meat-eating temperament to survive in the professional world. Both research findings and everyday experience suggest that women's ambitions express themselves differently from men's. The meaning of that difference is the hinge on which the arguments turn.

Economists Lise Vesterlund of the University of Pittsburgh and Muriel Niederle of Stanford University conducted a study in which they assembled 40 men and 40 women, gave them five minutes to add up as many two-digit numbers as they could, and paid them 50¢ for each correct answer. The subjects were not competing against one another but simply playing against the house. Later, the game was changed to a tournament in which the subjects were divided into teams of two men or two women each. Winning teams got $2 per computation; losers got nothing. Men and women performed equally in both tests, but on the third round, when asked to choose which of the two ways they wanted to play, only 35% of the women opted for the tournament format; 75% of the men did.

"Men and women just differ in their appetite for competition," says Vesterlund. "There seems to be a dislike for it among women and a preference among men."

To old-line employers of the old-boy school, this sounds like just one more reason to keep the glass ceiling polished. But other behavioral experts think Vesterlund's conclusions go too far. They say it's not that women aren't ambitious enough to compete for what they want; it's that they're more selective about when they engage in competition; they're willing to get ahead at high cost but not at any cost. "Primate-wide, males are more directly competitive than females, and that makes sense," says Sarah Blaffer Hrdy, emeritus professor of anthropology at the University of California, Davis. "But that's not the same as saying women aren't innately competitive too."

As with so much viewed through the lens of anthropology, the roots of these differences lie in animal and human mating strategies. Males are built to go for quick, competitive reproductive hits and move on. Women are built for the it-takes-a-village life, in which they provide long-term care to a very few young and must sail them safely into an often hostile world. Among some of our evolutionary kin—baboons, macaques and other old-world monkeys—this can be especially tricky since young females inherit their mother's social rank. The mothers must thus operate the levers of society deftly so as to raise both their own position and, eventually, their daughters'. If you think that kind of ambition-by-proxy doesn't translate to humans, Hrdy argues, think again. "Just read an Edith Wharton novel about women in old New York competing for marriage potential for their daughters," she says.

Import such tendencies into the 21st century workplace, and you get women who are plenty able to compete ferociously but are inclined to do it in teams and to split the difference if they don't get everything they want. And mothers who appear to be unwilling to strive and quit the workplace altogether to go raise their kids? Hrdy believes they're competing for the most enduring stakes of all, putting aside their near-term goals to ensure the long-term success of their line. Robin Parker, 46, a campaign organizer who in 1980 was already on the presidential stump with Senator Edward Kennedy, was precisely the kind of lifetime pol who one day finds herself in the West Wing. But in 1992, at the very moment a President of her party was returning to the White House and she might have snagged a plum Washington job, she decamped from the capital, moved to Boston with her family and became a full-time mom to her two sons.

"Being out in the world became a lot less important to me," she says. "I used to worry about getting Presidents elected, and I'm still an incredibly ambitious person. But what I want to succeed at now is managing my family, raising my boys, helping my husband and the community. In 10 years, when the boys are launched, who knows what I'll be doing? But for now, I have my world."

But even if something as primal as the reproductive impulse wires you one way, it's possible for other things to rewire you completely. Two of the biggest influences on your level of ambition are the family that produced you and the culture that produced your family.

There are no hard rules for the kinds of families that turn out the highest achievers. Most psychologists agree that parents who set tough but realistic challenges, applaud successes and go easy on failures produce kids with the greatest self-confidence.

What's harder for parents to control but has perhaps as great an effect is the level of privilege into which their kids are born. Just how wealth or poverty influences drive is difficult to predict. Grow up in a rich family, and you can inherit either the tools to achieve (think both Presidents Bush) or the indolence of the aristocrat. Grow up poor, and you can come away with either the motivation to strive (think Bill Clinton) or the inertia of the hopeless. On the whole, studies suggest it's the upper middle class that produces the greatest proportion of ambitious people—mostly because it also produces the greatest proportion of anxious people.

When measuring ambition, anthropologists divide families into four categories: poor, struggling but getting by, upper middle class, and rich. For members of the first two groups, who are fighting just to keep the electricity on and the phone bill paid, ambition is often a luxury. For the rich, it's often unnecessary. It's members of the upper middle class, reasonably safe economically but not so safe that a bad break couldn't spell catastrophe, who are most driven to improve their lot. "It's called status anxiety," says anthropologist Lowe, "and whether you're born to be concerned about it or not, you do develop it."

But some societies make you more anxious than others. The U.S. has always been a me-first culture, as befits a nation that grew from a scattering of people on a fat saddle of continent where land was often given away. That have-it-all ethos persists today, even though the resource freebies are long since gone. Other countries—where the acreage is smaller and the pickings are slimmer—came of age differently, with the need to cooperate getting etched into the cultural DNA. The American model has produced wealth, but it has come at a price—with ambition sometimes turning back on the ambitious and consuming them whole.

The study of high-achieving high school students conducted by Ohio State's Demerath was noteworthy for more than the stress he found the students were suffering. It also revealed the lengths to which the kids and their parents were willing to go to gain an advantage over other suffering students. Cheating was common, and most students shrugged it off as only a minor problem. A number of parents—some of whose children carried a 4.0 average—sought to have their kids classified as special-education students, which would entitle them to extra time on standardized tests. "Kids develop their own moral code," says Demerath. "They have a keen sense of competing with others and are developing identities geared to that."

Demerath got very different results when he conducted research in a very different place—Papua, New Guinea. In the mid-1990s, he spent a year in a small village there, observing how the children learned. Usually, he found, they saw school as a noncompetitive place where it was important to succeed collectively and then move on. Succeeding at the expense of others was seen as a form of vanity that the New Guineans call "acting extra." Says Demerath: "This is an odd thing for them."

That makes tactical sense. In a country based on farming and fishing, you need to know that if you get sick and can't work your field or cast your net, someone else will do it for you. Putting on airs in the classroom is not the way to ensure that will happen.

Of course, once a collectivist not always a collectivist. Marcelo Suárez-Orozco, a professor of globalization and education at New York University, has been following 400 families that immigrated to the U.S. from Asia, Latin America and the Caribbean. Many hailed from villages where the American culture of competition is alien, but once they got here, they changed fast.

As a group, the immigrant children in his study are outperforming their U.S.-born peers. What's more, the adults are dramatically outperforming the immigrant families that came before them. "One hundred years ago, it took people two to three generations to achieve a middle-class standard of living," says Suárez-Orozco. "Today they're getting there within a generation."

So this is a good thing, right? Striving people come here to succeed—and do. While there are plenty of benefits that undeniably come with learning the ways of ambition, there are plenty of perils too—many a lot uglier than high school students cheating on the trig final.

Human history has always been writ in the blood of broken alliances, palace purges and strong people or nations beating up on weak ones—all in the service of someone's hunger for power or resources. "There's a point at which you find an interesting kind of nerve circuitry between optimism and hubris," says Warren Bennis, a professor of business administration at the University of Southern California and the author of three books on leadership. "It becomes an arrogance or conceit, an inability to live without power."

While most ambitious people keep their secret Caesar tucked safely away, it can emerge surprisingly, even suddenly. Says Frans de Waal, a primatologist at the Yerkes Primate Center in Atlanta and the author of a new book, *Our Inner Ape:* "You can have a male chimp that is the most laid-back character, but one day he sees the chance to overthrow the leader and becomes a totally different male. I would say 90% of people would behave this way too. On an island with three people, they might become a little dictator."

But a yearning for supremacy can create its own set of problems. Heart attacks, ulcers and other stress-related ills are more common among high achievers—and that includes nonhuman achievers. The blood of alpha wolves routinely shows elevated levels of cortisol, the same stress hormone that is found in anxious humans. Alpha chimps even suffer ulcers and occasional heart attacks.

For these reasons, people and animals who have an appetite for becoming an alpha often settle contentedly into life as a beta. "The desire to be in a high position is universal," says de Waal. "But that trait has co-evolved with another skill—the skill to make the best of lower positions."

Humans not only make peace with their beta roles but they also make money from them. Among corporations, an increasingly well-rewarded portion of the workforce is made up of B players, managers and professionals somewhere below the top tier. They don't do the power lunching and ribbon cutting but instead perform the highly skilled, everyday work of making the company run. As skeptical shareholders look ever more askance at overpaid corporate A-listers, the B players are becoming more highly valued. It's an adaptation that serves the needs of both the corporation and the culture around it. "Everyone has ambition," says Lowe. "Societies have to provide alternative ways for people to achieve."

Ultimately, it's that very flexibility—that multiplicity of possible rewards—that makes dreaming big dreams and pursuing big goals worth all the bother. Ambition is an expensive impulse, one that requires an enormous investment of emotional capital. Like any investment, it can pay off in countless different kinds of coin. The trick, as any good speculator will tell you, is recognizing the riches when they come your way.

"Ambition: Why Some People Are Most Likely to Succeed" by Jeffrey Kluger, *Time*, November 6, 2005. © 2005 TIME Inc. reprinted by permission.

▶ Reflection Questions

1. What does Kluger mean when he says people can "make peace with their beta roles"? How does this relate to career choice? Be specific.

2. Do you think that high ambition comes from within one's self, from an outside source, or from some combination of the two? Give a specific example from your life, either from personal experience or from the experience of someone you know.

3. What motivates you? Are you an "alpha" or a "beta"? Are you comfortable with where you are? What is positive and negative about your level of motivation?

Reading Three

This reading describes what makes a good leader. Outstanding leaders are not always those who were expected to be at the top of their fields. Goleman studied many great leaders and found traits that were common to them. These characteristics include being aware of your own feelings, knowing your strengths and weaknesses, staying calm, having optimism, setting goals, being flexible, being sensitive, resolving conflicts, building and maintaining relationships, inspiring others, being a team player, and helping others to develop their abilities. As you read, think about great leaders you know (they can be from all walks of life).

Could You Be a Leader?

Daniel Goleman

It was just after the World Trade Center towers had collapsed, and a stunned nation was glued to a press conference with New York City Mayor Rudy Giuliani. Asked by a reporter how many people died in the collapse, Giuliani replied, "We don't know the exact number yet, but whatever the number, it will be more than we can bear."

In that moment, Giuliani performed a masterful act of leadership. He spoke with conviction, from the depths of his own heart, in a way that resonated with our own unspoken feelings.

Like Giuliani, great leaders move us deeply. They inspire us by touching our feelings. Leadership works through the emotions. And what makes a leader shine looks much the same whether he or she heads a major company, runs the corner store or leads the Wednesday-night church group.

WHAT MAKES A GOOD LEADER?

For the first time, research is bringing hard science to the question of leadership. As a psychologist and science journalist, I've been tracking the science of outstanding performance for the last decade. In recent years, I have collaborated on some of the research myself, teaming up with Prof. Richard Boyatzis of Case Western Reserve University's School of Management and Prof. Annie McKee of the University of Pennsylvania's School of Education.

In order to identify the elusive recipe for outstanding leadership, we've reviewed data ranging from neurology to measures of the emotional climate that a leader creates. Hundreds of studies in organizations of all kinds—from small family businesses to the largest companies, from religious groups to schools and hospitals—have yielded a set of 30 or so abilities that distinguish the best leaders. (See the box on page 67 to rate yourself on some of these essentials of leadership.)

These abilities shine through in any effective act of leadership. Take another event on Sept. 11, on an elevator in the World Trade Center: After a hijacked plane slammed into Tower One, the power went out, stopping the elevators cold. There were six men on one elevator—mostly executives and a window-washer, carrying his bucket and a squeegee on a pole. The men tried to figure out what to do. Who led the way to a solution? The window-washer, Jan Demczur.

Demczur (pronounced DEM-chur) realized the men could use the pole on his squeegee to pry open the elevator doors, and he directed the others in helping him. But as they finally pried open the doors, they faced a thick wall with a giant number "50" on it. Their elevator, they realized, was an express. It had no stop at the 50th floor and so no opening.

Undaunted, the window-washer again took the lead. Demczur used the sharp edge of the squeegee handle to scrape away at the wall. Under his direction, the men took turns at the wearisome task. They scratched a hole through three layers of drywall before breaking through to their freedom, surviving to tell the tale. That day Jan Demczur emerged not just as a hero but also as a leader. And in his display of self-confidence, initiative, optimism and teamwork, he demonstrated several of the traits that mark the very best leaders.

"EMOTIONAL INTELLIGENCE"

Just what are the essentials of leadership? My own work and that of hundreds of other researchers make clear that what sets the beloved leaders apart from the bosses we hate is excellence at things like handling upsets, listening and empathy. These abilities fall within the domain of emotional intelligence—an adeptness at managing ourselves and our interactions with others—not school smarts. This may explain why people who were only average students in school can blossom as leaders later in life.

A good example is Kent, whom I ran into at my 15th high school reunion. Though undistinguished as a student, Kent was extremely likable—considerate, fun, the kind of person who puts you at ease. Kent already was the senior vice president of America's largest cable TV company and the most successful grad in our class, surpassing both the valedictorian and the student with the highest scores on the college entrance exam.

New findings in brain science reveal that this kind of intelligence uses different parts of the brain than does the academic kind. Cognitive abilities such as verbal fluency or math skills reside in the neocortex, the wrinkled topmost layers, which are the most recent evolutionary addition to the human brain. But emotional intelligence relies largely on the ancient emotional centers deep in the midbrain between the ears, with links to the prefrontal cortex—the brain's executive center, just behind the forehead.

This may explain the fact that IQ and emotional intelligence are surprisingly independent. Of course, to be a great leader, you need enough intelligence to understand the issues at hand, but you need not be supersmart. By the same token, people who are intellectually gifted can be disasters as leaders.

That's what happened with a brilliant biochemist at a pharmaceutical company who was promoted to head a research team. Some of the habits that had helped him succeed as a biochemist defeated him as a leader. He had held himself to extremely high standards. Now he applied those same unrelenting standards to everyone on his team. Lavish in his criticisms, he never praised people when they did well. Ever impatient, he took over for people at the first sign of a lapse. The result? Within months, his team was dispirited, demoralized and failing.

The story is all too common in organizations everywhere. It happens when people are promoted for the wrong set of skills: IQ abilities rather than the emotional intelligence abilities that good leaders display.

YOU CAN LEARN TO LEAD

Unlike academic or technical skills, the aptitudes of leadership are learned in life, not in school. That's good news for all of us: If we are weak in leadership skills, we can get better at virtually any point in life with the right effort. But it takes motivation, a clear idea of what you need to improve and consistent practice.

For instance, good leaders are excellent listeners. Let's say you need to be a better listener. (Perhaps you tend to cut people off and take over the conversation without hearing them out.) The first step: Become aware of the moments you do this and stop yourself. Instead, let the other people speak their minds. Ask questions to be sure you understand their viewpoints. Then—and only then—give your own opinion.

At first, changing such a basic habit may feel forced. But if people use naturally occurring situations to practice the change and do so at every opportunity, it eventually becomes automatic. Leaders are made, not born.

MAKE THEM LAUGH

One of the most basic tasks of a leader is to help others stay in the positive emotional range, where they can do their best work. Research shows that the business leaders who achieve the best results get people to laugh three times more often than do the mediocre leaders. Laughter signals that people are not caught up in, say, toxic anger or paralyzing fear but rather are relaxed and enjoying what they do—and so they are more likely to be creative, focused and productive.

The artful execution of all the qualities of leadership can be seen in small, everyday acts. If done with a light touch, all the better.

Take what happened one Super Bowl Sunday on a plane that was several hours late. The passengers, mostly businessmen, were edgy and frustrated that the delays would mean missing the start of the big game. As the plane landed, it taxied toward the gate but mysteriously stopped several hundred yards away. At that, the passengers leaped to their feet, got their bags and crowded the aisle, waiting to deplane. But it's against federal regulations for the pilot to move the plane while passengers are standing.

So what did the flight attendant do? Instead of announcing in a stern tone, "You must sit down before we can taxi to the gate," she said—in a singsong voice, as

Continued on page 68

Leadership Skills: Rate Yourself

The best leaders have strengths in at least a half-dozen key emotional-intelligence competencies out of 20 or so. To see how you rate on some of these abilities, assess how the statements below apply to you. While getting a precise profile of your strengths and weaknesses requires a more rigorous assessment, this quiz can give you a rough rating. More important, we hope it will get you thinking about how well you use leadership skills—and how you might get better at it.

Statement	Seldom	Occasionally	Often	Frequently
1. I am aware of what I am feeling.	☐	☐	☐	☐
2. I know my strengths and weaknesses.	☐	☐	☐	☐
3. I deal calmly with stress.	☐	☐	☐	☐
4. I believe the future will be better than the past.	☐	☐	☐	☐
5. I deal with changes easily.	☐	☐	☐	☐
6. I set measurable goals when I have a project.	☐	☐	☐	☐
7. Others say I understand and am sensitive to them.	☐	☐	☐	☐
8. Others say I resolve conflicts.	☐	☐	☐	☐
9. Others say I build and maintain relationships.	☐	☐	☐	☐
10. Others say I inspire them.	☐	☐	☐	☐
11. Others say I am a team player.	☐	☐	☐	☐
12. Others say I helped to develop their abilities.	☐	☐	☐	☐
Total the number of checks in each column	___	___	___	___
Multiply this number by:	×1	×2	×3	×4
To get your score, add these four numbers:	= ___ +	___ +	___ +	___

Total: ____

Interpretation:

36+: An overall score of 36 or higher suggests you are using key leadership abilities well—but ask a co-worker or partner for his or her opinions, to be more certain. 30–35: Suggests some strengths but also some underused leadership abilities. 29 or less: Suggests unused leadership abilities and room for improvement.

Leaders are unique, and they can show their talent in different ways. To further explore your leadership strengths, you might ask people whose opinions you value: "When you have seen me do really well as a leader, which of these abilities am I using?" If a number of people tell you that you use the same quality when doing well, you have likely identified a leadership strength that should be appreciated and nurtured.

though talking to a lovable but mischievous 4-year-old—"You're staaaanding . . ." And the passengers laughed and sat down. Not only did she get them to comply but also, by the time they got off the plane, their frustration had melted into smiles.

That's real leadership.

"Could You Be a Leader?" by Daniel Goleman, *Parade Magazine,* June 16, 2002. © 2002 Daniel Goleman. Reprinted by permission. All rights reserved.

▶ Reflection Questions

1. Goleman suggests that students who are average in school can go on to be exceptional leaders. How? Describe someone you know of who meets this description.

2. Take the leadership skills test provided. How did you score? Given that these kinds of skills can be improved, what can you work on first? What are some specific ways that you can improve yourself in this area?

3. There is new evidence emerging from research on college students that "emotional intelligence" is related to success in school? Why do you think this might be true? Give two specific examples on how having good emotional intelligence might help a student to be successful.

◀ Writing Assignment ─────────────────

audience: Your instructor

purpose: To describe why a college student should develop strong emotional intelligence

length: Minimum of two typed pages, double-spaced

Anna Quindlen, a bestselling author and Pulitzer Prize winning columnist, wrote in a commencement speech at Villanova University, that when Senator Paul Tsongas was diagnosed with cancer and decided not to run for reelection he said, "No man ever said on his deathbed that I wish I had spent more time in the office." Clearly that is true, but if one wants to have a nice home, car, and time for vacations, we have to work, but must find balance. We must have ambition and be motivated to succeed. We must know our ourselves, our strengths and weakness, what motivates us, be able to work well with others, and have strong interpersonal relationships. One of the foundations of emotional intelligence is the ability to know yourself. It is important to know why we feel a particular way and be able to control our emotions as opposed to them controlling us. When we know why we feel the way we do, and deal with our emotions effectively, we are better able to be successful in whatever we do, whether it be in school, at work, or in relationships. If you were to design a one-hour presentation for students on the reasons why they should work on developing their emotional intelligence to be successful in school, what would you tell them?

 Journal Entries: DISCOVERY AND INTENTION STATEMENTS

Write about what you were thinking when you were writing the above essay. Were you thinking about what you should do in life, as opposed to what you think you will or want to do? Were you completely honest with yourself? Have you ever thought that you wanted to be like Donald Trump? Do you think it possible for someone like Donald Trump to have balance in life? Do you? Write down and describe any thoughts you had doing this exercise.

In this Power Process you have read about what it means to "Be here now." Write one or two sentences about what you have learned and what you intend to do as a result of this reading, what you will do to make it work, and what you risk by not doing what you intend to do.

Mastering Vocabulary

List five words that were new to you (more or less if necessary). For each, include which reading you found the word in, the definition, and where you got the definition from, as well as a time or place you might use the word again.

1.

2.

3.

4.

5.

 ## Additional Activities

1. Take five minutes to answer the following questions: When you are in class, are you thinking of other things or are you attending to the lecture? When you are at the movies, are you stressing about the fact that you didn't finish a paper or are you enjoying the show? Think of how you might get the most out of each segment of your day. Do you set goals to accomplish getting things done? Share your thoughts with other students in the class.

2. How do these readings relate to the Power Processes? After reading the questions above, can you see how they might connect? In groups of three or four, discuss the readings "How to Help Them Succeed," "Ambition: Why Some People Are Most Likely to Succeed," and "Could You Be a Leader?" and how they relate to "be here now." Choose one person in the group to report to the class.

3. Describe a perfect week in college. You might begin by writing a time log of when you will study, exercise, and go to bed. This may not be what you actually do, but write a time log that you want to be able to follow. Be sure to include leisure time. Is your perfect week realistic? Describe how you might feel "in the moment" of this perfect week. Either share this with a partner in the class or

keep it to yourself, but make sure you refer to it during the week. Could you keep up the schedule of the perfect week? Why or why not? Do you think first-year students have different schedules than upperclassmen? Why or why not? Consider adjusting the schedule for next week and subsequent weeks until you feel you have a schedule you can live with.

4. Write a short article for next year's incoming students about "be here now" and the connection between strong emotional intelligence and success in college. Use the article "Incorporating Emotional Skills Content in a College Transition Course Enhances Student Retention" by Nicola S. Schutte and John M. Matlouff (*Journal of the First-Year Experience* 14, no. 1 (2002): 7–21) as a reference. You may even want to submit this article to your school's newspaper.

Online Study Center **Improve Your Grade**
Visit the Online Study Center for resources and exercises to accompany this text
http://college.hmco.com/pic/msreader1e

CHAPTER THREE

Love Your Problems

Love it.

Accept it.

I can do this!

There are very few individuals, if any, who are good at everything. Of course, we all know a few people who we *think* are, but most often each of us has some barrier in life that he or she has to overcome. Successful college students don't let barriers stop them; rather they figure out ways to overcome them or get around them. Whether it be a fear of failure, a fear of standing up in front of a group, a learning disability, or simply struggling with how to memorize a wealth of information for a test, it is important to know that we are not alone in our fears and challenges. We can also look for ways to meet the challenges on our way to being a successful student.

The Power Process: Love Your Problems

We all have problems and barriers that block our progress or prevent us from moving into new areas. Often the way we respond to our problems puts boundaries on our experiences. We place limitations on what we allow ourselves to be, do, and have.

Our problems might include fear of speaking in front of a group, anxiety about math problems, or reluctance to sound ridiculous when learning a foreign language. We might have a barrier about looking silly when trying something new. Some of us even have anxiety about being successful.

Problems often work like barriers. When we bump up against one of our problems, we usually turn away and start walking along a different path. And all of a sudden—bump!—we've struck another barrier. And we turn away again. As we continue to bump into problems and turn away from them, our lives stay inside the same old boundaries. Inside these boundaries we are unlikely to have new adventures. We are unlikely to improve or to make much progress.

The word *problem* is a wonderful word coming from the ancient Greek word *proballein,* which means "to throw forward." In other words, problems are there to provide an opportunity for us to gain new skills. If we respond to problems by loving them instead of resisting them, we can expand the boundaries in which we live our lives. When approached with acceptance, and even love, problems can "throw us forward."

Three ways to handle a barrier

It's natural to have barriers, but sometimes they limit our experience so much that we get bored, angry, or frustrated with life. When this happens, consider the following three ways of dealing with a barrier. One way is to pretend it doesn't exist. Avoid it, deny it, lie about it. It's like turning your head the other way, putting on a fake grin, and saying, "See, there's really no problem at all. Everything is fine. Oh, that problem. That's not a problem—it's not really there."

In addition to making us look foolish, this approach leaves the barrier intact, and we keep bumping into it. We deny the barrier and might not even be aware that we're bumping into it. For example, a student who has a barrier about math might subconsciously avoid enriching experiences that include math.

A second approach is to fight the barrier, to struggle against it. This usually makes the barrier grow. It increases the barrier's magnitude. A person who is obsessed with weight might constantly worry about being fat. She might struggle with it every day, trying diet after diet. And the more she struggles, the bigger the problem gets.

The third alternative is to love the barrier. Accept it. Totally experience it. Tell the truth about it. Describe it in detail. When you do this, the barrier loses its power. You can literally love it to death.

The word *love* might sound like an overstatement. In this Power Process, the word means to accept your problems, to allow and permit them. When we fight a problem, it grows bigger. The more we struggle against it, the stronger it seems to become. When we accept the fact that we have a problem, we are more likely to find effective ways to deal with it.

Suppose one of your barriers is being afraid of speaking in front of a group. You can use any of these three approaches.

First, you can get up in front of the group and pretend that you're not afraid. You can fake a smile, not admitting to yourself or the group that you have any concerns about speaking—even though your legs have turned to rubber bands and your mind to jelly. The problem is that everyone in the room, including you, will know you're scared when your hands start shaking, your voice cracks, and you forget what you were going to say.

The second way to approach this barrier is to fight it. You can tell yourself, "I'm not going to be scared," and then try to keep your knees from knocking. Generally, this doesn't work. In fact, your knee knocking might get worse.

The third approach is to go to the front of the room, look out into the audience, and say to yourself, "I am scared. I notice that my knees are shaking and my mouth feels dry, and I'm having a rush of thoughts about what might happen if I say the wrong thing. Yup, I'm scared, and that's OK. As a matter of fact, it's just part of me, so I accept it and I'm not going to try to fight it. I'm going to give this speech even though I'm scared." You might not actually eliminate the fear; however, your barrier about the fear—which is what inhibits you—might disappear. And you might discover that if you examine the fear, love it, accept it, and totally experience it, the fear itself also disappears.

Applying this process

Applying this process is easier if you remember three ideas. First, loving a problem is not necessarily the same as enjoying it. Love in this sense means total and unconditional acceptance.

This can work even with problems as thorny as physical pain. When we totally experience pain, it often diminishes and sometimes it disappears. This strategy can work with emotions and even with physical pain. Make it your aim to love the pain, that is, to fully accept the pain and know all the details about it. Most pain has a wavelike quality. It rises, reaches a peak of intensity, and then subsides for a while. See if you can watch the waves as they come and go.

Second, unconditional acceptance is not the same as unconditional surrender. Accepting a problem does not mean escaping from it or giving up on finding a solution. Rather, this process involves freeing ourselves from the grip of the problem by diving *into* the problem headfirst and getting to know it in detail.

Third, love and laughter are allies. It's hard to resist a problem while you are laughing at it. Sure, that incident when you noticed the spinach in your teeth only *after* you got home from a first date was a bummer. But with the passage of time, you can admit that it was kind of funny. You don't have to wait weeks to gain that perspective. As long as you're going to laugh anyway, why wait? The sooner you can see the humor in your problems, the sooner you can face them.

When people first hear about loving their problems, they sometimes think it means being resigned to problems. Actually, loving a problem does not need to stop us from solving it. In fact, fully accepting and admitting the problem usually helps us take effective action—which can free us of the problem once and for all.

Readings

The readings in this chapter are about barriers and what individuals have done to get over and around them. There are also specific selections about what many of us struggle with and how our memory can sometimes fail us. The readings are chosen to encourage you to realize that barriers need to be identified and overcome or accepted. Before you read the following selections, think about barriers to higher education. Think of real barriers that have caused students to drop out of college or to never enroll.

Reading One

This reading is about how to overcome the fear of public speaking. A 2000 survey done by the Discovery Health Channel "put the fear of public speaking above the fear of hell, cancer, violent storm or fire." Many colleges require students to take a course in public speaking. While not everyone who completes such classes ultimately overcomes his fear of speaking (if he had the fear to begin with), he often finishes the class with some tips on how to deal with this type of anxiety.

Too Scared for Words: Fear of Public Speaking Can Be Overcome, Experts Insist

Mark Ellis

The fear of fire can't hold a candle to the fear of public speaking. Nor can the fear of hell.

Among phobias, public speaking always ranks with the heavy hitters.

A 2000 survey for the Discovery Health Channel put the fear of public speaking above the fear of hell, cancer, violent storms or fire.

"Most people would rather walk over hot coals," said Columbus psychologist and toastmaster Michael Brickey.

Prize-winning speaker David Fetters, 16, swallows his anxiety by fasting before a speech.

Top Fears
Snakes
Being buried alive
Heights
Being bound or tied up
Drowning
Public speaking
Hell
Cancer
Violent storms
Fire

Then he imagines that he doesn't have any listeners.

"When you get up there, it's nerve-racking," he said. "You can prepare, but you still have to cope with nervousness.

"I just pretend they're off doing their own thing. The whole nudity thing never worked for me."

The "nudity thing" refers to the idea of calming the nerves by picturing an audience undressed.

Preparation and practice, according to most experts, are better tactics.

Whatever Fetters does is working.

A member of the Upper Arlington High School speech and debate team, he has qualified, with three others, for the National Forensic League tournament in June.

He is raising money for the trip to Atlanta by competing in speech contests.

This month, after recently winning $450 from chapters of the Rotary and the Sons of the American Revolution, Fetters will move up the ladder and vie for state titles from both groups.

He stands to win $800 more.

"I could end up being very happy," he said.

The junior is taking a high-school course in public speaking.

"I think it's important we get the experience to be able to do this before we go out in the real world, where it counts.

"We really don't like it. People don't like to speak in front of groups."

His debate coach, Chris Goddard, teaches debate and public speaking.

Freshmen, he said, seem to do better in the required class because they tend to be good students willing to "face the fear."

"I hope that many will discover that they enjoy giving speeches," he said. "I work on having fun at the beginning."

The fear of public speaking is exaggerated, Goddard thinks.

"Every speech is a new chance to communicate," he said. "Most people don't try. People confuse nervousness with fear. You should be nervous. Nerves help us accomplish goals."

His suggestion? "Practice, practice, practice."

THE PSYCHOLOGIST

Many people who show up at the Ohio State University Anxiety and Stress Disorders Clinic to overcome public-speaking fears are facing a challenge on the job.

"Public speaking has become a major problem for them," said director Brad Schmidt, clinical psychologist and associate professor of psychology. "They've gotten a promotion or gotten in line for a promotion, and it involves . . . new things they've not been doing.

"Usually these people have had prior difficulties and have done some avoidance," he said. "Now, there's no way to avoid it."

People who suffer from this fear often lose sight of what will happen if they don't deliver "the most perfect speech," he said.

Public speaking is a type of social-anxiety disorder not helped much by medication.

But the anxiety can be managed through therapy. "Behavior rehearsals" are a common approach.

"They need to think more clearly . . . to readjust the attitude," he said.

"We'd like them to have the normal apprehension almost anyone will have in those kinds of performance-based situations."

THE EXPERT

After 3,000 speeches, Mike Frank is at ease in front of a crowd.

But he still finds it "very stressful" to stand and deliver at a National Speakers Association convention.

A good speech can hinge on knowing the audience and preparing well, and the country's top speakers invest heavily in preparation when called to address their peers. "I've done it twice," he said. "It's not worth the stress."

Frank, 59, started building a business on public speaking in 1971, when he created Speakers Unlimited. He was so impressed with a motivational seminar that he stopped selling insurance and started selling motivation.

Big, public motivational seminars faded in the 1990s, he said, after speakers raised fees. Speakers Unlimited evolved into the largest speakers bureau in Ohio, pairing speakers with "every kind of function."

"It's been my life," he said.

Public speaking is "still a major fear . . . inherent in most people," he said. "It's a fear of failure more than anything else."

Others are not afraid or have overcome the fear and become professionals, especially in Ohio. "There are more top-notch, reasonably priced speakers here than in any other state in the country," Frank said.

Talking Points

Select a familiar topic.

Practice the speech repeatedly.

Visualize yourself as a speaker. Imagine your voice loud, clear and assertive.

Ease tension by exercising.

Study the room by getting there early. Try the microphone.

Greet some members of the audience as they arrive.

Embrace the idea that people want you to succeed.

Focus attention on the message, not the anxiety.

Don't note your nervousness and any other problems by apologizing for them.

Turn nervous energy into vitality and enthusiasm.

Build confidence by gaining experience.

Tough Cases

Seek help.

Have a medical examination to ensure that your anxiety isn't related to a physical condition.

Address any mental-health issue, such as depression or obsessive-compulsive disorder, that might add to your problem.

Don't force yourself into a panic-inducing situation. Approach the fear through manageable steps.

Eat protein-rich foods before a stressful situation. Avoid processed foods high in sugar and caffeine.

Get regular exercise.

Get plenty of rest.

Avoid the added stress of tardiness.

Contacts

International Training in Communication: www.itcintl.com

Speakers Unlimited: 614-864-3703 or www.speakersunlimited.com

Toastmasters International: 949-858-8255 or www.toastmasters.org

Sources: Toastmasters International; the Public Speaking-Social Anxiety Disorder Center of New York; Penn, Schoen & Berland Associates for the Discovery Health Channel Research: Susan Stonick, Dispatch information specialist

A few naturals are out there, but most speakers work hard at it.

"You have to put together the pieces for each group," he said. "The key in every situation is preparation."

Frank suggests speakers practice 20 to 30 times "in front of the mirror, the spouse, the kids, the girlfriends and boyfriends."

Those who want to overcome fear or enhance skills can find courses, hire a coach or join a group such as Toastmasters International.

THE FELLOWSHIP

The applause is generous, the body language fluent and the eye contact relentless when the Mid-Day Club of Toastmasters International convenes at noon each Thursday.

The club is one of about 50 in central Ohio but among only a handful that meets weekly. At a recent session, 22 people showed up in a room at the Motorists Insurance building Downtown.

"People really enjoy each other and have a good time," Brickey said. The psychologist and author joined seven years ago to polish his public speaking.

"You do it on a regular basis to keep in practice," he said. "It keeps you in the rhythm of speaking every week or two."

The meeting is run by a toastmaster in the role of ringmaster. A time-keeper monitors three five- to seven-minute speeches—and this day all ran long. Evaluators are assigned for public critiques. A short humor speech and quick-hitting "table topics," for spontaneous discussion, round out a typical meeting.

Diane Grahovac scored points by leading the room in song, wrapping up her Hollywood-theme speech with Hooray for Hollywood—both verses.

Another group well-versed in public speaking is International Training in Communication, once the female answer to Toastmasters and now "fully coed," Marie Holland said.

The East Side woman is a retired software engineer. She joined 26 years ago and is now part of a fledgling club—the Diction Aires—that meets once a month at St. Philip Lutheran Church.

"I was very shy and introverted," she said. "I lived alone, which is not good for someone shy and introverted. I needed some help in that regard.

"I have a little more confidence."

Developing organizational skills is a feature of the group, and Holland took advantage to learn how to run meetings at her church.

"I like to serve in leadership roles. I can deliver a speech if I have to, but I don't want to deliver any more than I'm called on to do."

Her advice on overcoming the fear?

"Just doing it," she said. "Doing it and getting positive feedback."

Whatever she goes through is worth it.

"We all have opinions. We all have ideas," Holland said. "At times you need the confidence to stand up and let other people know how you feel."

"Too Scared for Words", by Mark Ellis, *The Columbus Dispatch*, April 30, 2003. Reprinted by permission.

▶ Reflection Questions

1. Summarize this reading by listing the suggestions for overcoming the fear of public speaking. Do you have a fear of public speaking? If so, how did this fear develop?

2. Can you think of a situation where you spoke to an audience and you did a good job? Can you also think of a time when you did not do well? What were the differences? Describe a presentation that you thought was delivered well (even if you were not that interested in the content) as opposed to one that was not. What was different about the two? What do you think accounted for the difference?

3. This selection lists the top fears from a Discovery Health Channel survey. Are you fearful of any items that are on the list? Which ones? How do you deal with these fears?

Reading Two

Even those individuals who are lucky to easily absorb and remember information can sharpen their skills. This article describes eleven different strategies (tricks, habits, and techniques) that can improve and expand your mind.

11 Steps to a Better Brain

Kate Douglas et al.

It doesn't matter how brainy you are or how much education you've had—you can still improve and expand your mind. Boosting your mental faculties doesn't have to mean studying hard or becoming a reclusive book worm. There are lots of tricks, techniques and habits, as well as changes to your lifestyle, diet and behaviour that can help you flex your grey matter and get the best out of your brain cells. And here are 11 of them.

SMART DRUGS

Does getting old have to mean worsening memory, slower reactions and fuzzy thinking?

Around the age of 40, honest folks may already admit to noticing changes in their mental abilities. This is the beginning of a gradual decline that in all too many of us will culminate in full-blown dementia. If it were possible somehow to reverse it, slow it or mask it, wouldn't you?

A few drugs that might do the job, known as "cognitive enhancement", are already on the market, and a few dozen others are on the way. Perhaps the best-known is modafinil. Licensed to treat narcolepsy, the condition that causes people to suddenly fall asleep, it has notable effects in healthy people too. Modafinil can keep a person awake and alert for 90 hours straight, with none of the jitteriness and bad concentration that amphetamines or even coffee seem to produce.

In fact, with the help of modafinil, sleep-deprived people can perform even better than their well-rested, unmedicated selves. The forfeited rest doesn't even need to be made good. Military research is finding that people can stay awake for 40 hours, sleep the normal 8 hours, and then pull a few more all-nighters with no ill effects. It's an open secret that many, perhaps most, prescriptions for modafinil are written not for people who suffer from narcolepsy, but for those who simply want to stay awake. Similarly, many people are using Ritalin not because they suffer from attention deficit or any other disorder, but because they want superior concentration during exams or heavy-duty negotiations.

The pharmaceutical pipeline is clogged with promising compounds—drugs that act on the nicotinic receptors that smokers have long exploited, drugs that work on the cannabinoid system to block pot-smoking-type effects. Some drugs have also been specially designed to augment memory. Many of these look genuinely plausible: they seem to work, and without any major side effects.

So why aren't we all on cognitive enhancers already? "We need to be careful what we wish for," says Daniele Piomelli at the University of California at Irvine. He is studying the body's cannabinoid system with a view to making memories less emotionally charged in people suffering from post-traumatic stress disorder. Tinkering with memory may have unwanted effects, he warns. "Ultimately we may end up remembering things we don't want to."

Gary Lynch, also at UC Irvine, voices a similar concern. He is the inventor of ampakines, a class of drugs that changes the rules about how a memory is encoded and how strong a memory trace is—the essence of learning (see *New Scientist*, 14 May, p 6). But maybe the rules have already been optimized by evolution, he suggests. What looks to be an improvement could have hidden downsides.

Still, the opportunity may be too tempting to pass up. The drug acts only in the brain, claims Lynch. It has a short half-life of hours. Ampakines have been shown to restore function to severely sleep-deprived monkeys that would otherwise perform poorly. Preliminary studies in humans are just as exciting. You could make an elderly person perform like a much younger person, he says. And who doesn't wish for that?

FOOD FOR THOUGHT

You are what you eat, and that includes your brain. So what is the ultimate mastermind diet?

Your brain is the greediest organ in your body, with some quite specific dietary requirements. So it is hardly surprising that what you eat can affect how you think. If you believe the dietary supplement industry, you could become

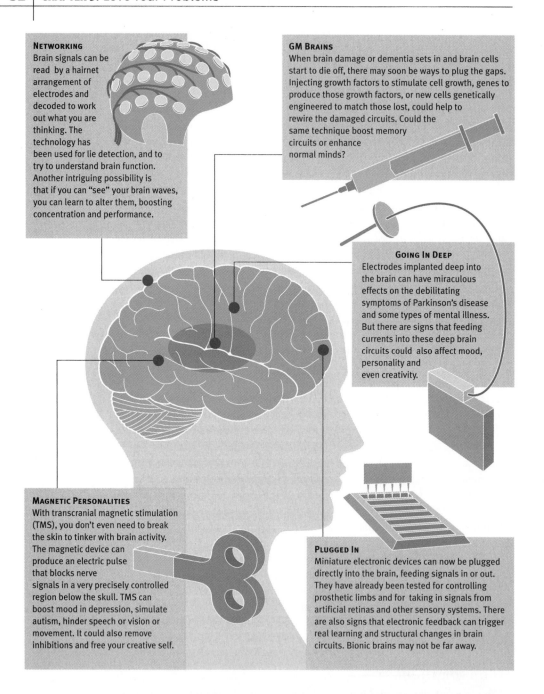

NETWORKING
Brain signals can be read by a hairnet arrangement of electrodes and decoded to work out what you are thinking. The technology has been used for lie detection, and to try to understand brain function. Another intriguing possibility is that if you can "see" your brain waves, you can learn to alter them, boosting concentration and performance.

GM BRAINS
When brain damage or dementia sets in and brain cells start to die off, there may soon be ways to plug the gaps. Injecting growth factors to stimulate cell growth, genes to produce those growth factors, or new cells genetically engineered to match those lost, could help to rewire the damaged circuits. Could the same technique boost memory circuits or enhance normal minds?

GOING IN DEEP
Electrodes implanted deep into the brain can have miraculous effects on the debilitating symptoms of Parkinson's disease and some types of mental illness. But there are signs that feeding currents into these deep brain circuits could also affect mood, personality and even creativity.

MAGNETIC PERSONALITIES
With transcranial magnetic stimulation (TMS), you don't even need to break the skin to tinker with brain activity. The magnetic device can produce an electric pulse that blocks nerve signals in a very precisely controlled region below the skull. TMS can boost mood in depression, simulate autism, hinder speech or vision or movement. It could also remove inhibitions and free your creative self.

PLUGGED IN
Miniature electronic devices can now be plugged directly into the brain, feeding signals in or out. They have already been tested for controlling prosthetic limbs and for taking in signals from artificial retinas and other sensory systems. There are also signs that electronic feedback can trigger real learning and structural changes in brain circuits. Bionic brains may not be far away.

the next Einstein just by popping the right combination of pills. Look closer, however, and it isn't that simple. The savvy consumer should take talk of brain-boosting diets with a pinch of low-sodium salt. But if it is possible to eat your way to genius, it must surely be worth a try.

First, go to the top of the class by eating breakfast. The brain is best fuelled by a steady supply of glucose, and many studies have shown that skipping breakfast reduces people's performance at school and at work.

But it isn't simply a matter of getting some calories down. According to research published in 2003, kids breakfasting on fizzy drinks and sugary snacks performed at the level of an average 70-year-old in tests of memory and attention. Beans on toast is a far better combination, as Barbara Stewart from the University of Ulster, UK, discovered. Toast alone boosted children's scores on a variety of cognitive tests, but when the tests got tougher, the breakfast with the high-protein beans worked best. Beans are also a good source of fibre, and other research has shown a link between a high-fibre diet and improved cognition. If you can't stomach beans before midday, wholemeal toast with Marmite makes a great alternative. The yeast extract is packed with B vitamins, whose brain-boosting powers have been demonstrated in many studies.

A smart choice for lunch is omelette and salad. Eggs are rich in choline, which your body uses to produce the neurotransmitter acetylcholine. Researchers at Boston University found that when healthy young adults were given the drug scopolamine, which blocks acetylcholine receptors in the brain, it significantly reduced their ability to remember word pairs. Low levels of acetylcholine are also associated with Alzheimer's disease, and some studies suggest that boosting dietary intake may slow age-related memory loss.

A salad packed full of antioxidants, including beta-carotene and vitamins C and E, should also help keep an ageing brain in tip-top condition by helping to mop up damaging free radicals. Dwight Tapp and colleagues from the University of California at Irvine found that a diet high in antioxidants improved the cognitive skills of 39 ageing beagles—proving that you can teach an old dog new tricks.

Round off lunch with a yogurt dessert, and you should be alert and ready to face the stresses of the afternoon. That's because yogurt contains the amino acid tyrosine, needed for the production of the neurotransmitters dopamine and noradrenalin, among others. Studies by the US military indicate that tyrosine becomes depleted when we are under stress and that supplementing your intake can improve alertness and memory.

Don't forget to snaffle a snack mid-afternoon, to maintain your glucose levels. Just make sure you avoid junk food, and especially highly processed goodies such as cakes, pastries and biscuits, which contain trans-fatty acids. These not only pile on the pounds, but are implicated in a slew of serious mental disorders, from dyslexia and ADHD (attention deficit hyperactivity disorder) to autism. Hard evidence for this is still thin on the ground, but last year researchers at the annual Society for Neuroscience meeting in San Diego, California, reported that rats and mice raised on the rodent equivalent of junk food struggled to find their way around a maze, and took longer to remember solutions to problems they had already solved.

It seems that some of the damage may be mediated through triglyceride, a cholesterol-like substance found at high levels in rodents fed on trans-fats.

When the researchers gave these rats a drug to bring triglyceride levels down again, the animals' performance on the memory tasks improved.

Brains are around 60 per cent fat, so if trans-fats clog up the system, what should you eat to keep it well oiled? Evidence is mounting in favour of omega-3 fatty acids, in particular docosahexaenoic acid or DHA. In other words, your granny was right: fish is the best brain food. Not only will it feed and lubricate a developing brain, DHA also seems to help stave off dementia. Studies published last year reveal that older mice from a strain genetically altered to develop Alzheimer's had 70 per cent less of the amyloid plaques associated with the disease when fed on a high-DHA diet.

Finally, you could do worse than finish off your evening meal with strawberries and blueberries. Rats fed on these fruits have shown improved coordination, concentration and short-term memory. And even if they don't work such wonders in people, they still taste fantastic. So what have you got to lose?

THE MOZART EFFECT

Music may tune up your thinking, but you can't just crank up the volume and expect to become a genius

A decade ago Frances Rauscher, a psychologist now at the University of Wisconsin at Oshkosh, and her colleagues made waves with the discovery that listening to Mozart improved people's mathematical and spatial reasoning. Even rats ran mazes faster and more accurately after hearing Mozart than after white noise or music by the minimalist composer Philip Glass. Last year, Rauscher reported that, for rats at least, a Mozart piano sonata seems to stimulate activity in three genes involved in nerve-cell signalling in the brain.

This sounds like the most harmonious way to tune up your mental faculties. But before you grab the CDs, hear this note of caution. Not everyone who has looked for the Mozart effect has found it. What's more, even its proponents tend to think that music boosts brain power simply because it makes listeners feel better—relaxed and stimulated at the same time—and that a comparable stimulus might do just as well. In fact, one study found that listening to a story gave a similar performance boost.

There is, however, one way in which music really does make you smarter, though unfortunately it requires a bit more effort than just selecting something mellow on your iPod. Music lessons are the key. Six-year-old children who were given music lessons, as opposed to drama lessons or no extra instruction, got a 2 to 3-point boost in IQ scores compared with the others. Similarly, Rauscher found that after two years of music lessons, pre-school children scored better on spatial reasoning tests than those who took computer lessons.

Maybe music lessons exercise a range of mental skills, with their requirement for delicate and precise finger movements, and listening for pitch and rhythm, all combined with an emotional dimension. Nobody knows for sure.

Neither do they know whether adults can get the same mental boost as young children. But, surely, it can't hurt to try.

BIONIC BRAINS
If training and tricks seem too much like hard work, some technological short cuts can boost brain function

YOU MUST REMEMBER THIS

REMEMBER	FORGET
Glucose	Fatty foods
Chewing gum	Excess alcohol
Aerobic exercise	Sleep deprivation
Music	Poor hearing
Word association	Bad eyesight

GAINFUL EMPLOYMENT
Put your mind to work in the right way and it could repay you with an impressive bonus

Until recently, a person's IQ—a measure of all kinds of mental problem-solving abilities, including spatial skills, memory and verbal reasoning—was thought to be a fixed commodity largely determined by genetics. But recent hints suggest that a very basic brain function called working memory might underlie our general intelligence, opening up the intriguing possibility that if you improve your working memory, you could boost your IQ too.

Working memory is the brain's short-term information storage system. It's a workbench for solving mental problems. For example if you calculate $73 - 6 + 7$, your working memory will store the intermediate steps necessary to work out the answer. And the amount of information that the working memory can hold is strongly related to general intelligence.

A team led by Torkel Klingberg at the Karolinska Institute in Stockholm, Sweden, has found signs that the neural systems that underlie working memory may grow in response to training. Using functional magnetic resonance imaging (fMRI) brain scans, they measured the brain activity of adults before and after a working-memory training programme, which involved tasks such as memorising the positions of a series of dots on a grid. After five weeks of training, their brain activity had increased in the regions associated with this type of memory (*Nature Neuroscience*, vol 7, p 75).

Perhaps more significantly, when the group studied children who had completed these types of mental workouts, they saw improvement in a range of cognitive abilities not related to the training, and a leap in IQ test scores of 8 per cent (*Journal of the American Academy of Child and Adolescent Psychiatry*, vol 44, p 177). It's early days yet, but Klingberg thinks working-memory training could be a key to unlocking brain power. "Genetics determines a lot and so does the early gestation period," he says. "On top of that, there is a few per cent—we don't know how much—that can be improved by training."

MEMORY MARVELS

Mind like a sieve? Don't worry. The difference between mere mortals and memory champs is more method than mental capacity

An auditorium is filled with 600 people. As they file out, they each tell you their name. An hour later, you are asked to recall them all. Can you do it? Most of us would balk at the idea. But in truth we're probably all up to the task. It just needs a little technique and dedication.

First, learn a trick from the "mnemonists" who routinely memorise strings of thousands of digits, entire epic poems, or hundreds of unrelated words. When Eleanor Maguire from University College London and her colleagues studied eight front runners in the annual World Memory Championships they did not find any evidence that these people have particularly high IQs or differently configured brains. But, while memorising, these people did show activity in three brain regions that become active during movements and navigation tasks but are not normally active during simple memory tests.

This may be connected to the fact that seven of them used a strategy in which they place items to be remembered along a visualised route (*Nature Neuroscience*, vol 6, p 90). To remember the sequence of an entire pack of playing cards for example, the champions assign each card an identity, perhaps an object or person, and as they flick through the cards they can make up a story based on a sequence of interactions between these characters and objects at sites along a well-trodden route.

Actors use a related technique: they attach emotional meaning to what they say. We always remember highly emotional moments better than less emotionally loaded ones. Professional actors also seem to link words with movement, remembering action-accompanied lines significantly better than those delivered while static, even months after a show has closed.

Helga Noice, a psychologist from Elmhurst College in Illinois, and Tony Noice, an actor, who together discovered this effect, found that non-thesps can benefit by adopting a similar technique. Students who paired their words with previously learned actions could reproduce 38 per cent of them after just 5 minutes, whereas rote learners only managed 14 per cent. The Noices believe that having two mental representations gives you a better shot at remembering what you are supposed to say.

Strategy is important in everyday life too, says Barry Gordon from Johns Hopkins University in Baltimore, Maryland. Simple things like always putting your car keys in the same place, writing things down to get them off your mind, or just deciding to pay attention, can make a big difference to how much information you retain. And if names are your downfall, try making some mental associations. Just remember to keep the derogatory ones to yourself.

SLEEP ON IT
Never underestimate the power of a good night's rest

Skimping on sleep does awful things to your brain. Planning, problem-solving, learning, concentration, working memory and alertness all take a hit. IQ scores tumble. "If you have been awake for 21 hours straight, your abilities are equivalent to someone who is legally drunk," says Sean Drummond from the University of California, San Diego. And you don't need to pull an all-nighter to suffer the effects: two or three late nights and early mornings on the trot have the same effect.

Luckily, it's reversible—and more. If you let someone who isn't sleep-deprived have an extra hour or two of shut-eye, they perform much better than normal on tasks requiring sustained attention, such taking an exam. And being able to concentrate harder has knock-on benefits for overall mental performance. "Attention is the base of a mental pyramid," says Drummond. "If you boost that, you can't help boosting everything above it."

These are not the only benefits of a decent night's sleep. Sleep is when your brain processes new memories, practises and hones new skills—and even solves problems. Say you're trying to master a new video game. Instead of grinding away into the small hours, you would be better off playing for a couple of hours, then going to bed. While you are asleep your brain will reactivate the circuits it was using as you learned the game, rehearse them, and then shunt the new memories into long-term storage. When you wake up, hey presto! You will be a better player. The same applies to other skills such as playing the piano, driving a car and, some researchers claim, memorising facts and figures. Even taking a nap after training can help, says Carlyle Smith of Trent University in Peterborough, Ontario.

There is also some evidence that sleep can help produce moments of problem-solving insight. The famous story about the Russian chemist Dmitri Mendeleev suddenly "getting" the periodic table in a dream after a day spent struggling with the problem is probably true. It seems that sleep somehow allows the brain to juggle new memories to produce flashes of creative insight. So if you want to have a eureka moment, stop racking your brains and get your head down.

BODY AND MIND
Physical exercise can boost brain as well as brawn

It's a dream come true for those who hate studying. Simply walking sedately for half an hour three times a week can improve abilities such as learning, concentration and abstract reasoning by 15 per cent. The effects are particularly noticeable in older people. Senior citizens who walk regularly perform better on memory tests than their sedentary peers. What's more, over several years their scores on a variety of cognitive tests show far less decline than those of non-walkers. Every extra mile a week has measurable benefits.

It's not only oldies who benefit, however. Angela Balding from the University of Exeter, UK, has found that schoolchildren who exercise three or four times a week get higher than average exam grades at age 10 or 11. The effect is strongest in boys, and while Balding admits that the link may not be causal, she suggests that aerobic exercise may boost mental powers by getting extra oxygen to your energy-guzzling brain.

There's another reason why your brain loves physical exercise: it promotes the growth of new brain cells. Until recently, received wisdom had it that we are born with a full complement of neurons and produce no new ones during our lifetime. Fred Gage from the Salk Institute in La Jolla, California, busted that myth in 2000 when he showed that even adults can grow new brain cells. He also found that exercise is one of the best ways to achieve this.

In mice, at least, the brain-building effects of exercise are strongest in the hippocampus, which is involved with learning and memory. This also happens to be the brain region that is damaged by elevated levels of the stress hormone cortisol. So if you are feeling frazzled, do your brain a favour and go for a run.

Even more gentle exercise, such as yoga, can do wonders for your brain. Last year, researchers at the University of California, Los Angeles, reported results from a pilot study in which they considered the mood-altering ability of different yoga poses. Comparing back bends, forward bends and standing poses, they concluded that the best way to get a mental lift is to bend over backwards.

And the effect works both ways. Just as physical exercise can boost the brain, mental exercise can boost the body. In 2001, researchers at the Cleveland Clinic Foundation in Ohio asked volunteers to spend just 15 minutes a day thinking about exercising their biceps. After 12 weeks, their arms were 13 per cent stronger.

NUNS ON A RUN

If you don't want senility to interfere with your old age, perhaps you should seek some sisterly guidance

The convent of the School Sisters of Notre Dame on Good Counsel Hill in Mankato, Minnesota, might seem an unusual place for a pioneering brain-science experiment. But a study of its 75 to 107-year-old inhabitants is revealing more about keeping the brain alive and healthy than perhaps any other to date. The "Nun study" is a unique collaboration between 678 Catholic sisters recruited in 1991 and Alzheimer's expert David Snowdon of the Sanders-Brown Center on Aging and the University of Kentucky in Lexington.

The sisters' miraculous longevity—the group boasts seven centenarians and many others well on their way—is surely in no small part attributable to their impeccable lifestyle. They do not drink or smoke, they live quietly and communally, they are spiritual and calm and they eat healthily and in moderation. Nevertheless, small differences between individual nuns could reveal the key to a healthy mind in later life.

Some of the nuns have suffered from Alzheimer's disease, but many have avoided any kind of dementia or senility. They include Sister Matthia, who was mentally fit and active from her birth in 1894 to the day she died peacefully in her sleep, aged 104. She was happy and productive, knitting mittens for the poor every day until the end of her life. A post-mortem of Sister Matthia's brain revealed no signs of excessive ageing. But in some other, remarkable cases, Snowdon has found sisters who showed no outwards signs of senility in life, yet had brains that looked as if they were ravaged by dementia.

How did Sister Matthia and the others cheat time? Snowdon's study, which includes an annual barrage of mental agility tests and detailed medical exams, has found several common denominators. The right amount of vitamin folate is one. Verbal ability early in life is another, as are positive emotions early in life, which were revealed by Snowdon's analysis of the personal autobiographical essays each woman wrote in her 20s as she took her vows. Activities, crosswords, knitting and exercising also helped to prevent senility, showing that the old adage "use it or lose it" is pertinent. And spirituality, or the positive attitude that comes from it, can't be overlooked. But individual differences also matter. To avoid dementia, your general health may be vital: metabolic problems, small strokes and head injuries seem to be common triggers of Alzheimer's dementia.

Obviously, you don't have to become a nun to stay mentally agile. We can all aspire to these kinds of improvements. As one of the sisters put it, "Think no evil, do no evil, hear no evil, and you will never write a best-selling novel."

ATTENTION SEEKING

You can be smart, well-read, creative and knowledgeable,
but none of it is any use if your mind isn't on the job

Paying attention is a complex mental process, an interplay of zooming in on detail and stepping back to survey the big picture. So unfortunately there is no single remedy to enhance your concentration. But there are a few ways to improve it.

The first is to raise your arousal levels. The brain's attentional state is controlled by the neurotransmitters dopamine and noradrenalin. Dopamine encourages a persistent, goal-centred state of mind whereas noradrenalin produces an outward-looking, vigilant state. So not surprisingly, anything that raises dopamine levels can boost your powers of concentration.

One way to do this is with drugs such as amphetamines and the ADHD drug methylphenidate, better known as Ritalin. Caffeine also works. But if you prefer the drug-free approach, the best strategy is to sleep well, eat foods packed with slow-release sugars, and take lots of exercise. It also helps if you are trying to focus on something that you find interesting.

The second step is to cut down on distractions. Workplace studies have found that it takes up to 15 minutes to regain a deep state of concentration after a distraction such as a phone call. Just a few such interruptions and half the day is wasted.

Music can help as long as you listen to something familiar and soothing that serves primarily to drown out background noise. Psychologists also recommend that you avoid working near potential diversions, such as the fridge.

There are mental drills to deal with distractions. College counselors routinely teach students to recognise when their thoughts are wandering, and catch themselves by saying "Stop! Be here now!" It sounds corny but can develop into a valuable habit. As any Zen meditator will tell you, concentration is as much a skill to be lovingly cultivated as it is a physiochemical state of the brain.

POSITIVE FEEDBACK

Thought control is easier than you might imagine

It sounds a bit New Age, but there is a mysterious method of thought control you can learn that seems to boost brain power. No one quite knows how it works, and it is hard to describe exactly how to do it: it's not relaxation or concentration as such, more a state of mind. It's called neurofeedback. And it is slowly gaining scientific credibility.

Neurofeedback grew out of biofeedback therapy, popular in the 1960s. It works by showing people a real-time measure of some seemingly uncontrollable aspect of their physiology—heart rate, say—and encouraging them to try and change it. Astonishingly, many patients found that they could, though only rarely could they describe how they did it.

More recently, this technique has been applied to the brain—specifically to brain wave activity measured by an electroencephalogram, or EEG. The first attempts were aimed at boosting the size of the alpha wave, which crescendos when we are calm and focused. In one experiment, researchers linked the speed of a car in a computer game to the size of the alpha wave. They then asked subjects to make the car go faster using only their minds. Many managed to do so, and seemed to become more alert and focused as a result.

This early success encouraged others, and neurofeedback soon became a popular alternative therapy for ADHD. There is now good scientific evidence that it works, as well as some success in treating epilepsy, depression, tinnitus, anxiety, stroke and brain injuries.

And to keep up with the times, some experimenters have used brain scanners in place of EEGs. Scanners can allow people to see and control activity of specific parts of the brain. A team at Stanford University in California showed that people could learn to control pain by watching the activity of their pain centers (*New Scientist*, 1 May 2004, p 9).

But what about outside the clinic? Will neurofeedback ever allow ordinary people to boost their brain function? Possibly. John Gruzelier of Imperial College London has shown that it can improve medical students' memory and make them feel calmer before exams. He has also shown that it can improve musicians' and dancers' technique, and is testing it out on opera singers and surgeons.

Neils Birbaumer from the University of Tübingen in Germany wants to see whether neurofeedback can help psychopathic criminals control their impulsiveness. And there are hints that the method could boost creativity, enhance our orgasms, give shy people more confidence, lift low moods, alter the balance between left and right brain activity, and alter personality traits. All this by the power of thought.

"11 Steps to A Better Brain," by Kate Douglas et al, *New Scientist,* May 28, 2005. Reprinted by permission.

▶ Reflection Questions

1. Of the eleven different strategies that are suggested in this reading, which are the two that you think would make the most difference for you? Why?

2. College, especially the first year, can be a time when good eating habits become a thing of the past. Whether it is grabbing a quick bite on the run between your job and school or simply choosing the wrong foods in the cafeteria, food causes weight gain and, according to this reading, changes in the way your mind responds. Think of what you eat within a three-day period. Are you getting the right fuel for your brain? How do your eating habits affect your daily performance? What can you do to make proper eating a priority?

3. According to this reading, "The difference between mere mortals and memory champs is more method than mental capacity." Do you agree with this assertion? Which of the suggestions given do you think might help you? On what subjects would you use this as a study technique?

Reading Three

This reading is about Brian Morrow, a young man who overcame a learning disability (keep in mind, learning disabilities don't go away) to achieve a clinical doctorate in physical therapy. He describes his educational journey, from repeating first grade to struggling throughout his educational career with reading and comprehension among other challenges, and what he did to overcome the obstacles along the way.

He Has Become a Turtle with a Tailwind

Bill Moor

"You know those really good readers in grade school who are called the rabbits?" Brian says. "Well, I was one of the turtles. I still am, for that matter."

Back then, he also believed he was something else.

"I thought I was just stupid," admits the graduate of Penn High School and Lake Forest College. "I felt inferior to other kids."

His parents, David and Janet Morrow, made the hard decision to have him repeat first grade.

He had a learning disability, after all.

"I still do," says Brian, 27. "There isn't any pill that is going to make that go away."

He still struggles with reading and comprehension, and left-and-right determinations and learning numbers in sequence.

And yet earlier this month, he earned his clinical doctorate in physical therapy and already has started work for the Marianjoy Medical Group in Palos Heights outside Chicago.

Think about that—from flunking first grade to earning a doctorate.

"I couldn't have done it without the wonderful support of my parents and some really great teachers," he says.

Janet Morrow says this success story is a testament to Brian's strength, motivation and guts.

"He always has tried so very hard," says Janet, now the head of Penn's special education department. "When he was little, it was as if you could see the smoke coming off his head, he was working so hard to learn how to read."

"I think there was some concern that I might never learn to properly read or even get through high school," Brian adds. "But as time went by, I sort of figured some things out and basically learned how to learn."

Much of it was writing everything down, repeating it over and not being afraid to seek help.

"He took ownership of his own education," says his mother, whose younger son, Chris, is in law school at Michigan State.

When Brian was in eighth grade, the Morrows moved from the Indianapolis area to South Bend, where David became the pastor at First Presbyterian Church.

"And that was about the time that my mom taught me how to sing," Brian says. "I wasn't going to become the fourth tenor, but I at least became pretty good. It didn't have anything to do with my learning disability, and it really gave me some self-esteem that I hadn't had before."

He eventually sang in the Penn High school's choir, joined the swim team and started making friends.

"I also took advantage of my teachers' kindness and would be in school early and then there late to get all the tutoring I could. I guess I was a bit of a nerd."

But a very determined nerd.

By high school, he was mainstreamed into all his classes. Then during his junior year, he made the National Honor Society.

Yet nothing ever became easy for him. When he took a difficult astronomy class, he came home one day and told his mom he had correctly named 49 out of 50 constellations.

"But then he said, 'I bet I could find most of the constellations out in the sky, too, if I could determine which way was north and which way was south,'" his mom recalls.

When he was with the Penn chamber choir and the guys were to wear top hats and carry canes, he brought the cane home and practiced the routine because of his problems with left and right.

"He actually went down in the basement and turned off the lights," Janet says. "He figured if he could do the moves in the dark, he would be OK during the performance."

He was A-OK.

Before Brian went off to college, Janet found a piece of paper in a waste basket on which Brian had written his dorm telephone number down almost 100 times so he would remember it.

"I had a lot of tutors who helped me through college," he admits, "And then getting my doctorate (at Lake Forest) was one of the hardest things I ever had to do in my life."

He had to stretch the 2 1/2-year program an extra year and figures he had to study twice as long as other students.

A special friend in the program, Kristina Nielsen, was also great help and now has become his girlfriend and a fellow physical therapy graduate.

Brian looks forward to the next chapter of his life. But he won't forget his journey—and those who are on similar paths.

"I have talked several times to high school students with learning disabilities and have also given lectures at IUSB, Notre Dame, Loyola and DePaul," he says. "I want others to know what is possible, but I also want the teachers to know how important they are in the education of students like me. Without my teachers, I'm not sure where I would be right now."

Brian already had helped his mom, who became a special education teacher because of him.

"I guess I walked the walk with Brian, and now I talk the talk," she says.

Sometimes, she shares her son's story with other families—if she can hold back her tears of joy.

Brian, meanwhile, remains a turtle. A turtle with a tailwind.

"He Has Become a Turtle with a Tailwind", by Bill Moor, *South Bend Tribune*, December 21, 2004. Reprinted by permission.

▶ Reflection Questions

1. Brian Morrow took the initiative to discover and overcome barriers brought on by his learning disability. Do you feel there are any barriers in your life that are out of your control? Using lessons learned from Brian, how could you meet and overcome these barriers?

2. Sometimes we feel it is easier not to try, as opposed to putting in effort and failing. What may have driven Brian Morrow to challenge himself and those around him?

3. Describe Brian and describe his personality. What qualities were vital to his success?

4. What resources are available on your campus to a person who feels she may have a learning disability?

Writing Assignment

audience: Your instructor

purpose: To choose and support a position: Do you believe that students with learning disabilities should be excused from having to take certain subjects?

length: Minimum of three typed pages, double-spaced

Write a position paper for or against how students with disabilities are accommodated in classes. For example, if a student who has dyslexia reverses numbers and letters, should he be exempt from math? Should students who stutter be exempt from public speaking? What about deaf or hard of hearing students? Should they not be required to present? How about people who may have trouble with memory? Argue for or against accommodations for students with learning disabilities.

Include information about the laws regarding students with disabilities, what constitutes a disability, and how it is documented. Take a look at the policy for students with learning disabilities. This information may help guide your thinking. Be very specific when it comes to what you recommend.

 Journal Entries: DISCOVERY AND INTENTION STATEMENTS

Describe some of the barriers that you believe stop you from achieving what you want. Take one and step by step think of some ways you might get over or around the barrier; also, write about someone you know who has a barrier larger than yours. Has he or she figured out a way around or over it? Describe it.

Write one or two sentences about what you have discovered and what you intend to do as a result of these readings, what you will do to make it work, and what you risk if you don't do what you intend to do. How do your discoveries relate to the Power Process? What are your problems? If they are things that you cannot change, have you accepted them? If they are things you can change, how will you work to overcome them?

 ## Mastering Vocabulary

List five words that were new to you (more or less if necessary). For each, include which reading you found the word in, the definition, and where you got the definition from, as well as a time or place you might use the word again.

1.

2.

3.

4.

5.

Additional Activities

1. List some information from one of your classes that you have to memorize, and develop a technique for learning the list that you will share with the class.

2. Look back at your journal entry, choose one barrier that you can feel proud about overcoming, and think how you can do that. Share this with the class.

3. Using one of the search engines on the Internet (Google, for example), find ten famous people who have learning disabilities. You may be surprised to find out who is on the list.

4. Give a speech to the class on one of the topics listed above: tips to help memorize, how to overcome a barrier as successful public speakers may have, or famous individuals who have overcome learning disabilities. Use PowerPoint. Be sure to investigate some of the principles behind developing a good PowerPoint presentation. For help in creating your PowerPoint presentation, you can access the PowerPoint Tutorial on the Master Student Reader website: college.hmco. com/pic/msreader1e.

Online Study Center **Improve Your Grade**
Visit the Online Study Center for resources and exercises to accompany this text
http://college.hmco.com/pic/msreader1e

CHAPTER FOUR

Notice Your Pictures and Let Them Go

Pictures can leave lasting impressions in our minds. The impressions can be positive—a beautiful sunset at the beach—or negative. Who can forget the image of the World Trade Center collapsing? Sometimes negative images can prevent us from seeing another side of an issue. In Chapter One we read about critical thinking. Think about dualism (two ways to view the world) and the fact that at this low level of critical thinking, individuals may see only one side of an issue. If a child is raised to believe that poor people are poor because they are lazy, he might balk at volunteering in a soup kitchen. If one is raised in a household were she is taught that individuals with a different sexual orientation are bad, her "picture" of these individuals is bad. In these cases, an individual has a picture of what he or she believes is right and may not be able to let it go.

The Power Process: Notice Your Pictures and Let Them Go

One of the brain's primary jobs is to manufacture images. We use mental pictures to make predictions about the world, and we base much of our behavior on those predictions.

When a cook adds chopped onions, mushrooms, and garlic to a spaghetti sauce, he has a picture of how the sauce will taste and measures each ingredient according to that picture. When an artist is creating a painting or sculpture, he has a mental picture of the finished piece. Novelists often have mental images of the characters that they're about to bring to life. Many parents have a picture about what they want their children to become.

These kinds of pictures and many more have a profound influence on us. Our pictures direct our thinking, our conversations, and our actions—all of which help create our immediate circumstances. That's amazing, considering that we often operate with little, if any, conscious knowledge of our pictures.

Just about any time we feel a need, we conjure up a picture of what will satisfy that need. A baby feels hunger pangs and starts to cry. Within seconds, his mother appears and he is satisfied. The baby stores a mental picture of his mother feeding him. He connects that picture with stopping the hunger pangs. Voilà! Now he knows how to solve the hunger problem. The picture goes on file.

According to psychiatrist William Glasser, our minds function like a huge photo album.[1] Its pages include pictures of all the ways we've satis-

---

[1] William Glasser, *Take Effective Control of Your Life* (New York: Harper & Row, 1984).

fied needs in the past. Whenever we feel dissatisfied, we mentally search the album for a picture of how to make the dissatisfaction go away. With that picture firmly in mind, we act in ways to make the world outside our heads match the pictures inside.

Remember that pictures are not strictly visual images. They can involve any of the senses. When you buy a CD, you have a picture of how it will sound. When you buy a sweater, you have a picture of how it will feel.

A problem with pictures

The pictures we make in our heads are survival mechanisms. Without them, we couldn't get from one end of town to the other. We couldn't feed or clothe ourselves. Without a picture of a socket, we couldn't screw in a light bulb.

Pictures can also get in our way. Take the case of a student who plans to attend a school he hasn't visited. He chose this school for its strong curriculum and good academic standing, but his brain didn't stop there. In his mind, the campus has historic buildings with ivy-covered walls and tree-lined avenues. The professors, he imagines, will be as articulate as Bill Moyers and as entertaining as Oprah Winfrey. His roommate will be his best friend. The cafeteria will be a cozy nook serving delicate quiche and fragrant teas. He will gather there with fellow students for hours of stimulating, intellectual conversation. The library will have every book, while the computer lab will boast the newest technology.

The school turns out to be four gray buildings downtown, next to the bus station. The first class he attends is taught by an overweight, balding professor, who is wearing a purple-and-orange bird of paradise tie and has a bad case of the sniffles. The cafeteria is a nondescript hall with machine-dispensed food, and the student's apartment is barely large enough to accommodate his roommate's tuba. This hypothetical student gets depressed. He begins to think about dropping out of school.

The problem with pictures is that they can prevent us from seeing what is really there. That happened to the student in this story. His pictures prevented him from noticing that his school is in the heart of a culturally vital city—close to theaters, museums, government offices, clubs, and all kinds of stores. The professor with the weird tie is not only an expert in his field, but is also a superior teacher. The school cafeteria is skimpy because it can't compete with the variety of inexpensive restaurants in the area. There might even be hope for a tuba-playing roommate.

Anger and disappointment are often the results of our pictures. We set up expectations of events before they occur, which can lead to disappointment. Sometimes we don't even realize that we have these expectations. The next time you discover you are angry, disappointed, or frustrated, look to see which of your pictures aren't being fulfilled.

Take charge of your pictures

Having pictures is unavoidable. Letting these pictures control our lives *is* avoidable. Some techniques for dealing with pictures are so simple and effortless, they might seem silly.

One way to deal with pictures is to be aware of them. Open up your mental photo album and notice how the pictures there influence your thoughts, feelings, and actions. Just becoming aware of your pictures— how they affect you—can help you take a huge step toward dealing with them effectively.

When you notice that pictures are getting in your way, then in the most gentle manner possible, let your pictures go. Let them drift away like wisps of smoke picked up by a gentle wind.

Pictures are persistent. They come back over and over. Notice them again and let them go again. At first a picture might return repeatedly and insistently. Pictures are like independent beings. They want to live. If you can see the picture as a thought independent from you, you will likely find it easier to let it go.

You are more than your pictures. Many images and words will pop into your head in the course of a lifetime. You do not have to identify with these pictures. You can let pictures go without giving up yourself.

If your pictures are interfering with your education, visualize them scurrying around inside your head. See yourself tying them to a brightly colored helium balloon and letting them go. Let them float away again and again.

Sometimes we can let go of old pictures and replace them with new ones. We stored all of those pictures in the first place. We can replace them. Our student's new picture of a great education can include the skimpy cafeteria, the professor with the weird tie, and the roommate with the tuba.

We can take charge of the images that float through our minds. We don't have to be ruled by an album of outdated pictures. We can stay aware of our pictures and keep looking for new ones. And when *those* new pictures no longer serve us, we can also let them go.

Readings

The readings in this chapter are about how we develop images of people and places on the basis of what we hear, see, and are taught. The readings are also chosen to show multiple perspectives. Before you read them, think about some of your own stereotypes (we all have them) and how they may have prevented you from getting to know someone. Some individuals are members of groups that are not the majority, but the minority. Keep in mind that the term *minority* is certainly relative to the setting and circumstances; the majority in one place could easily be the minority in another. Think about when you have been in the minority group (be it based on race, religion, ethic background, sexual orientation, class, ability, or ideology). How does that experience feel?

Reading One

This reading by Malcolm X is a powerful piece that chronicles his desire to learn to read and write. As a young man he was convicted of robbery and sentenced to jail. During his imprisonment he learned from fellow African American inmates about the struggles of his people. Driven to learn more about the history of African Americans, he knew that he had to learn to read and write to acquire more knowledge. In this piece he describes, among other things, how he painstakingly copied words from the dictionary in an effort to learn.

Learning to Read

Malcolm X

It was because of my letters that I happened to stumble upon starting to acquire some kind of a homemade education.

I became increasingly frustrated at not being able to express what I wanted to convey in letters that I wrote, especially to Mr. Elijah Muhammad. In the street, I had been the most articulate hustler out there—I had commanded attention when I said something. But now, trying to write simple English, I not only wasn't articulate, I wasn't even functional. How would I sound writing in slang, the way I would *say* it, something such as, "Look, daddy, let me pull your coat about a cat, Elijah Muhammed—"

Many who today hear me somewhere in person, or on television, or those who read something I've said, will think I went to school far beyond the eighth grade. This impression is due entirely to my prison studies.

It had really begun back in the Charlestown Prison, when Bimbi first made me feel envy of his stock of knowledge. Bimbi had always taken charge of any conversations he was in, and I had tried to emulate him. But every book I picked up had few sentences which didn't contain anywhere from one to nearly all of the words that might as well have been in Chinese. When I just skipped those words, of course, I really ended up with little idea of what the book said. So I had come to the Norfolk Prison Colony still going through only book-reading motions. Pretty soon, I would have quit even these motions, unless I had received the motivation that I did.

I saw that the best thing I could do was get hold of a dictionary—to study, to learn some words. I was lucky enough to reason also that I should try to improve my penmanship. It was sad. I couldn't even write in a straight line. It was both ideas together that moved me to request a dictionary along with some tablets and pencils from the Norfolk Prison Colony school.

I spent two days just riffling uncertainly through the dictionary's pages. I'd never realized so many words existed! I didn't know *which* words I needed to learn. Finally, just to start some kind of action, I began copying.

In my slow, painstaking, ragged handwriting, I copied into my tablet everything printed on that first page, down to the punctuation marks.

I believe it took me a day. Then, aloud, I read back, to myself, everything I'd written on the tablet. Over and over, aloud, to myself, I read my own handwriting.

I woke up the next morning, thinking about those words—immensely proud to realize that not only had I written so much at one time, but I'd written words that I never knew were in the world. Moreover, with a little effort, I also could remember what many of these words meant. I reviewed the words whose meanings I didn't remember. Funny thing, from the dictionary first page right now, that "aardvark" springs to my mind. The dictionary had a picture of it, a long-tailed, long-eared, burrowing African mammal, which lives off termites caught by sticking out its tongue as an anteater does for ants.

I was so fascinated that I went on—I copied the dictionary's next page. And the same experience came when I studied that. With every succeeding page, I also learned of people and places and events from history. Actually the dictionary is like a miniature encyclopedia. Finally the dictionary's A section had filled a whole tablet—and I went on into the B's. That was the way I started copying what eventually became the entire dictionary. It went a lot faster after so much practice helped me to pick up handwriting speed. Between what I wrote in my tablet, and writing letters, during the rest of my time in prison I would guess I wrote a million words.

I suppose it was inevitable that as my word-base broadened, I could for the first time pick up a book and read and now begin to understand what the book was saying. Anyone who has read a great deal can imagine the new world that opened. Let me tell you something: from then until I left that prison, in every free moment I had, if I was not reading in the library, I was reading on my bunk. You couldn't have gotten me out of books with a wedge. Between Mr. Muhammad's teachings, my correspondence, my visitors, . . . and my reading of books, months passed without my even thinking about being imprisoned. In fact, up to then, I never had been so truly free in my life.

The Norfolk Prison Colony's library was in the school building. A variety of classes was taught there by instructors who came from such places as Harvard and Boston universities. The weekly debates between inmate teams were also held in the school building. You would be astonished to know how worked up convict debaters and audiences would get over subjects like "Should Babies Be Fed Milk?"

Available on the prison library's shelves were books on just about every general subject. Much of the big private collection that Parkhurst had willed to the prison was still in crates and boxes in the back of the library—thousands of old books. Some of them looked ancient: covers faded, old-time parchment-looking binding. Parkhurst . . . seemed to have been principally interested in history and religion. He had the money and the special interest to have a lot of books that you wouldn't have in a general circulation. Any college library would have been lucky to get that collection.

As you can imagine, especially in a prison where there was heavy emphasis on rehabilitation, an inmate was smiled upon if he demonstrated an unusually intense interest in books. There was a sizable number of well-read inmates, especially the popular debaters. Some were said by many to be practically walking encyclopedias. They were almost celebrities. No university would ask any student to devour literature as I did when this new world opened to me, of being able to read and *understand.*

I read more in my room than in the library itself. An inmate who was known to read a lot could check out more than the permitted maximum number of books. I preferred reading in the total isolation of my own room.

When I had progressed to really serious reading, every night at about ten P.M. I would be outraged with the "lights out." It always seemed to catch me right in the middle of something engrossing.

Fortunately, right outside my door was a corridor light that cast a glow into my room. The glow was enough to read by, once my eyes adjusted to it. So when "lights out" came, I would sit on the floor where I could continue reading in that glow.

At one-hour intervals the night guards paced past every room. Each time I heard the approaching footsteps, I jumped into bed and feigned sleep. And as soon as the guard passed, I got back out of bed onto the floor area of that light-glow, where I would read for another fifty-eight minutes—until the guard approached again. That went on until three or four every morning. Three or four hours of sleep a night was enough for me. Often in the years in the streets I had slept less than that.

The teachings of Mr. Muhammad stressed how history had been "whitened"— when white men had written history books, the black man simply had been left out. Mr. Muhammad couldn't have said anything that would have struck me much harder. I had never forgotten how when my class, me and all of those whites, had studied seventh-grade United States history back in Mason, the history of the Negro had been covered in one paragraph, and the teacher had gotten a big laugh with his joke, "Negroes' feet are so big that when they walk, they leave a hole in the ground."

This is one reason why Mr. Muhammad's teachings spread so swiftly all over the United States, among *all* Negroes, whether or not they became followers of Mr. Muhammad. The teachings ring true—to every Negro. You can hardly show me a black adult in America—or a white one, for that matter— who knows from the history books anything like the truth about the black man's role. In my own case, once I heard of the "glorious history of the black man," I took special pains to hunt in the library for books that would inform me on details about black history.

I can remember accurately the very first set of books that really impressed me. I have since bought that set of books and I have it at home for my children to read as they grow up. It's called *Wonders of the World.* It's full of pictures of archeological finds, statues that depict, usually, non-European people.

I found books like Will Durant's *Story of Civilization.* I read H. G. Wells' *Outline of History. Souls of Black Folk* by W. E. B. Du Bois gave me a glimpse into the black people's history before they came to this country. Carter G. Woodson's *Negro History* opened my eyes about black empires before the black slave was brought to the United States, and the early Negro struggles for freedom.

J. A. Rogers' three volumes of *Sex and Race* told about race-mixing before Christ's time; and Aesop being a black man who told fables; about Egypt's Pharaohs; about the great Coptic Christian Empires; about Ethiopia, the earth's oldest continuous black civilization, as China is the oldest continuous civilization.

Mr. Muhammad's teaching about how the white man had been created led me to *Findings in Genetics* by Gregor Mendel. (The dictionary's G section was where I had learned what "genetics" meant.) I really studied this book by the Austrian monk. Reading it over and over, especially certain sections, helped me to understand that if you started with a black man, a white man could be produced; but starting with a white man, you never could reproduce a black man—because the white chromosome is recessive. And since no one disputes that there was but one Original Man, the conclusion is clear.

During the last year or so, in the *New York Times,* Arnold Toynbee used the word "bleached" in describing the white man. His words were: "White (i.e., bleached) human beings of North European origin. . . ." Toynbee also referred to the European geographic area as only a peninsula of Asia. He said there is no such thing as Europe. And if you look at the globe, you will see for yourself that America is only an extension of Asia. (But at the same time Toynbee is among those who have helped to bleach history. He has written that Africa was the only continent that produced no history. He won't write that again. Every day now, the truth is coming to light.)

I never will forget how shocked I was when I began reading about slavery's total horror. It made such an impact upon me that it later became one of my favorite subjects when I became a minister of Mr. Muhammad's. The world's most monstrous crime, the sin and the blood on the white man's hands, are almost impossible to believe. Books like the one by Frederick Olmsted opened my eyes to the horrors suffered when the slave was landed in the United States. The European woman, Fanny Kemble, who had married a Southern white slaveowner, described how human beings were degraded. Of course I read *Uncle Tom's Cabin.* In fact, I believe that's the only novel I have ever read since I started serious reading.

Parkhurst's collection also contained some bound pamphlets of the Abolitionist Anti-Slavery Society of New England. I read descriptions of atrocities, saw those illustrations of black slave women tied up and flogged with whips; of black mothers watching their babies being dragged off, never to be seen by their mothers again; of dogs after slaves, and of the fugitive slave catchers, evil white men with whips and clubs and chains and guns. I read about the slave preacher Nat Turner, who put the fear of God into the white slavemaster. Nat Turner wasn't going around preaching pie-in-the-sky and "non-violent" freedom for the black man. There in Virginia one night in 1831, Nat and seven other slaves started out at his master's home and through the night they went from one plantation "big house" to the next, killing, until by the next morning

57 white people were dead and Nat had about 70 slaves following him. White people, terrified for their lives, fled from their homes, locked themselves up in public buildings, hid in the woods, and some even left the state. A small army of soldiers took two months to catch and hang Nat Turner. Somewhere I have read where Nat Turner's example is said to have inspired John Brown to invade Virginia and attack Harper's Ferry nearly thirty years later, with thirteen white men and five Negroes.

I read Herodotus, "the father of History," or, rather, I read about him. And I read the histories of various nations, which opened my eyes gradually, then wider and wider, to how the whole world's white men had indeed acted like devils, pillaging and raping and bleeding and draining the whole world's non-white people. I remember, for instance, books such as Will Durant's *The Story of Oriental Civilization,* and Mahatma Gandhi's accounts of the struggle to drive the British out of India.

Book after book showed me how the white men had brought upon the world's black, brown, red, and yellow peoples every variety of the sufferings of exploitation. I saw how since the sixteenth century the so called "Christian trader" white man began to ply the seas in his lust for Asian and African empires, and plunder, and power. I read, I saw, how the white man never has gone among the nonwhite peoples bearing the Cross in the true manner and spirit of Christ's teachings—meek, humble, and Christlike.

I perceived, as I read, how the collective white man had been actually nothing but a piratical opportunist who used Faustian machinations to make his own Christianity his initial wedge in criminal conquests. First, always "religiously," he branded "heathen" and "pagan" labels upon ancient nonwhite cultures and civilizations. The stage thus set, he then turned upon his nonwhite victims his weapons of war.

I read how, entering India—half a *billion* deeply religious brown people—the British white man, by 1759, through promises, trickery, and manipulations, controlled much of India through Great Britain's East India Company. The parasitical British administration kept tentacling out to half of the subcontinent. In 1857, some of the desperate people of India finally mutinied—and, excepting the African slave trade, nowhere has history recorded any more unnecessary bestial and ruthless human carnage than the British suppression of the nonwhite Indian people.

Over 115 million African blacks—close to the 1930's population of the United States—were murdered or enslaved during the slave trade. And I read how when the slave market was glutted, the cannibalistic white powers of Europe next carved up, as their colonies, the richest areas of the black continent. And Europe's chancelleries for the next century played a chess game of naked exploitation and power from Cape Horn to Cairo.

Ten guards and the warden couldn't have torn me out of those books. Not even Elijah Muhammad could have been more eloquent than those books were in providing indisputable proof that the collective white man had acted like a devil in virtually every contact he had with the world's collective nonwhite man. I listen today to the radio, and watch television, and read the headlines about the collective white man's fear and tension concerning China. When the white man professes ignorance about why the Chinese hate him so, my mind can't help flashing back to what I read, there in prison, about how the blood forebears of this same white man raped China at a time when China was trusting and helpless. Those original white "Christian traders" sent into China millions of pounds of opium. By 1839, so many of the Chinese were addicts that China's desperate government destroyed twenty thousand chests of opium. The first Opium War was promptly declared by the white man. Imagine! Declaring *war* upon someone who objects to being narcotized! The Chinese were severely beaten, with Chinese-invented gunpowder.

The Treaty of Nanking made China pay the British white man for the destroyed opium; forced open China's major ports to British trade; forced China to abandon Hong Kong; fixed China's import tariffs so low that cheap British articles soon flooded in, maiming China's industrial development.

After a second Opium War, the Tientsin Treaties legalized the ravaging opium trade, legalized a British-French-American control of China's customs. China tried delaying that Treaty's ratification; Peking was looted and burned.

"Kill the foreign white devils!" was the 1901 Chinese war cry in the Boxer Rebellion. Losing again, this time the Chinese were driven from Peking's choicest areas. The vicious, arrogant white man put up the famous signs, "Chinese and dogs not allowed."

Red China after World War II closed its doors to the Western white world. Massive Chinese agricultural, scientific, and industrial efforts are described inside a book that *Life* magazine recently published. Some observers inside Red China have reported that the world never has known such a hate-white campaign as is now going on in this nonwhite country where, present birth-rates continuing, in fifty more years Chinese will be half the earth's population. And it seems that some Chinese chickens will soon come home to roost, with China's recent successful nuclear tests.

Let us face reality. We can see in the United Nations a new world order being shaped, along color lines—an alliance among the nonwhite nations. America's U.N. ambassador Adlai Stevenson complained not long ago that in the United Nations "a skin game" was being played. He was right. He was facing reality. A "skin game" *is* being played. But Ambassador Stevenson sounded like Jesse James accusing the marshal of carrying a gun. Because who in the world's history ever has played a worse "skin game" than the white man?

Mr. Muhammad, to whom I was writing daily, had no idea of what a new world had opened up to me through my efforts to document his teaching in books.

When I discovered philosophy, I tried to touch all the landmarks of philosophical development. Gradually, I read most of the old philosophers, Occidental and Oriental. The Oriental philosophers were the ones I came to prefer; finally, my impression was that most Occidental philosophy had largely been borrowed from the Oriental thinkers. Socrates, for instance, traveled in Egypt. Some sources even say that Socrates was initiated into some of the Egyptian mysteries. Obviously Socrates got some of his wisdom among the East's wise men.

I have often reflected upon the new vistas that reading opened to me. I knew right there in prison that reading had changed forever the course of my life. As I see it today, the ability to read awoke inside me some long dormant craving to be mentally alive. I certainly wasn't seeking any degree, the way a college confers a status symbol upon its students. My homemade education gave me, with every additional book that I read, a little bit more sensitivity to the deafness, dumbness, and blindness that was afflicting the black race in America. Not long ago, an English writer telephoned me from London, asking questions. One was, "What's your alma mater?" I told him, "Books." You will never catch me with a free fifteen minutes in which I'm not studying something I feel might be able to help the black man.

Yesterday I spoke in London, and both ways on the plane across the Atlantic I was studying a document about how the United Nations proposes to insure the human rights of the oppressed minorities of the world. The American black man is the world's most shameful case of minority oppression. What makes the black man think of himself as only an internal United States issue is just a catch-phrase, two words, "civil rights." How is the black man going to get "civil rights" before first he wins his *human* rights? If the American black man will start thinking about his *human* rights, and then start thinking of himself as part of one of the world's great peoples, he will see he has a case for the United Nations.

I can't think of a better case! Four hundred years of black blood and sweat invested here in America, and the white man still has the black man begging for what every immigrant fresh off the ship can take for granted the minute he walks down the gangplank.

But I'm digressing. I told the Englishman that my alma mater was books, a good library. Every time I catch a plane, I have with me a book that I want to read—and that's a lot of books these days. If I weren't out here every day battling the white man, I could spend the rest of my life reading, just satisfying my curiosity—because you can hardly mention anything I'm not curious about. I don't think anybody ever got more out of going to prison than I did. In fact, prison enabled me to study far more intensively than I would have if my life had gone differently and I had attended some college. I imagine that one of the biggest troubles with colleges is there are too many distractions, too much panty-raiding, fraternities, and boola-boola and all of that. Where else but in a prison could I have attacked my ignorance by being able to study intensely sometimes as much as fifteen hours a day?

▶ Reflection Questions

1. From this reading, it is clear Malcolm X was motivated to learn, to know more about himself and his people. He describes how history has been distorted by the majority in power and how this distortion influences our perception today of issues, national and global. Can you think of instances where your perception of events has been changed by something you read or something you were taught? How did you react?

2. How did Malcolm X use education to either eliminate or enhance the pictures he had in his mind? What are your perceptions of race and human rights? How does this reading affect you?

3. Malcolm X describes his time in prison as a period that enabled him to study far more intensively than if his life had been different and he had gone to college. Do you believe his concentrated focus was better than going to college where he may have had distractions? How did his self-guided study differ from the structure he may have encountered in a college setting? How can you take ownership of your experiences and education while you are in college? Explain your answer.

Reading Two

Richard Light, a professor at Harvard, spent ten years interviewing college seniors. In this article about diversity, students discuss what it means to them. Some students talk about the importance of being a reflective student, while others discuss the positive and negative experiences of wrestling with issues of diversity. In all cases, the student-to-student interaction provided a rich forum for learning.

Making the Most of College: Students Speak Their Minds

Richard J. Light

DIVERSITY AT COLLEGE

Undergraduates differentiate between two types of learning. One is academic learning, in which academic topics and perspectives and ways of thinking are the focus of student interactions. The other is interpersonal learning. Here student interactions are built around learning about, and from, one another's different backgrounds and perspectives about life as well as school.

Responses to questions about the impact of diversity are sharp, clear, and overwhelmingly positive. One Latina student told interviewer Shu-Ling Chen:

Learning from diversity depends so much on being a reflective student. I feel like for the first eighteen years of my life there has been a veil. Coming to college has taken off that veil. It takes your ideals and forces you to look back and reconsider them. That's how this education affects my life. It affects how I treat people and how I think about my relationship with those people. I learn a lot from this real-world experience.

White students are the most positive about how fellow undergraduates from other races and ethnic groups have taught them much they would not have learned or even thought of otherwise. They are closely followed in a three-way tie by Asian-American, Latino, and African-American students. When I pressed the 120 students I interviewed on this topic for examples of something they had learned because of the diversity among undergraduates, only 9 students were unable to think of such an example. The other 111 found it pretty easy.

About 20 percent of the specific examples came from classroom discussions. Many students mention situations in which, in a small class or seminar, a person whose ethnic background is different from their own interprets an idea or a written work or a historical document in a way they did not expect. Often students recall fellow students making arguments that clearly flowed from different assumptions or different starting points, and there is a clear correlation between these unexpected arguments and different ethnic backgrounds. While not all professors seem able to capitalize on such educational moments, many do well at it, and this is when maximum learning takes place.

The other 80 percent of the examples come from events or interactions or conversations outside of classes. They may be from a discussion in a residence hall, or over a meal, or at a rehearsal for a dramatic production or a singing or dance performance.

I took a class on Jerusalem, which dealt with biblical archaeology. As a Muslim, this was my first encounter with reading the Bible and learning about the view of Christianity and Judaism. A friend of mine who was taking the class is Christian. I asked him a lot of questions about the early stories of Jesus. He also described how his brother was baptized in Bethlehem. These conversations, mostly outside of class but initiated by class discussions and the assigned readings, helped me to understand why the course material we were studying is significant.

They helped me to understand the personal and emotional connections that people attribute to these sites, which can be very different from the "objective" and sometimes sterile academic view that textbooks and even lectures can present. So they gave me a context in which to make sense of what I was learning.

A large number of students mention situations in which students from different ethnic and racial backgrounds work together to arrange and supervise an event. This may involve arranging a speakers' series on campus co-sponsored by students from different ethnic groups. It may involve arranging public debates on politically controversial topics. The very process of planning such a debate offers a great opportunity for undergraduates to engage with one another on topics about which they may disagree, while they are simultaneously working together to make a public debate work well and to make a positive contribution to the entire campus community. A Latina senior talked about such a situation:

> I think one of the reasons our Forums are so well attended and so successful is that we always try to get several co-sponsors together for each event. I am not exactly sure how that started historically, but I heard that a few years ago a couple of student groups, working entirely alone, invited speakers whose sole redeeming value seemed to be their capacity to preach anger and even hatred of other ethnic groups.
>
> Understandably, that enraged different groups. Things got pretty tense, apparently. I can hardly believe those stories, they are so offensive. If I thought that some other ethnic organization had specifically chosen to invite a speaker whose main focus is preaching contempt for other groups, I would be pretty outraged too. What are we here, ten years old?
>
> Apparently after that happened, two deans and the president held a series of meetings among student leaders to try to change the way such events are developed and organized. They sure seem to have succeeded. In my few years here, nearly every night there are speakers who arrive here with a joint invitation from blacks and whites, Latinos and Asians.
>
> We have a Latin American policy series that is co-sponsored by about six groups, two of which are Latino, yet the groups include both Democrats and Republicans as well as different ethnic groups. And of course Cultural Rhythms is pretty much everyone's favorite activity—it features snippets of many different cultures, and it seems like just about every ethnic group on campus is sponsoring it. It really is a healthy atmosphere. Maybe it is a virtuous circle.

MEANINGS OF DIVERSITY

One finding that I did not expect is the emphasis some students, especially non-white students, put on the word "diversity" as conveying disagreements within their own ethnic or racial community. These students stressed that for them these disagreements are yet another source of learning and personal maturation. They note that a great strength of studying in a college with a substantial number of members of their own racial group is that they can learn from disagreements with their fellow students.

One graduating senior, an African American, told me about a class he took. He asked that if I chose to share his example I should characterize it as his "journey of discovery."

> I will guess that most people you interview tell you how diversity on campus, for them, means interacting with students from different backgrounds. In my case, the learning from diversity came in an entirely different way. It has little to do with whites or Latinos or Asians. It happened when I became

very upset about how a fellow black student approached discussions in our sociology class.

The topic of the class was, roughly speaking, "Who gets ahead in America?" We studied works by Jencks and Riesman, and as sociology concentrators we all had pretty good backgrounds in statistics. So I was eager to read some pretty controversial texts, including The Bell Curve *and* The Shape of the River. *As you know, these two books put forth very different perspectives on the role of race in understanding who gets ahead in America. I did not expect to agree with much in* The Bell Curve, *but I was eager to read it, and fully prepared that what I read might upset me.*

Well, I was far more surprised by our class discussion than by any analyses in these two books. One day in class we were discussing illegitimate birth rates, broken down by race. The professor rather matter-of-factly presented birth rates for several ethnic groups. Those data included the fact that for blacks the illegitimate birth rate has hovered around 70 percent for the past ten years. I was stunned when one of my black classmates became visibly angry and accused the professor of not realizing how much it hurt him to hear such information presented in class. Thank goodness he did it politely and not accusingly. But he was obviously upset. And his upset got me very upset, but in the opposite direction.

This was the whole reason I had signed up to take this course. I need to grapple with unpleasant realities. I can't imagine that ignoring them helps anyone. I hope to help my community in future work. Yet it seems kind of obvious to me that the first step in improving any situation is facing the facts squarely, even when they are awkward and uncomfortable. Then, once we recognize a problem, we can try to think of ways to improve the situation. And work our butts off to do so. But my fellow black student really made it awkward—both for the professor and for me. I actually wanted to hear more details about those demographics. Not because I am happy about them, but because I absolutely need to understand them as well as I can. Illusions are definitely no help.

Well, frankly, I didn't know quite what to do. My fellow student was simply shooting the messenger. The professor seemed as taken aback as I was. Thank goodness there was a third African-American student in the class. He had the courage to speak right up, and to thank the professor for sharing this awkward but real data. This guy basically said what I was thinking, except I didn't have the courage to verbalize it out loud.

The student who had complained to the professor seemed surprised that a fellow black student would criticize him. But this other student was so diplomatic that I think he somehow succeeded in getting the complainer to take a deep breath and to pause and reconsider his views. It took some courage for that black student to criticize another black student who clearly was upset. And in the context of a mostly white class.

I think a lot of learning took place in that seminar. First, the fellow who was offended by hearing the real-world data quickly learned that two other black students not only weren't offended, they felt exactly the opposite. They wanted more discussion of this unpleasant topic, not less. I think that led him to at least reconsider his assumptions.

Second, all the other students saw for themselves that there is some diversity of perspectives among the black students here. I think that is a good thing. Especially because it is really true. And of course it isn't only true among black students—it is true among all subsets of students from all backgrounds.

I guess you could say that a truly awkward moment became a positive learning experience for most of the class. I learned something from that exchange. The two other black students learned something. And I'm pretty sure most of the white students learned something important just watching our brief exchange of comments. For me, as an African-American guy, this idea of learning from disagreement within a group is one benefit of the word "diversity" that too often gets overlooked.

BRINGING DIFFERENT PERSPECTIVES TO COLLEGE

If, on average, students who are African American, Asian American, Latino, and white all arrived on campus having read the same books, with the same distribution of political perspectives, with the same distribution of future hopes and dreams, and with the same distribution of perspectives on history—then it would be hard to argue that racial and ethnic diversity enhanced the academic component of a college education. Perhaps personal relationships across groups would be enhanced, but it would take some differences among groups in an academic sense to invigorate classroom learning.

Students from different subgroups actually do bring several such differences. Students' backgrounds often result in their exposure to different literature, different perspectives about societal institutions such as police protection and crime control, and different expectations about how the leadership of a college or university will treat them. These differences challenge everyone on campus to respond constructively. As long as students interact across groups both in classes and in situations of living, working, studying, and socializing, they can learn something different, something more, than what they would learn on a campus without those racial and ethnic differences.

"Diversity at College" reprinted by permission of the publisher from MAKING THE MOST OF COLLEGE: STUDENTS SPEAK THEIR MINDS by Richard J. Light, pp. 145–152, Cambridge, Mass.: Harvard University Press, © 2001 by Richard J. Light.

▶ Reflection Questions

1. Light suggests that in his numerous interviews with students he found some things that he did not expect. He tells us that some students, especially nonwhites, learned by having disagreements within their own ethnic or racial community. What does he mean by this?

2. Students from different subgroups arrive on campus with experiences that are different from each other's. What is the value of having a diverse group of individuals discuss a controversial topic such as affirmative action?

3. Students in Light's book were asked what current books were especially important. Students did not agree. What accounted for their different choices? Who was right? How would you have answered this question?

Reading Three

College is a time of self-discovery. Especially during the first critical year of college, students begin to examine their sense of self. It is not unusual for an individual who has struggled with his own sexual identity to "come out" during college. This next reading is a powerful letter from a son to his mother about his sexual orientation.

Coming Out Letter, from Troy to His Mother

This letter was written to my Mother in 1989 following a phone call. I admitted to her that I was Gay after she asked during a phone call. When I said yes I was, she hung up on me and we did not speak for several weeks. I then wrote this letter:

Dear Mom,

I am sorry for the pain I have caused you. It was not intentional. There are some things in life that you cannot control and this is one of them. Don't blame yourself for any part of this, you had nothing to do with it. I have known about this for years. I tried to fight it but it just grew truer.

I wanted to come to you so many times but I couldn't imagine your reaction. When you came right out and asked me I couldn't lie to you any longer. I know this is hard for you and I wish there was something I could do to help.

I'm still the same person you loved and were proud of. I am only admitting who I want to be with. It's none of the World's business what I do at home or in my own time and I really don't think that I deserve a title for being myself and the way I am. I really wish you could understand Mom. I know that your biggest concern is what could happen, but I think you know that I am a smart person and I wouldn't do something to mess up my life.

I am taking very good care of myself and I take a lot of precautions. Please try to understand—not accept—but just try to understand. It's really going to hurt me if you are not here to share my graduation with me. It's kind of my chance to show you that I can still be successful and you can still be proud of me regardless of my personal life. When I mentioned you staying in a Hotel room—it wasn't to hide anything. I only suggested it because our place is small—I have nothing to hide. If you want to stay with me there would be no problem with that. If you wanted to stay in a Hotel, I would stay with you if you wanted. If you don't want to come to my graduation—I will understand. Please let me know.

Love Always,
Your Son
Troy

Mother never made it to graduation. After a period of consulting with her Pastor and a Therapist, my Mother began to understand and come around. We are now closer than ever and we share every aspect of our lives, even though we live over 3,000 miles from each other.

Reprinted by permission.

▶ Reflection Questions

1. In his letter to his mother, Troy says that "her biggest concern" is what could happen to him. Why would this be her biggest concern?

2. How may Troy's perception of his mother affect how he handled the situation? How did concealing his sexuality affect their relationship? Are there circumstances in your life where the fear of someone's reaction led you to hide things? How could you have handled the situation differently?

3. Have you ever thought about how quickly life can change? What do you think led Troy to write his letter at this time? What do you think led his mother to reconcile with him when she did? Think about the victims of 9/11 and how when they left for work that fateful morning, they never knew or dreamed of what was to come. Have you ever experienced adversity in your life that made you appreciate people and things differently than you had before this adversity? Do you know of anyone who did?

⬆ Writing Assignment

audience: Your college's Board of Trustees

purpose: To support the expansion of hiring faculty and staff with diverse backgrounds (race, ethnicity, sexual orientation, or disability)

length: Minimum of two typed pages, double-spaced

Write a letter to the Board of Trustees, including information from the Malcolm X article indicating that we have a moral responsibly to provide role models for the diverse college population that is becoming ever more ethnically diverse. Include how we may tend to stereotype individuals (our pictures of people) who cannot read or write as stupid and interchange the words *illiterate* and *stupid,* when in fact they are not the same. Discuss the need to include how we tend to stereotype those with a different sexual orientation as well. Conclude your letter by discussing the benefits of a diverse faculty in an institution of higher education.

Journal Entries: DISCOVERY AND INTENTION STATEMENTS

In the beginning of this chapter we discussed the fact that we all have preconceived notions about people, both positive and negative, based on our own experiences. Think back to a time when you thought something about an individual or group of individuals and later you discovered something different about them. Go back to the Kurfiss reading on critical thinking in Chapter One. Do you think this experience enabled you to move from dualistic thinking to a different level of critical thinking? The Power Process in this chapter states, "One way to deal with pictures is to be aware of them. Open up your mental photo album and notice how the pictures there influence your thoughts, feelings, and actions." What are some of your pictures? Can you change how they influence your behavior?

Mastering Vocabulary

List five words that were new to you (more or less if necessary). For each, include which reading you found the word in, the definition, and where you got the definition from, as well as a time or place you might use the word again.

1. _____

_____

2. _____

_____

3. _____

_____

4. _____

_____

5. _____

_____

 ## Additional Activities

1. Look at the list of clubs on your campus. You can find the list of these by going to your student activity center. If you don't have a center on campus, look in your college student handbook or your college website. Are you able to tell which clubs are most recent? If you can't find this out, can you guess which five may be the most recent? Why did you choose these? Are the groups visible? Why or why not?

2. Identify at least three sentences in the readings of this chapter that were particularly powerful. Why did you choose these? Compare your choices with those of someone in your class. Did you find any similar sentences or themes?

3. Take a look at your college mission statement. How are individuals from all groups supported and given a voice? Look at mission statements from other institutions across the country. What are some of the differences in how specific groups are treated?

Online Study Center **Improve Your Grade**
Visit the Online Study Center for resources and exercises to accompany this text
http://college.hmco.com/pic/msreader1e

CHAPTER FIVE

I Create It All

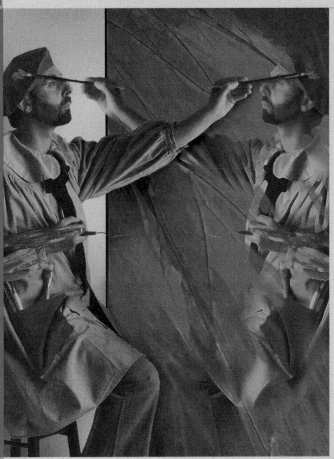

117

In this chapter we see how individuals create something positive out of negative circumstances. "When life gives you lemons, make lemonade." This concept has been proven to help cancer patients (those with an optimistic attitude have been known to physically do better). Also, those who dwell on the negative often find themselves angry and paralyzed, unable to move on. It is important to recognize that we are the masters of our destiny. We choose whether we want to study or to pay attention in class. Often we hear students say, "Professor X gave me a D." What they mean is "I earned a D in Professor X's class." We have the choice of how we behave and what we think. We create it all.

The Power Process: I Create It All

This is a powerful tool in times of trouble. In a crisis, "I create it all" can lead the way to solutions. "I create it all" means treating experiences, events, and circumstances in your life as if you created them.

For example, when your dog tracks fresh tar on the white carpet, when your political science teacher is a crushing bore, when your spouse dents the car, when your test on Latin American literature focuses on an author you've never read—it's time for a Power Process. Tell yourself, "I created it all."

"Baloney!" you shout. "I didn't let the dog in, that teacher really is a bore, I wasn't even in the car, and nobody told me to read Gabriel García Márquez. I didn't create these disasters."

Good points. Obviously, "I create it all" is one of the most unusual and bizarre suggestions in this book. It certainly is not an idea that is easily believed. In fact, believing it can get you into trouble. "I create it all" is strictly a practical idea. Use it when it works. Don't when it doesn't.

Keeping that caution in mind, consider how powerful this Power Process can be. It is really about the difference between two distinct positions in life: being a victim or being self-responsible. A victim of circumstances is controlled by outside forces. We've all felt like victims at one time or another. When tar-footed dogs tromped on the white carpets of our lives, we felt helpless. In contrast, we can take responsibility. *Responsibility* is the important word. It does not mean "blame."—Far from it. Responsibility is "response-ability"—the ability to choose a response.

Practicing resignation

By not taking responsibility, we are acknowledging that the power to determine what happens in our lives is beyond our grasp. When we feel as if we don't have control over our lives, we feel resigned. The opposite of practicing "I create it all" is practicing resignation.

There is a phenomenon called *learned resignation.* An interesting experiment with dogs demonstrates how learned resignation works. A dog is put in a caged pen with a metal floor that can be electrified. When the cage door is left open and the dog is given a mild shock, she runs out of the cage to escape the discomfort. Then the dog is put back into the cage, the door is shut and locked, and a mild shock is given again. The dog runs around, looking for an escape. When she doesn't find one, she just lies down, sits, or stands there, and quits trying to find a way out. She has no control over her circumstances and is learning to be resigned.

Now, here comes the interesting part. After the dog has consistently stopped trying to escape the shock, the door is opened and the dog is led in and out several times. Then the dog is left in the cage, the door is left open, and the shock is administered once again. Amazingly, the dog doesn't even try to escape, even though the open door is right there in front of her. Instead, the dog continues to endure the shock. She has learned to be resigned.

A variety of this phenomenon can occur in human beings as well. When we consistently give control of our lives over to other people and to circumstances, we run the risk of learning to give up. We might develop the habit of being resigned, even though there is abundant opportunity all around us.

Applying this process

Many students approach grades from the position of being victims. When a student who sees the world this way gets an F, she reacts something like this:

"Oh, no!" (Slaps forehead)

"Rats!" (Slaps forehead again) (Students who get lots of F's often have flat foreheads.)

"Another F! That teacher couldn't teach her way out of a wet paper bag. She can't teach English for anything. And that textbook—what a bore! How could I read it with a houseful of kids making noise all the time? And then friends came over and wanted to party, and . . ."

The problem with this viewpoint is that in looking for excuses, the student is robbing herself of the power to get any grade other than an F. She's giving all of her power to a bad teacher, a boring textbook, noisy children, and friends.

There is another way, called *taking responsibility.* You can recognize that you choose your grades by choosing your actions. Then you are the source, rather than the result, of the grades you get. The student who got an F could react like this:

"Another F! Oh, shoot! Well, hm . . . how did I choose this F? What did I do to create it?"

Now, that's power. By asking "How did I contribute to this outcome?" you give yourself a measure of control. You are no longer the victim. This student might continue by saying, "Well, let's see. I didn't review my notes after class. That might have done it." Or "I studied in the same room with my children while they watched TV. Then I went out with my friends the night before the test. Well, that probably helped me fulfill some of the requirements for getting an F."

The point is this: When the F is the result of your kids, your friends, the book, or the teacher, you probably can't do anything about it. However, if you *chose* the F, you can choose a different grade next time. You are in charge.

Choosing our thoughts

There are times when we don't create it all. We do not create earthquakes, floods, avalanches, or monsoons. Yet if we look closely, we discover that we *do* create a larger part of our circumstances than most of us are willing to admit.

For example, we can choose our thoughts. And thoughts can control our perceptions by screening information from our senses. We can never be aware of every single thing in our environment. If we could, we'd go crazy from sensory overload. Instead, our brains filter out most sensory inputs. This filtering colors the way we think about the world.

Choosing our behaviors

Moment by moment we make choices about what we will do and where we will go. The results of these choices are where we are in life. A whole school of psychology called *control theory* is based on this idea, and the psychiatrist William Glasser has written extensively about it.[1]

All of those choices help create our current circumstances—even those circumstances that are not "our fault." After a car accident, we tell ourselves, "It just happened. That car came out of nowhere and hit me." We forget that driving 5 miles per hour slower and paying closer attention might have allowed us to miss the driver who was "to blame."

Some cautions

The presence of blame is a warning that this Power Process is being misused. "I create it all" is not about blaming yourself or others.

---

[1] William Glasser, *Take Effective Control of Your Life* (New York: Harper & Row, 1984).

Feeling guilty is another warning signal. Guilt actually involves the same dynamic as blame. If you are feeling guilty, you have just shifted the blame from another person to yourself.

Another caution is that this Power Process is not a religion. Saying that you "create it all" does not mean that you have divine powers. It is simply a way to expand the choices you already have. This Power Process is easy to deny. Tell your friends about it, and they're likely to say, "What about world hunger? I didn't cause that. What about people who get cancer? Did they create that?"

These are good arguments—and they miss the point. Victims of rape, abuse, incest, and other forms of violence can still use "I create it all" to choose their response to the people and events that violated them.

Some people approach world hunger, imprisonment, and even cancer with this attitude: "Pretend for a moment that I am responsible for this. What will I do about it?" These people see problems in a new way, and they discover choices that other people miss.

"I create it all" is not always about disaster. It also works when life is going great. We often give credit to others for our good fortune when it's actually time to pat ourselves on the back. By choosing our behavior and thoughts, we can create A's, interesting classes, enjoyable relationships, material wealth, and ways to contribute to a better world.

Readings

The readings in this chapter are about individuals who took adversity and turned it into something positive. The readings give examples of individual's attitudes and how their choice of how to respond dictated their outcomes. They chose not to give up, but rather found the strength within themselves to change the outcome of what might have been. Before you read the selections here, think about negative experiences you have had. For example, when you failed a test or scored lower then you should have, did you give up or simply work harder? Think also about the flow state and the ideas behind working hard at something and achieving it.

Reading One

In this reading Sam fails an important medical exam and struggles with which lesson he is supposed to learn from failure. At first he struggles with the fact that he failed, but he examines his life and makes a choice. He decides to figure out a way to forge on. At the end of this reading, Sam says, "When you've failed repeatedly and think you're done, that last try—the one that requires every ounce of will and strength you have—is often the one to pull you through."

The Pact: Three Young Men Make a Promise and Fulfill a Dream

Drs. Sampson Davis, George Jenkins, and Rameck Hunt

SAM ON PERSEVERANCE

Medical school was one of the roughest periods of my life. Something unexpected was always threatening to knock me out of the game: family distractions, the results of my first state board exam, the outcome of my initial search for a residency. But through determination, discipline, and dedication, I was able to persevere.

I call them my three D's, and I believe that they are the perfect formula for survival, no matter what you are going through.

Determination is simply fixing your mind on a desired outcome, and I believe it is the first step to a successful end in practically any situation. When I made the pact with George and Rameck at the age of seventeen, I was desperate to change my life. Going to college and medical school with my friends seemed the best way to make that happen.

But, of course, I had no idea of the challenges awaiting me, and many times over the years I felt like giving up. Trust me, even if you're the most dedicated person, you can get weary when setbacks halt or interfere with your progress. But determination means nothing without the discipline to go through the steps necessary to reach your goal—whether you're trying to lose weight or finish college—and the dedication to stick with it.

When I failed the state board exam, the light in the tunnel disappeared. But I just kept crawling toward my goal. I sought counseling when I needed it, and I found at least one person with whom I could share the range of emotions I was experiencing. If you're going through a difficult time and can't see your way out alone, you should consider asking for help. I know how difficult that is for most guys. We're raised to believe that it's a sign of weakness even to display emotions, let alone ask for help. But reaching out to counselors I had come to trust over the years and talking to my roommate Camille helped me unload some of the weight I was carrying. Only then was I able to focus clearly on what I needed to do to change my circumstances.

I'm grateful that I took kung fu lessons as a kid, because the discipline I learned back then really helped me to stay consistent once I started meditating, working out, and studying every single day. It wasn't easy, but those were the steps required to get where I wanted to be. Concentrating on getting through each day kept me from feeling overwhelmed. And reflection helped me to see that I had overcome tremendous barriers. In the beginning, during a trying adolescence, I'd felt like I was a good kid caught up in a bad situation and truly had to work diligently to overcome obstacles. You can't choose the circumstances that you're born in. However, you can use your insight and hunger to push forward. Life's challenges helped me to maintain my focus and remain humble.

Family matters—my brother's injury, my sister's diagnosis, my mother's financial struggles back home—sometimes competed for my full attention. There is no one-size-fits-all way to handle family issues. Everbody's family and circumstances are different. But I realized that to remain focused on my goal I couldn't focus so much on my family, especially when the energy I expended worrying about them didn't change a thing.

Another important ingredient of perseverance is surrounding yourself with friends who support your endeavor. I can't tell you how much it helped me to have George and Rameck in my life to help me reach my goal. Even though things were awkward between us for a while after I failed the state boards, just knowing they were there and that they expected me to succeed motivated me.

I found motivation wherever I could. One of my college professors once told me that I didn't have what it takes to be a doctor, and I even used that to motivate me. I love being the underdog. I love it when someone expects me to fail. That, like nothing else, can ignite my three D's.

And when success comes, I'm the one who's not surprised.

My motto is simply: no one can tell me that I can't succeed. I've come to believe that every goal in life is obtainable and that the only limitations are the ones you set for yourself. For some, the road to success is merely based on taking advantage of opportunities provided to them. For others, the road is much more difficult because they have to create opportunities for themselves. When you have to find a way where there seems to be none, as I sometimes had to do, success in the end is even sweeter.

I had to keep getting up when life knocked me down. There is nothing sweeter than stealing victory from the jaws of defeat. The closest I ever came to giving up was when I didn't match at any of the hospitals I had listed. But again, something on the inside wouldn't let me quit. And my last try, on the Internet, brought amazing results.

That's how life is sometimes. When you've failed repeatedly and think you're done, that last try—the one that requires every ounce of will and strength you have—is often the one to pull you through.

"Sam on Perseverance", from THE PACT by Sampson Davis, George Jenkins and Rameck Hunt, with Liza Frazier Page, © 2002 by Three Doctors LLC. Used by permission of Riverhead Books, an imprint of Penguin Group (USA) Inc.

▶ Reflection Questions

1. When Sam failed, he took it on himself to find ways to help himself get through it. What lessons can you learn from how Sam handled his obstacles? How could you use what he did to persevere through your own challenges?

2. Sam says that in order to finish, he had to focus on his goals. At times this meant he couldn't focus on other things in his life, such as his family. Why was this

sacrifice necessary? Should he deserve any blame for having to focus less on those he cares about? Explain what his reasons may have been. Do you agree that this was his only option?

3. Was there ever a time that you failed something and just gave up? Look back at that experience. Do you think, if you had the chance to do it over, you would do things differently? How would you approach that situation now?

Reading Two

This reading chronicles the stories of two individuals over eighty who survived the devastation of Hurricane Katrina. These elderly people bounced back "from extraordinary adversity more quickly than young people." A number of studies are summarized that report the ability of older individuals to withstand adversity. For example, according to the psychologist Robert E. Reichlin, "older adults do bounce back well because they have seen a lot and they have lived though a lot. Psychologically, they can take a lot more in stride than young people." Read on to see what we can learn from the "experienced" generation.

With Age Comes Resilience, Storm's Aftermath Proves

Blaine Harden

Winsboro, La.—As captured by searing images on television, Hurricane Katrina seemed to single out the elderly for particular punishment—people such as 86-year-old Pearline Chambers.

She spent two days alone in her one-story house in the submerged Ninth Ward of New Orleans, with hurricane floodwater up to her neck. She lost her false teeth, her wig and her cats.

"I just waded around and waded around, trying to get up in my attic," said Chambers, a widow. "I kept climbing and slipping and falling in that water."

After she was rescued—two men floating by on a board heard her screams—she spent two more semiconscious days in the city, struggling to walk, severely dehydrated and hungry. As she recalled, "I didn't know where I was. I laid somewhere, I'm not sure where, and people walked around me."

Two weeks after the storm, though, Chambers feels fine. Living now with her sister's family in this small town in northern Louisiana, she said she has nobody but "my stubborn self" to blame for ignoring hurricane warnings and refusing to flee New Orleans in her blue Chevrolet Corsica.

Her rapid recovery and emotional balance do not surprise experts who study the elderly. A large and growing body of research shows that healthy elderly people are often able to bounce back from extraordinary adversity more quickly than younger people.

"Study after study has shown that for older people, negative emotions have less of an effect than with young people—and for the elderly those effects dissipate faster," said Gene D. Cohen, a geriatric psychiatrist at George Washington University who for 20 years directed research on aging at the National Institutes of Health.

Research on the resilience of the elderly squares with the impressions of half a dozen psychiatrists, psychologists and social workers who in the past two weeks have treated several hundred elderly people displaced by Hurricane Katrina. They agreed that when elderly evacuees were given water, food, clothes and a secure place to sleep, they tended to be less anxious and had higher morale than younger adults. This was especially true, they said, if elderly people were reunited with family.

"You don't live to 80 without being tough," said Robert E. Reichlin, a clinical psychologist and specialist on early onset Alzheimer's disease at Baylor College of Medicine in Houston. He treated elderly evacuees at the Astrodome. "Older adults do bounce back well because they have seen a lot and they have lived through a lot. Psychologically, they can take a lot more in stride than young people."

There is, however, an important medical caveat to the toughness of the elderly, Reichlin said.

"Physically, they are much less resilient than the young," he said. "When they are maxed out by an event like Hurricane Katrina—dehydrated, malnourished and exhausted—they often show signs of something that looks like dementia, which is sometimes called 'acute confusion syndrome.'" That confusion—the glazed and lost look that many Americans saw in the televised images of elderly evacuees from New Orleans—usually goes away in a day or two with rest and nutrition, Reichlin said, assuming they do not have a preexisting medical problem, such as Alzheimer's.

When 24 elderly and middle-age evacuees arrived by van at the psychiatric center of the American Legion Hospital in Rayne, La., one of the elderly people was immediately diagnosed with Alzheimer's, according Charles E. Bramlet Jr., a psychiatrist who runs the center.

"In 24 hours, we were surprised to see that it cleared up," Bramlet said. "We saw a much better outcome with the elderly patients than I thought we would when they were taken out of that van. We have released most of the elderly to their families, while many of the younger adults are still in the hospital."

According to Cohen, the psychiatrist at George Washington University, recent CT-scan research on a structure of the inner brain called the amygdala, which is believed to process emotions, suggests that older people tend to filter out painful experiences more than young people.

"Most people would intuitively think that older people would not be able to handle adversity," Cohen said. "But they have survived the death of a significant other, loss of prestigious work, loss of health. They are very high on the scale of creatively adapting to adversity."

Harold Gerkin, 82, knows adversity as only hurricanes can dish it out. Counting Katrina, he has lived through five major hurricanes while refusing to leave his home in Pilot Town, La., the southernmost human habitation in the swampy archipelago that juts south of New Orleans.

"I survived Camille in '69, with 200-mile [per hour] winds, so I figured I could handle this one," Gerkin said.

Katrina, though, demolished his house under 25-foot waves. When he saw water rising on the road near that house, he and his son, Charles, 47, fled to a nearby two-story structure protected by hurricane-storm sheathing.

Katrina, though, tore much of that structure apart.

"The damn building kept shaking so much, pilings were rammed through the floor and waves broke over the balcony on the second floor," Harold said. "At dawn, with the wind blowing like it blew with Camille, we saw two houses and a big barge float past us. If that barge would a hit us, we were gone."

After Katrina passed, the Gerkins were rescued by a Coast Guard helicopter and are now living as evacuees in a hotel in Baton Rouge. Friends say that Charles seems numb since the storm and has had a hard time calming down.

But Harold, his father, said he does not have nightmares about the storm and he does not regret having tried to weather it.

"To tell you the truth, I never even thought about that stuff," he said.

"With Age Comes Resilience, Storm's Aftermath Proves", by Blaine Harden, washingtonpost. com, September 14, 2005. © 2005, *The Washington Post,* reprinted with permission.

▶ Reflection Questions

1. Pearline Chambers says she has nobody but "my stubborn self" to blame for ignoring warnings about the hurricane. Harold Gerkin doesn't have nightmares about his ordeal or any regrets about weathering the storm. He never "thought about that stuff [being killed]." What can we learn from these two individuals? Describe a scenario where a college student might make use of what you learned from Pearline and Harold.

2. What makes older individuals able to filter out painful experiences? When are there times when we should filter out painful experiences and when should we deal with them directly? Give examples.

3. Can a positive attitude impact student success? Explain your answer. (You may want to refer back to the discussion of emotional intelligence in Chapter Two.)

Reading Three

This reading was written by Bill Moon as part of his reflection on the heroes of 9/11 and the thoughts expressed by his students at Texas A&M University–Commerce. He describes heroes as not only firefighters, police officers, journalists, and rescue personnel but also the nameless and faceless everyday heroes.

September 11, 2001: Answering the Call

Bill Moon

When the Pentagon was seriously damaged and the twin towers of the World Trade Center were physically leveled by the terrorist attack on September 11, 2001, I was emotionally leveled myself. My fellow students and I had believed that the terrorism that occurs on a daily basis in many places could not happen here, and we were outraged to hear that terrorists had flown fuel-filled passenger planes into these buildings. As Americans, we are not accustomed to being on the defensive. We pick and choose our battles, deciding when and where we will have a confrontation. But we didn't have that option on that fateful Tuesday.

In spite of the initial shock, or perhaps because of it, this tragic event has become an enormous opportunity for the renewal of heroism, patriotism, and unity in our nation: Indeed, the events surrounding those first shocking moments have helped us all see not only the heroic actions of our fellow citizens but also the heroic potential within ourselves. In his book *The Hero with a Thousand Faces*, Joseph Campbell describes the pattern of heroic action—a pattern that begins with a call to action, a "summons [that] may be to live . . . or to die," but one that "rings up the curtain, always, on a mystery of transfiguration—a rite, or moment, of spiritual passage, which, when complete, amounts to a dying and a rebirth." The attacks on America were indeed a call to action on the part of our nation. Those involved—from the firefighters to the police officers to the passengers on Flight 93—had a choice between accepting or refusing the call. An amazing number of individuals answered the call, and the reactions of these many heroic individuals are an inspiration to all of us as we continue to attempt to understand exactly what occurred and why.

Many of the heroes of September 11 are nameless faces on the pages of weekly news magazines and local newspapers: people who donated blood, money, or water for the victims and workers; the doctors and nurses who worked around the clock to provide medical attention for those who needed it most; and the crews who dug for weeks to clear away the smoldering razor-sharp debris and recover the remains of the dead. The very wise author Anonymous once said, "Character is made up of small duties faithfully performed—of self-denials, of self-sacrifices, of kindly acts of love and duty." On that terrible day the most memorable heroic responses came from two particular groups who indeed sacrificed themselves for love and duty—the firefighters and rescue personnel of the cities involved and the passengers on United Airlines Flight 93.

On that terrible day, firefighters and rescue personnel rushed to the scenes at the Pentagon and the World Trade Center, but it was at the WTC where the most lives—about 3,000—were lost. Two of the over 300 firefighters who lost their lives at what has come to be known as "Ground Zero" were Ray Downey and the Rev. Mychal Judge. The chief of special operations in New York City,

63-year-old Downey was in the first tower trying to save those still trapped inside when the second tower collapsed and he disappeared. Downey had a history of being a hero: in 1993 he answered the call at the first World Trade Center bombing; in 1995 he was in Oklahoma City answering the call there; and in 1996 he had responded to the TWA Flight 800 explosion. He stepped into the crumpled Trade Center on September 11 knowing full well what potential danger lay ahead, but he also knew that there were people in the building who needed to be rescued. He answered the call. The Rev. Mychal Judge also responded to the call to heroism on September 11. When a fellow Franciscan monk told him about the attack, he immediately rushed to where he could be of most service. Eyewitnesses say that he was administering last rites and comforting the wounded when he was killed by falling rubble. He, too, answered the call.

Another group of individuals called into action on September 11 were the passengers on United Airlines Flight 93, who apparently rushed hijackers who had also taken over their plane with intentions to use it as another missile. We don't know—and may never know—exactly what went on during those few minutes before the plane slammed into a rural Pennsylvania field. However, we can be fairly sure that a few courageous passengers saved the lives of hundreds of potential terrorist targets—many of whom may have been government officials—and perhaps preserved an American landmark such as the White House. In phone calls to relatives, Jeremy Glick, Tom Burnett, and Mark Bingham all revealed their plans to rush the hijackers, and Todd Beamer was heard on an onboard phone call giving the signal, "Let's roll." These men also answered the call, sacrificing their lives in the process.

After accepting the call to service, the potential hero undergoes a rigorous challenge. The firefighters literally had to go through what Campbell describes as "dark and devious ways" as they climbed through the ruins of the Pentagon and the World Trade Center. Because they had more time to think about their decision, the passengers of Flight 93 must have traveled the hero path that Campbell says is "fundamentally inward rather than outward." But all of these heroes left their comfort zones, giving their lives unselfishly, unswervingly. They pressed on into dark, frightening places. Some crawled through black, billowing smoke and falling debris into tight airless passages to pull out victims; others grappled both physically and psychologically with crazed and determined terrorists, wrestling them and therefore the plane itself to the ground. All faced death.

In the traditional hero tale, the successful adventurer returns to his or her society with a "boon" of some kind—either physical treasure or spiritual knowledge. The stories of many of the heroes of September 11 do not have happy endings for the individuals involved, for in giving of themselves, many gave the ultimate sacrifice of their lives. However, the gift they bestowed on society is far greater than anything they could have lived for. Drawing on their own inner resources, these heroes revived the heroic potential in all of us and made it available for "the transfiguration of the world." Even though they died in the process, these heroes live on in our memories, in the lives of those they saved, and in the renewed sense of patriotism our nation has experienced.

Indeed, those individuals who answered the call on September 11 have renewed our belief in heroism itself. Campbell believes that the hero of the fairy tale "prevails over his personal oppressors" whereas the hero of myth "brings back from his adventure the means for the regeneration of his society as a whole." As countless numbers of quiet heroes continue to sift through the ashes of the World Trade Center and as Americans throughout the country give of their blood, tears, and prayers, we need both kinds of heroes. Our country must prevail over our attackers, and our citizens must have the courage, diligence, and faith to continue the process of regeneration our society has already begun.

▶ Reflection Questions

1. Do you remember where you were on 9/11? What was your first reaction? What were your thoughts concerning people living in the New York or Washington areas, whether you had specific friends and family there or not?

2. What can we learn from the heroes in this essay? How does this change your thoughts about who heroes are and what they do? Does this affect your thoughts on how you could be a hero?

3. In the Power Process "I create it all," a caution is suggested: "'I create it all' is not about blaming yourself or others." How do you think the heroes described in this reading approached feelings of guilt? What may their guilt have been about? Are they justified in these feelings?

◆ Writing Assignment

audience: A friend or family member who is struggling with some problem (illness, financial burden, divorce, etc.) in life

purpose: To help her or him see the value of a positive attitude

length: Minimum of three typed pages, double-spaced

Write a letter to a friend or family member who is struggling with some problem in life; include excerpts from the three readings. Share how Sam would not give up and how the elderly who seem most vulnerable are often most resilient. Convince your reader that she, or he, must take control of the situation whatever it may be and not let the situation control her. Suggest some strategies that she can use and include some information that you have found (either on the Web or from some organization) related to the problem that your friend or relative is facing.

Include in this letter specific examples of what you learned from the three readings. Can you think of a situation that you have experienced similar to that of any of these individuals? Share this in your letter.

If you are fortunate enough to know no one who has a problem, think of a problem that someone might face and develop your paper the same way.

 ## Journal Entries: DISCOVERY AND INTENTION STATEMENTS

For this journal entry, think about a person you know or an individual from history who against all odds chose to live a life of purpose. For example, MADD (Mother's Against Drunk Drivers) was started by a group of mothers who chose to take the horror of losing their children and channel it into an organization that can help others.

According to the Power Process "I create it all," what is meant by choosing your own thoughts or choosing your behaviors? How does this Power Process relate to these readings? Write one or two sentences about what you have learned and what you intend to do as a result of the readings, what you will do to make it work, and what you risk if you don't do what you intend to do.

Mastering Vocabulary

List five words that were new to you (more or less if necessary). For each, include which reading you found the word in, the definition, and where you got the definition from, as well as a time or place you might use the word again.

1.

2.

3.

4.

5.

 ## Additional Activities

1. How might the way we approach everyday kinds of stress be helpful or hinder our success in college? Have you ever been under stress and then gotten sick? What kind of stress was it? Was there anything you could do about it? Share with other class members what your particular situation was and what you did about it.

2. Pair up with someone in class and share with them one thing that you want to work on. For example, you might want to quit smoking or stop biting your nails. Visualize yourself doing the behavior you want to have happen and then describe to your classmate what it would feel like if you were able to overcome the behavior you want to work on. Talk about the obstacles you might encounter and brainstorm ways you might get support. Consider being email buddies for the week to support each other as you try to change the behavior.

3. Research the mind-body connection and the actual physiological changes that occur in individuals with positive attitudes. Develop a PowerPoint presentation on what you have discovered.

Online Study Center   **Improve Your Grade**
Visit the Online Study Center for resources and exercises to accompany this text
http://college.hmco.com/pic/msreader1e

CHAPTER SIX

Detach

Why is it that some people seem to handle many stressful events with ease? How is it that others seem to juggle work, school, and family commitments and are able to smile and appear composed? Recent evidence suggests that the most successful college students are those who are in touch with their emotions. They know themselves, they know what stresses them, and they know what makes them angry or sad. They have figured out ways to handle their emotions in appropriate ways. In fact, in a study by Parker, et al[1], it was found that students with strong emotional intelligence (EI) had higher GPA's than students who did not have strong EI. This study suggests that strong social and emotional competence helps students make the transition into college. Specifically, they found that handling stress and being flexible were two important traits connected to college success. Successful college students can let go of things and not obsess. They control their emotions; they don't let their emotions control them.

The Power Process: Detach

This Power Process helps you release the powerful, natural student within you. It is especially useful whenever negative emotions are getting in the way of your education.

Attachments are addictions. When we are attached to something, we think we cannot live without it, just as a drug addict feels he cannot live without drugs. We believe our well-being depends on maintaining our attachments.

We can be attached to just about anything—expectations, ideas, objects, self-perceptions, people, results, rewards. The list is endless.

One person, for example, might be so attached to his car that he takes an accident as a personal attack. Pity the poor unfortunate who backs into this person's car. He might as well back into the owner himself.

Another person might be attached to his job. His identity and sense of well-being depend on it. He could become suicidally depressed if he gets fired.

We can be addicted to our emotions as well as to our thoughts. We can identify with our anger so strongly that we are unwilling to let it go. We can also be addicted to our pessimism and reluctant to give it up. Rather than perceive these emotions as liabilities, we can see them as indications that it's time to practice detachment.

Most of us are addicted, to some extent, to our identities. We are Americans, veterans, high achievers, bowlers, loyal friends, business owners, humanitarians, devoted parents, dancers, hockey fans, or bird watchers. If we are attached to these roles, they can dictate who we think we are.

---

[1] Parker, J.D.A., Duffy, Jon., M., Wood, Laura M., Bond, Barbara J., Hogan, Marjorie J., Academic Achievement and Emotional Intelligence. *Journal of the First-Year Experience.* 2005. Vol. 17, No. 1.

When these identities are threatened, we might fight for them as if we were defending our lives. The more addicted we are to an identity, the harder we fight to keep it.

Ways to recognize an attachment

When we are attached and things don't go our way, we might feel irritated, angry, jealous, confused, fatigued, bored, frightened, or resentful.

Suppose you are attached to getting an A on your physics test. You feel as though your success in life depends on getting an A. It's not just that you want an A. You *need* an A. During the exam, the thought "I must get an A" is in the back of your mind as you begin to work a problem. And the problem is difficult. The first time you read it, you have no idea how to solve it. The second time around, you aren't even sure what it's asking. The more you struggle to understand it, the more confused you get. To top it all off, this problem is worth 40 percent of your score.

As the clock ticks away, you work harder, getting more stuck, while that voice in your head gets louder: "I must get an A. I MUST get an A. I MUST GET AN A!"

At this point, your hands begin to sweat and shake. Your heart is pounding. You feel nauseated. You can't concentrate. You flail about for the answer as if you were drowning. You look up at the clock, sickened by the inexorable sweep of the second hand. You are doomed.

Now is a time to detach.

Ways to use this process

Detachment can be challenging. In times of stress, it might seem like the most difficult thing in the world to do. You can practice a variety of strategies to help you move toward detachment.

Practice observer consciousness. This is the quiet state above and beyond your usual thoughts, the place where you can be aware of being aware. It's a tranquil spot, apart from your emotions. From here, you can observe yourself objectively, as if you were someone else. Pay attention to your emotions and physical sensations. If you are confused and feeling stuck, tell yourself "Here I am, confused and stuck." If your palms are sweaty and your stomach is one big knot, admit it.

Practice perspective. Put current circumstances into a broader perspective. View personal issues within the larger context of your community, your nation, or your planet. You will likely see them from a different point of view. Imagine the impact your present problems will have 20 or even 100 years from now.

Take a moment to consider the worst that could happen. During that physics exam, notice your attachment to getting an A. Realize that even flunking the test will not ruin your life. Seeing this helps you put the test in perspective.

Practice breathing. Calm your mind and body with breathing or relaxation techniques.

Note: It might be easier to practice these techniques when you're not feeling strong emotions. Notice your thoughts, behaviors, and feelings during neutral activities such as watching television or taking a walk.

Practice detaching. The key is to let go of automatic emotional reactions when you don't get what you want.

Rewrite the equation

To further understand this notion of detaching, we can borrow an idea from mathematics. An equation is a set of symbols joined by an equal sign ($=$) that forms a true statement. Examples are $2 + 2 = 4$ and $a + b = c$.

Equations also work with words. In fact, our self-image can be thought of as a collection of equations. For example, the thought "I am capable" can be written as the equation "I $=$ capable." "My happiness depends on my car" can be written as "happiness $=$ car." The statement "My well-being depends on my job" becomes "well-being $=$ job." Each equation is a tip-off to an attachment. When we're upset, a closer look often reveals that one of our attachments is threatened. The person who believes that his happiness is equal to his current job will probably be devastated if his company downsizes and he's laid off.

Once we discover a hidden equation, we can rewrite it. In the process, we can watch our upsets disappear. The person who gets laid off can change his equation to "my happiness $=$ my happiness." In other words, his happiness does not have to depend on any particular job.

People can rewrite equations under the most extreme circumstances. A man dying from lung cancer spent his last days celebrating his long life. One day his son asked him how he was feeling.

"Oh, I'm great," said the man with cancer. "Your mom and I have been having a wonderful time just rejoicing in the life that we have had together."

"Oh, I'm glad you're doing well," said the man's son. "The prednisone you have been taking must have kicked in again and helped your breathing."

"Well, not exactly. Actually, my body is in terrible shape, and my breathing has been a struggle these last few days. I guess what I'm saying is that my body is not working well at all, but I'm still great."

The dying man rewrote the equation "I $=$ my body." He knew that he had a body and that he was more than his body. This man lived this Power Process and gave his son—the author of this book—an unforgettable lesson about detachment.

Some cautions

Giving up an addiction to being an A student does not mean giving up being an A student. And giving up an addiction to a job doesn't mean getting rid of the job. It means not investing your entire well-being in the grade or the job. Keep your desires and goals alive and healthy while detaching from the compulsion to reach them.

Notice also that detachment is different from denial. Denial implies running away from whatever you find unpleasant. In contrast, detachment includes accepting your emotions and knowing the details of them—down to every last thought and physical sensation involved. It's OK to be angry or sad. Once you accept and fully experience your emotions, you can more easily move beyond them.

Being detached is not the same as being apathetic. We can be 100 percent detached and 100 percent involved at the same time. In fact, our commitment toward achieving a particular result is usually enhanced by being detached from it.

Detach and succeed

When we are detached, we perform better. When we think everything is at stake, the results might suffer. Without anxiety and the need to get an A on the physics test, we are more likely to recognize the problem and remember the solution.

This Power Process is useful when you notice that attachments are keeping you from accomplishing your goals. Behind your attachments is a master student. By detaching, you release that master student. Detach.

Readings

Have you been unable to let go of something? Have you ever thought "I just have to get an A on this test" or "If I don't get a new DVD player, I just won't be happy"? Sometimes we get caught up in events or things and can't put them in the proper perspective. Assuming you did your best preparing for the test, if you go into the test stressing about getting an A, chances are you become preoccupied with getting the A and can't give the test your full attention. What if you just think and think about the DVD player, to the point that you use money you need for college expenses like books and food to buy it? In this chapter's Power Process we learned that attachments can be like addictions. For example, if we think that we can't live without something, or what we want to happen doesn't, then we don't think we will be happy. This Power Process highlights the value in learning to think about the worst that can happen if what you want doesn't occur by stopping our stress and detaching. What we want or think we need may not be what is best. In addition, the readings highlight some specific, easily changed causes of stress, and how to manage it.

Reading One

Stress is something that we all experience in our lives. The difference is how we respond to the stress. In this article Hook suggests ways to help identify the sources of stress and ways to reduce and cope with stress. One suggestion includes how to detach and how not to "awfulize" by asking "What is the worst that can happen" and seeing troubles as temporary—"This will pass." In addition, think back to some of the readings about emotional intelligence and the need to be in touch with our emotions.

Stress Management: Rolling with the Punch

John R. Hook

TYPICAL SITUATION

Mary Turner, assistant V.P. of a regional bank, walks into her office, ten minutes late (again) for the morning staff meeting. The new child-care arrangement isn't working out well. Her daughter, Kelly, doesn't like the new sitter, and the location is all wrong for Ned (her husband) to take her occasionally. The days start out hectic and don't get better. No time to exercise anymore, boring business lunches that eat up time, always running behind on work. Then as the day ends, on to the sitter, the store, try to get dinner together. At night often irritable, too tired to sleep. Stress has a lock on her. What can she do?

CENTRAL IDEAS

Stress is caused by three emotions: fear, anger, or sadness. The bad news is that you can't avoid some stressors. They will always be part of life. What's important is how you react to them. You trigger negative responses when you doubt your ability to cope with what life presents you. The good news is that we all have available to us many approaches to help reduce the harmful impact of stress.

On the next page is a descriptive model for an integrated stress-management program. It identifies major sources of stress and some of the typical coping mechanisms. Take time to study this diagram.

Stress has professional consequences in that it alters performance, usually in a negative way. It also has personal and social consequences causing illness, divorce, and sometimes crime. Yet stress is an inevitable part of life. The key is not to avoid stress but to learn to recognize your own personal stressors and to develop coping mechanisms that will help you deal with unavoidable stress.

> *"Learn to let go. That is the key to happiness."*
>
> **—The Buddha**

There is a lot of literature available on coping techniques. Here is a sequence of three steps that have been helpful to me, and that I have seen work for others.

- *Self-Monitoring.* Lie down and get comfortable. Then mentally scan your body head to toe. Become a witness to your own stress responses by reflecting on any tension and on your emotions: fear, anger, or sadness.
- *Detach.* Try to make a sudden break with the stressful situation by saying to yourself: "Stop!"
- *Meditation/Deep Relaxation.* Slow your breathing, and count your breaths from ten to zero several times. Then again scan your body head-to-toe, first tensing then relaxing each part of the body. Let yourself feel inert (heavy or like jelly). Finally, focus on a pleasant thought, place, or image.

Integrated Stress Management Program

SOURCES OF STRESS

Work Setting	Personal Situation	Home Setting
Heavy workload	Feeling alone	Marital problems
Time pressure	Poor health	Problems with children
Goal/role ambiguity	Low physical fitness	Problems with relatives
Political climate	Worry	Illness in the family
Lack of feedback	Physical pain	Financial problems

STRESS REDUCERS AND COPING MECHANISMS

Exercise and Nutrition	Support Systems	Improved Professional Skills
Diet	Family	Goal setting
Vitamins	Friends	Role clarification
Walking	Pastor	Time management
Biking	Doctor	Delegation
Running	Team	Team building
Swimming		
Team sports		

Self-Awareness	Relaxation Techniques
Awareness of stress	Time alone
Self-assessment	Talk with others
Who am I?	Meditate
How do I fit in?	Massage
What do I want?	Yoga
What can I do?	

One other thing that has proven helpful to many is to develop some of the following habits of stress hardy people:

—Recognize your unique stressors.

—Don't let problems in one life area spill over to other areas.

—See troubles as temporary ("This will pass").

—See meaning in troubles.

—Focus on immediate matters ("What do I do right now?").

—Don't "awfulize." Ask: "What's the worst that can happen and how likely is that?"

—Ignore others' "shoulds"—as in, "You should . . ." Turn inward. Trust yourself.

—Know you are not alone. Take consolation from knowing others face similar or worse problems.

—Trust you can cope. Seek options. Don't get trapped.

—See the opportunity in troubles.

Focusing on stress-hardy characteristics and practicing the coping techniques above are good places to start. But I recommend you go beyond this. Buy a good book on stress management and experiment with the variety of techniques you'll find there. If you do that, I am confident that in short order your life will change for the better. And, while you're at it, think about the things you do that create stress for others. Acting on some of those findings will improve the lives of those around you and possibly improve both your family life and your organization.

SITUATION REVISITED

Mary knows there's a lot she can do about her stress. Her friend, Joan, teaches stress management at a local college. They had a good talk. Joan gave her some things to read.

Now, heading for the airport on Wednesday for a business trip, she's determined and optimistic: I'll have two long plane rides and two nights alone at the hotel. Thinking time. I'll figure it out, get a grip on it.

Friday night Ned meets a "new" Mary at the airport.

"You look different, Mary."

"How so?"

"Relaxed?"

"I am relaxed, but not as relaxed as I'm gonna be."

> *"Courage is the price life exacts for granting peace."*
>
> **—Amelia Earhart**

"So it worked."

"Yep. Simpler than I thought. Let's get home. Tell you later."

Friday night they sit up late. Mary tells her story:

"You know, Ned, I've been crazy, and dumb too. I really used the free time on this trip to think it out. First off, my situation is pretty typical. I took a look around the plane and picked out a dozen women that I bet have the same stress problems I do, probably worse in some cases."

"Why worse?"

"Because I had a chance to count my blessings. I, we, have it very good: good marriage, great kid, enough money, nice home, good friends. My stress problems are all work related, and I'm going to solve them at work."

"Tell me more."

"Well, Monday I'm informing them I'm going on flex time, coming in an hour later. That will give me time to take Kelly back to her old sitter who she loves. They won't love that at work, but you, Kelly, and I will. That's what counts. Also I'm going to stop saying yes to every request thrown at me. A big stressor for me is work overload, and it's my own fault. I say yes to everything. With the time I create

> *"There is nothing either good or bad but thinking makes it so."*
>
> **—William Shakespeare**

I'm going to take a swim at noon every day. Pool's right in the building. I use to do it and loved it. But I got lured into the 'let's have lunch' trap. Career enhancing maybe, boring definitely! That too changes next week. Get the idea?"

"I love it. And I'm proud of you."

"If it doesn't pan out at work, you can support me."

"You bet."

APPLICATION

- **Examine the following list of typical warning signs of stress:**
  - —irritability
  - —fatigue
  - —anxiety
  - —upset stomach
  - —impatience
  - —headache
  - —nervousness
  - —difficulty sleeping
  - —difficulty concentrating
  - —daydreaming, preoccupation
  - —short temper & anger
  - —doing more or less eating or drinking

  What are your top three warning signs? How do you react to them?

- **We can be stressed by many different things, including:**
  - —time deadlines
  - —family difficulties
  - —poor work or attitudes of subordinates
  - —poor interpersonal relationships
  - —fear of failure or tasks beyond our ability
  - —lack of information
  - —surprises
  - —new job demands
  - —frequent moves
  - —multiple top priorities
  - —frustration at not being able to change "the organization"
  - —special life events: divorce, vacations, illness

  What are your top three stressors?

  In what environment (home or work) and under what circumstances do they occur?

- **Some of the most effective approaches in controlling stress are:**
  - —physical exercise
  - —talking to someone
  - —developing a plan
  - —confronting the problem
  - —doing something pleasant
  - —self-imposed cool-off

—change in a routine

—rest

—quiet time/private place

—reflection

—being with family

What things do you habitually do when experiencing stress that seem to aggravate the situation? What three things could you do to reduce your stress?

- **Give yourself a stress check-up each month for a while. Ask yourself the following questions:**

    —What are my personal and professional goals?

    —Are my goals realistic?

    —Am I using my time, energy, and resources appropriately to achieve my goals?

    —Am I trying to do too much?

    —What stressful events, disappointments, or losses have I experienced recently? What problems have I experienced with my work or relationships?

    —How have I reacted?

    —What coping mechanisms have I used?

    —Have I been coping adequately?

    —What more could I do to cope?

    —How can I become more stress hardy?

BOTTOM LINES

- Stress can come from many sources: work, home, other personal situations.
- Sometimes professional help is needed. But often self-help is sufficient.
- There are many stress reducers and coping mechanisms: exercise, nutrition, relaxation techniques—all can be learned fairly easily.
- Self-assessment and the determination to act are key to reducing stress.

From *Developing Executive Skills: Managing Yourself, Others and Organizations* by John Hook. © 2001. Reprinted with permission of Thomson Learning: www.thomsonrights.com. Fax 800 730-2215.

▶ Reflection Questions

1. Hook suggests three categories of stress: work, personal, and home. Look at his list and see if you can add to it. You might consider his category of the work setting comparable to school. Or, if you are working and in school at the same time, try developing a new category and list the causes of stress related to the challenges of juggling work and school.

2. Hook lists a number of stress reducers. Have you ever tried any of them? Did they work? If so, what exactly did you do and how did you feel while or after doing it? If you have never tried a stress reducer, try one the next time you are stressed.

3. What does Hook mean by "stress hardy people"? Do you know any? Are you stress hardy? Describe someone you know (or yourself) who is stress hardy. After describing her or him, pick one thing in particular that makes this person stress hardy and explain it in detail. What techniques for reducing stress do you think could be best employed by this person?

Reading Two

This reading describes the importance of a consistent good night's sleep. It makes us smarter and healthier. Some high schools are delaying start times for students and giving them an extra hour to sleep in. Most reports indicate that students are livelier and participate more in class. In addition, there seems to be some hard evidence that the brain does something while we sleep that helps us to learn. Clearly, lack of sleep can lead to increased stress.

The Secrets of Sleep

Nell Boyce and Susan Brink

Health education teacher Pacy Erck remembers what it was like back when Edina High School students had to show up by 7:25 a.m. "The kids were always very tired," she recalls. But these days, Erck rarely has a kid nod off in class. That's because in the fall of 1996, officials at this Minnesota school decided to ring the first bell an hour later, at 8:30 a.m. Sleep researchers had reported that teens' natural slumber patterns favor a later bedtime, and the school wanted to ensure that its high schoolers weren't being shortchanged by an early wake-up call. The change means that students average five more hours of sleep a week, and teachers can see a difference. "You don't have the kids putting their heads down," Erck says. "The class is livelier."

Research confirms real benefits not only at Edina but also at many other high schools that have made similar scheduling switches, says Kyla Wahlstrom, an education policy expert at the University of Minnesota-Twin Cities. Grades have gone up, and dropout rates have declined. The results are impressive enough that other school systems have started to take notice. In Poquoson, Va., the school board has held public hearings over the past few months to consider making the first bell later. "We do believe our children aren't getting as much sleep as they ought to," says Jonathan Lewis, superintendent of schools in Poquoson. "We have children getting up at 5:30, quarter of 6 in the morning."

But what is it about getting more sleep that's actually helping students do better? Is it just that sleepy kids can't concentrate in class because they're dozing off over their books, or does something happen in dreamland that affects the brain's ability to learn and remember?

A growing number of scientists suspect that sleepless students may suffer more than just feeling dragged out during the day. Many intriguing studies in both humans and animals suggest that the sleeping brain does something to solidify memories and process newly learned lessons. The brain work of sleep may even allow people to form insights that they can't achieve while awake, according to research that gives new weight to the old notion of taking a tough problem and "sleeping on it." With most Americans routinely getting far less sleep than they should, some experts are starting to wonder if widespread sleep deprivation is having a real but unrecognized effect on society's brainpower and creativity.

Sleep is clearly important—after all, people and animals slumber away a third of their lives—but no one knows why. The special learning potential of sleep is an idea that has long held sway in the popular culture: Consider those sketchy "learn while you sleep" audiotapes that promise to "tap into the power of your unconscious." But hard scientific evidence has been scant until recently. Most sleep research has focused on health, and sleep has been viewed mainly as a period of rest and rejuvenation for the body.

That's why, for decades, most experts dismissed sleep as a boring, idle time for the brain. What they didn't realize is that while sleeping bodies lie motionless in bed, the brain's neurons continue to buzz and chatter. Only with the 1953 discovery of rapid eye movement (REM) sleep and the development of new machines to monitor brain activity did researchers begin to see what, exactly, was going on at night. Suddenly they could watch as the brain moved through predictable cycles of REM sleep—with its sometimes vivid dream imagery—and deeper "slow wave" sleep.

Before long, some labs noticed that amounts of REM sleep increased as animals learned various tasks but went back to normal after tasks got mastered. What's more, experiments that deprived animals of REM sleep by disrupting them during this sleep stage found that they didn't learn as well as animals that got in plenty of dreaming. But the idea that sleep might aid smarts didn't catch fire. "Sleep wasn't supposed to be for that. It was supposed to be for restoration," recalls Carlyle Smith of Trent University in Ontario, who has studied sleep and learning for over 30 years.

Slowly, though, the idea has attracted more interest, especially since the early 1990s. Part of the change is that scientists have redesigned experiments to counter critics' early objections, such as the possibility that the sleepless learn less because of stress and fatigue, not the loss of sleep-specific brain work. They've also realized that certain kinds of learning seem more linked to sleep than others. Memorizing lists of words or facts—what's called "declarative" memory—doesn't seem all that dependent on sleep. But scientists have lately gathered compelling evidence that people's "how to" learning, or "procedural memory," gets a boost from a bout of sleep.

Last October, for example, Kimberly Fenn and colleagues at the University of Chicago showed sleep's benefits for this type of learning with the help of an annoying, outdated speech synthesizer. When Fenn's computer says "smart," the word comes out sounding more like "smote," and it's hard to figure out what word it's actually saying. "When people first come into the lab, they're really bad," Fenn says, but 30 minutes of training vastly improves their understanding of the garbled speech. What happens over the next 12 hours depends on whether they are allowed to sleep or not. In a series of carefully controlled studies, Fenn showed that while people's learned ability seems to fade away over the course of the day, a night's sleep brings it back. Test-takers who slept showed nearly twice as much improvement as those who did not.

Timing. Similar effects have appeared in other laboratory learning tests of "how to" motor skills (typing a string of numbers as fast as possible) and visual perception (spotting rare diagonal lines in a sea of horizontal and vertical ones). For example, Harvard Medical School's Robert Stickgold trained people to quickly find diagonal lines; then he either let them sleep that night or kept them awake. Both groups got to sleep normally for two nights before being retested, to make sure they weren't fatigued. Only those who got sleep soon after their training showed improvement over their pretraining test scores. "You absolutely have to sleep the first night," says Stickgold.

Other studies hint that in addition to solidifying learned skills, sleep lets the brain forge brand-new strategies that it might never develop while awake. Earlier this year, scientists in Germany described an experiment in which they taught volunteers how to do a math problem. But there was also a shortcut solution to the problem, which wasn't mentioned. After either letting people sleep for eight hours or keeping them up, the researchers found that the sleepers were more than twice as likely to discover the mathematical trick on their own. Jan Born of the University of Lubeck, who led the study, thinks that the sleeping brain may process and repackage learned information so that, upon awaking, the brain can suddenly "see" it in new ways.

How exactly this mental magic happens isn't clear. It does seem that some kinds of learning can take place without long snoozes. Indeed, Stickgold's group found that a 60-to-90-minute nap works as well as a full night's sleep—as long as sleepers get both REM and non-REM sleep. Indeed, recent research indicates that despite the historical interest in dreamy REM sleep, the less sexy deep sleep may also play an essential role in learning.

In one recent study, rats were allowed to explore novel objects like a golf ball mounted on a spring. Then, using tiny electrodes in the rats' brains, the researchers monitored over 100 neurons for several days. Duke University's Sidarta Ribeiro found that electrical patterns recorded as the rats first encountered the objects later got replayed over and over during the next two days, mainly during sleep. The mental reverberation was, surprisingly, most common during the slow-wave sleep. This kind of replay during sleep, has also been seen in finches learning new songs and in brain scans of people learning to anticipate a pattern of flashing lights, suggesting that during sleep, the brain goes over new information again and again.

Another way to probe the sleeping brain is to use drugs that interfere with certain chemical changes that occur over the course of sleep. During slow-wave sleep, levels of a chemical called acetylcholine normally drop to low levels, but Born and his colleague Steffen Gais recently tested the effect of this chemical with the help of an Alzheimer's drug that keeps levels artificially high. The scientists gave the drug to half of a group that was taught to memorize a list of word pairs before going to sleep. After a while, everyone woke up and took the test again. People who got the drug did worse, suggesting that the normal chemical changes in slow-wave sleep aid learning.

There are sleep researchers who don't buy any of this. The University of California-Los Angeles's Jerry Siegel, an outspoken critic of the sleep-learning hypothesis, argues that many of these studies simply contradict each other. In the acetylcholine study, for example, he points out that many researchers haven't seen a link between memorizing word lists and sleep. Plus, the drug might just have taken away the normal restful effect of sleep, and fatigued people would do more poorly on any cognitive test. In addition, he notes, people on many common antidepressants get far less REM sleep than normal but don't seem to suffer big learning gaps. And regarding the mathematical insights reported in Born's study, he points out that people get many, many insights during their waking hours, not just during sleep.

Proponents of the sleep-learning theory in the end fall back on a basic fact: Sleep's total isolation from the waking world seems designed to focus attention inward, on information already obtained that needs to get organized. "It's frankly the only biological role for sleep that makes much sense for me," says Stickgold, who notes that the body can rest during quiet wakefulness and that shutting off awareness from the rest of the world is actually a pretty dangerous act that must serve some important function.

Even as debate continues on sleep and learning, new research is showing that sleep is essential not only to brain function but to the proper function of every bodily organ. From a central command post in the hypothalamus, the brain tells us when to go to bed and when to wake up, all the while regulating body temperature, blood pressure, hormone production, digestive secretion, and immune activity. But in addition to the brain's central circadian rhythm control, researchers now know there are at least eight other clock genes in the body's cells that occasionally go off on riffs of their own.

Out of sync. Consider the gut. "When I go to Europe or Japan, my sleep-wake cycle gets back in sync before my digestive system," says Richard Stevens, cancer epidemiologist at the University of Connecticut Health Center. Without getting too graphic about regular morning digestive tract functions, every time-zone crosser can relate to a gut that seems to have its own strong circadian rhythm. In addition to explaining why the first cup of coffee doesn't have the same effect upon landing in Paris that it did the morning before at home, these other clock genes might explain why heart attacks peak in the morning or why the timing of cancer chemotherapy may improve the odds of survival.

Researchers can point to a whole list of diseases connected to sleep deprivation. A 67-year-old man with prostate problems wakes up to go to the bathroom half a dozen times a night, and one morning he has a heart attack. A 19-year-old college student with a diagnosis of bipolar disorder has too much energy to sleep for five nights running and spins into an episode of uncontrolled mania. A healthy man of 30 gets half his required sleep—four hours a night—for a week and ends up in a prediabetic state with the metabolism of his grandfather. An 82-year-old woman falls and breaks her hip, possibly for the same reason that a 42-year-old truck driver slams into a barrier at 3 a.m.—inattention and slowed response because of chronic partial sleep deprivation.

The need for sleep is so strong that without enough of it "people can't even muster enough willpower to stay awake to save their lives," says Carol Everson, who studies sleep in laboratory rodents at the Medical College of Wisconsin in Milwaukee. Inadequate sleep comes with a high cost.

Perhaps the most graphic example of the link between sleep and illness is bipolar disorder, or manic-depression. "I've always believed the mania caused the lack of sleep, and the lack of sleep worsened the mania," says Alexis Maislen, 27, who was diagnosed with the disorder at the age of 19. It is a disease that cycles moods between boundless highs and incapacitating lows. During the highs, she had so much energy that she'd put on her in-line skates and zip around Boston during the wee hours of the morning. She slept maybe a half an hour a night and couldn't talk fast enough to keep up with her crackling ideas. Finally the words came faster than the thoughts behind them. Friends told her she didn't make sense.

Sleep deprivation itself, without underlying illness, won't cause mania. "People [with bipolar disorder] can trigger an episode of mania with sleep deprivation. And mania is preceded by an episode of insomnia," says Ruth Benca, a professor of psychiatry at the University of Wisconsin. Once mania is diagnosed, adequate sleep becomes one of the most important parts of treatment.

James Swinney, a retired developer on the board of the Depression and Bipolar Support Alliance, knows it. He's been able to regulate his sleep with drugs, including sleeping pills, though he still can't sleep more than six hours a night and often sleeps only in two-hour snatches. "I make sure I get six hours in a 24-hour period," he says.

The six hours Swinney gets is the best he's been able to do, but it isn't enough. Some rare individuals do fine on six hours or fewer, but most people who claim to need less are kidding themselves. They've simply gotten used to chronic drowsiness the way people get used to constant pain. "Everything we know would suggest that the vast, vast majority of people need more than six hours of sleep a night—somewhere between seven and eight," says David Dinges, chief of the Division of Sleep and Chronobiology at the University of Pennsylvania School of Medicine.

During those seven to eight hours, the cardiovascular system gets a break. "Most people, about 85 percent of those with normal or high blood pressure, have a 20 to 30 percent reduction in blood pressure and a 10 to 20 percent reduction in heart rate during sleep," says William White, professor of medicine at the University of Connecticut Health Center. He has monitored blood pressure for 24 hours in about 5,000 people. "It's amazing when you look at people who sleep like a log. Their blood pressure goes down to about 110 over 70."

But what if you're one of those people whose blood pressure, because of some abnormality, doesn't drop at night? Says White: "There's fairly good evidence that you'll develop more damage to your heart, arteries, and kidneys because your blood pressure is elevated 100 percent of the time, instead of 65 percent of the time for those spending one third of their time sleeping," says White.

Morning misery. With a good night's sleep under their belt, people should be expected to wake up with a heart that's raring to go, right? Yet the incidence of heart attacks and strokes peaks between 6 a.m. and 11 a.m. "We don't know why, but maybe the platelets are more sticky," says Virend Somers, a cardiologist at the Mayo Clinic. And sticky platelets are more likely to clot and clog arteries.

Heart attacks generally don't happen to people with no underlying risk factors, such as hypertension or diabetes. But when those are there, waking up during REM sleep may pose dangers. REM is the one stage of sleep that doesn't lower blood pressure. Indeed, during REM sleep, the sympathetic nervous system gets excited, and sleeping blood pressure and heart rate actually rise. Someone getting up during that dream phase might awaken with a pounding heart. And a fast heartbeat and higher blood pressure coupled with waking activity can put added stress on the heart.

That's a theory anyway. Another possibility for the morning spike is that endothelial cells—the cells that line blood vessels and are important in preventing clots and narrowing of arteries—don't seem to work as well in the morning. Somers measured this in his lab and found just that: The 6 a.m. level is dramatically lower than at other times of day—comparable to what one would expect to see in a smoker or diabetic.

Chest pains and abnormal heart rhythms also tend to occur during REM sleep. "It's not because REM is bad," says Somers. But if people already have an abnormality in their cardiovascular system, the instability of REM sleep may bring on a disaster. Some blood pressure medications can help keep the heart on an even keel during all phases of sleep and into the morning hours.

Those most at risk for heart problems due to bad sleep are people with apnea, a disease that obstructs the airway. The brain responds by signaling for hyperventilation, and the sleeper breathes harder and faster—heard as snoring. "Every time they do that, it causes a surge in blood pressure and heart rate," says White. Blood pressure can shoot up to 240 over 130, and it can happen dozens, even hundreds, of times a night for years. The damage done over time may put people with apnea at higher risk for hypertension, heart failure, and stroke.

When Douglas Bradley studied people with uncontrollable high blood pressure, he found that fully 85 percent of them suffered from sleep apnea. When treated with a mask that forces air into the airway, blood pressure dropped by 10 points on average. The same treatment can also improve heart function in people with congestive heart failure. The National Heart, Lung, and Blood Institute last year included sleep apnea as an identifiable cause of high blood pressure, but the medical community has been slow to embrace the idea.

The field of cancer treatment is even further behind in recognizing, and using, the body's sleep-wake clock to advantage. William Hrushesky published a paper in *Science* in 1985 on the circadian timing of cancer chemotherapy. In a group of patients with advanced ovarian cancer, women who took their drugs at one time of day had twice as many complications—and were much more likely to die within five years—as women on a different medication schedule.

Do these differences justify altering standard medical practice? Hrushesky has spent his career trying to answer that question, and his research suggests

THE RHYTHMS OF HEALTH AND DISEASE

12 Midnight Ulcer crises	**12 Noon**
2 a.m. Hormonal level use Asthma Hay fever	**3 p.m.** Respiratory rate climax
	4 p.m. Body temperature, blood pressure rise

6 a.m.
Heart rate, blood pressure
   begin to surge
Migraine headache
Stroke, heart attack,
   chest pain
	6 p.m.
	Urine output peaks
	Osteoarthritis
	Cerebral hemorrhage
	Intractable pain

Sources: Block Center for Integrative Cancer Care, M.H. Smolensky Rod Little—USN&WR

that the answer is yes. Cancer cells don't die when they're supposed to, and they don't stop dividing. "It's hard to even think about cancer without thinking about timing," says Hrushesky. But few oncologists use what is known about treatment timing. "These ideas may be popping, but they're not in vogue," he says.

Someday, scientists may finally figure out what's so special about sleep, for both the workings of the mind and the body. But until they do, experts say the bottom line remains the same: Get your sleep or suffer the consequences. That's why Erck, the health teacher, has sleep specialists visit her classes to talk to students about the many ways that sleep improves the body and the mind, so that they can start to see a good night's rest as a priority. But sleep still has to compete with the call of work, television, video games, and more; and adults and children alike increasingly find it hard to give shut-eye the respect it deserves. "Unfortunately," says Erck, "most kids and adults don't do the right thing to help them get a better night's sleep."

"The Secrets of Sleep," by Nell Boyce and Susan Brink, *U.S. News & World Report,* May 17, 2004. Copyright 2004 U.S. News & World Report, L.P. Reprinted with permission.

▶ Reflection Questions

1. Do you get enough sleep (some suggest around eight hours a night)? What prevents you from getting a good night's sleep? What changes can you make in your lifestyle to see that you get the appropriate amount of sleep?

2. Not everyone agrees that there is a sleep-learning connection. After reading this selection, what do you think about the sleep-learning connection? What evidence (either pro or con) can you cite from this reading to support your position? What connection do you think there is between the lack of sleep and stress?

3. Sometimes our schedule (whether it be class, life, or work) does not permit us to get enough sleep. If you believe that a good night's sleep helps your performance in class, what can you do to get enough sleep even if you can't change your early classes?

Reading Three

This short essay is written by Brian Drake, a contemporary college student from Ohio State University. He talks of a trip to the library that changed his life. He describes a way that he addressed stress (at the bottom of a bottle), later to emerge when he found his path to self-discovery. His process of finding himself was through books, but it encourages all of us to look for and find our own path.

Looking Life in the Eyes: Finding a Path to Self-Discovery

Brian Drake

I stumbled upon what would become my principal source of solace from the hardships of college life on a sweltering May afternoon in Columbus, Ohio. Students spilled onto the lush spring grass of the Oval as I meandered to the William Oxley Thompson Library. The towering statue of Mr. Thompson had seen little of me my freshman year at Ohio State and I hesitated to look at the eyes of his stern, bronze face. Intent on cramming for finals, I sped inside and along the dim corridors, glancing at a blur of colorful book spines that lined the walls. I searched for the nearest open desk. Little did I know that among this vast collection of paper, ink and binding, lay the keys that would shape my morals and transform my life.

Five months earlier I had begun to perceive the world around me in a different light. I was struck with a feeling of ill-defined uneasiness and soon the realities of my new milieu and beyond sent me into a state of anxiety. I was caught in a maelstrom of curiosity and disillusionment. Why were the slimy credit card recruits allowed to crouch on every campus corner ready to pounce on an innocent student who would graduate with debt that would take years to pay off? Why were so many students brimming with ceaseless animosity and hatred? Why was there an incessant, worldwide epidemic of conflict and warfare? Why would one desire to harness the power of atomic nuclei to decimate thousands of innocent lives in a split second? Why does an indifference to nature exist? How can one loathe another solely based on skin pigment? These and a bombardment of similar questions furiously collided in my brain. I struggled to find answers beyond my reach and I began to search for solutions at the bottom of a bottle. Of course I was unsuccessful and my freshman year ended as I found myself back where I started, none the wiser.

So how does this trip to the library factor into my transformation? While searching for that desk to study on, a stout book caught my eye: *The Journals of Sylvia Plath.* I remembered how captivated I had been reading *The Bell Jar* in high school. Lacking in time now, I tossed the book in my bag for summer reading. It was time to hit the books for finals.

Home in Cincinnati a few weeks later, I opened Plath's *Journals* and delved into her psyche. I always felt a passion for reading but had never been so engrossed in literature as I was with her journal. It was as if she clenched her hands around the edge of this diary and pulled herself out just to have a chat with me about all of the fascinating convictions that were the driving force behind her writing. I began to adopt Plath's dreary vision of life and by the time my sophomore year started, my mind's eye foresaw a bleak future.

Before long, I realized reading Plath's work may not have been the best idea. Considering it was anything but soft and fluffy, I found myself in a mood of dark depression and anxiety. I constantly mused about the state of the world and wondered why I was lucky enough to have regular nourishment and protection from inclement weather while the less fortunate struggled to find a scrap of food or a tattered jacket to divide among them. Distress swirled thick as fog through my hollow insides and soon enough, I could function no more. My life took a horrific nosedive. I lost all my physical and mental appetites. I began to experience alarming panic attacks. Like Plath, I wondered, "why the hell [are we] conditioned into the smooth strawberry-and-cream Mother-Goose-world . . . only to be broken on the wheel as we grow older and become aware of ourselves as individuals with a dull responsibility in life?" (1998, p. 21) The most striking aspect of her diary was her accurate portrayal of the hurdles she experienced in college, so many of the same feelings and issues that I was encountering. Much of what she wrote in the 1950's was equally relevant in present times. Why had so little changed? I admired her ability to tell it how it was—a very risky business in her day. She organized my chaotic thoughts on paper and almost every entry seemed strikingly similar to my own emotions. Awed, Plath spoke to me with an uncanny accuracy when she wrote about these enormous contradictions: "Be aware that you must compete somehow, and yet that wealth and beauty are not in your realm. To learn that a boy will make a careless remark about 'your side of town' as he drives you to a roadhouse in his father's latest chromium-plated convertible. To learn that you might have been more of an artist than you are if you had been born into a family of wealthy intellectuals. To learn that you can never learn anything valid for truth, only momentary, transitory sayings that apply to you in your moment, your locality, and your present state of mind [. . .] to realize that most American males worship woman as a sex machine with rounded breasts and a convenient opening in the vagina, as a painted doll who shouldn't have a thought in her pretty head other than cooking a steak dinner and comforting him in bed after a hard 9–5 day at a routine business job." (p. 21)

To some, this may sound like the whiny ramblings of a self-pitying woman, but her jumbled ideas resonated with me and dramatically altered my way of thinking. Unfortunately, the more I read, the more my life began to unravel. Once again, you are probably speculating as to why I claim that specific trip to the library as a revelation. To this point, it had left me comfortless, worried and weary. Soon enough I became fed up with wallowing in a bottomless pit of despair and decided that an urgent change was in order if I would ever successfully escape these feelings.

My junior year brought forth this crucial turning point. I had a revelation. Considering that I had shared a multitude of Plath's viewpoints, why wouldn't other authors affect my life in the same manner, only in a positive way? In an uncertain but hopeful move, I switched my major to English when I was more than half finished with a degree in Business Administration. Not long after, I crossed paths with Flaubert, Chopin, Bellow and Quinn and found "wisdom that could dispel my disillusionment and bewilderment." (1992, p. 5) Literature, I discovered was the richest, most vibrant form of communication.

Ultimately, this essay aims to prove three simple points. First, a path to one's self-discovery exists for everyone, everywhere. Harold Bloom, an acclaimed critic of literature, writes: " . . . we read in order to strengthen the self, and to learn its authentic interests." (2000, p. 22) Through the study of literature, I have learned my personal tendencies, weaknesses and strengths. It has taught me to question any situation or concept from multiple facets. Also, reading has opened my eyes to serenity in a world full of upheaval. No one puts this better than Virginia Woolfe. She wrote about what it means "to look life in the face, always, to look life in the face, and to know it for what it is. At last to know it, to love it, for what it is, and then, to put it away." She is also rumored to have uttered: "You cannot find peace by avoiding life," which I find extremely meaningful. There comes a time in every adolescent's life when one realizes that MTV's "Real World" is anything but real. My point is that disillusionment does not have to be a negative trait. In fact, it is almost indispensable to the genesis of one's ethical development. One of the foremost ways to find salvation in this chaotic world is to recognize and embrace the existence of all aspects of life, whether negative or positive. I can "look life in the face" through words on paper. Lastly, literature provides me with insights I may have never thought about. These insights might slightly modify or completely change my moral code. A short story altered my view of homeless people and was the catalyst that forced me to reevaluate my social responsibilities. A poem taught me to fully appreciate nature and the repercussions of careless action. These epiphanies can be reached many ways, through music, history, sociology, psychology, martial arts or any form of careful observation, concentration and thought.

The process of finding oneself is extremely personal and literature just happened to be my specific path to self-discovery. Find your path. Find yourself.

> In his preface to the legendary *Leaves of Grass,* Walt Whitman wrote: "A great poem is no finish to a man or woman but rather a beginning." (2003, p. 33) I like to think of life as a great poem.
>
> ─────────
>
> *Looking Life in the Eyes: Finding a Path to Self-Discovery,* by Brian Drake, Ohio State University. Reprinted by permission.

▶ Reflection Questions

1. Do you think that reading Plath's journals was the only way Drake could have come to terms with his depression and anxiety? If not, speculate about another path that might have led him to self-discovery.

2. Have you ever thought "Why me?" Why do I have to work so hard and others don't? Why can't I have money like my roommate or someone else? Have you ever thought life is not fair? What role do these questions play in the path to self-discovery? Explain.

3. Drake writes that "disillusionment does not have to be a negative trait." What does he mean? Do you agree? Why or why not?

4. Have you ever read a book, or even a quote, that has influenced you? If so, what is it and how and why did it impact you?

◤ Writing Assignment _____

audience: A student who is experiencing stress in his or her first semester of college

purpose: To share stressors about college and how to deal with them

length: Minimum of three typed pages, double-spaced

Often, colleges have a mentoring program where new students are paired with upper-level students to assist with the first-year students' transition into college. Often, this happens during the summer, prior to the start of the fall semester. (Check into your colleges' activity offerings. Mentoring programs are often under or part of Student Affairs or New Student Orientation. See if such a program exists on your campus for possible volunteer opportunities.) Write a hypothetical letter to a new student who might be coming to campus. First, point out how you are looking forward to meeting him or her. Next, discuss a few of the positive things that you experienced the first semester, but then share things that have stressed you and your friends. Describe to the student some of the things that no one told you might happen related to stress and what you or someone you know did to deal effectively with it.

Convince the student that he or she must take control of the situation, whatever it may be, and not let the situation control him or her. Suggest some strategies that you or your friends used and include some information that you have found (either on the Web or from some organization) related to the problem that the student is facing. Highlight some of the on-campus support for these problems.

Include in this letter specific examples of what you learned from the three readings. Can you think of a situation that you have experienced similar to any of these individuals? Share this in your letter too.

Journal Entries: DISCOVERY AND INTENTION STATEMENTS

We all have times when we think "Why me?" Write a journal entry that lists all of the things that are positive in your life. We all have positive things in our lives, particularly when we put them in the proper perspective. For example, when we think about the victims of the Tsunami or 9/11, our struggles may pale in comparison.

How do these readings relate to the Power Process "detach"? What are some of the tools that you will need to succeed in college on the basis of the readings? Can you think of some specific examples of situations where you might use these tools? Write one or two sentences about what you have learned and what you intend to do as a result of these readings, what you will do to make it work, and what you risk if you don't do what you intend to do.

Mastering Vocabulary

List five words that were new to you (more or less if necessary). For each, include which reading you found the word in, the definition, and where you got the definition from, as well as a time or place you might use the word again.

1.

2.

3.

4.

5.

 ## Additional Activities

1. Find Erma Bombeck's article online entitled "If I Had to Live My Life Over." Read it and then write about your own life. If you could, what would you do over? Anything? Is it possible to change the result of what you did now?

2. Develop a brochure of tips for college students on how to manage stress. Share it with the class.

3. Find a buddy in class, and share with each other one thing that stresses you. Brainstorm with each other and come up with a strategy or strategies that each of you will try during the next week to reduce your stress. Come back to class to share your thoughts.

Online Study Center **Improve Your Grade**
Visit the Online Study Center for resources and exercises to accompany this text
http://college.hmco.com/pic/msreader1e

CHAPTER SEVEN

Find a Bigger Problem

155

Have you ever felt that the busier you were the more you accomplished? If you really wanted to go somewhere or do something, you quickly completed tasks you needed to do so you could do what you wanted. Sometimes we perceive tasks that we need to do, whether they are large or small, as barriers or problems to achieve what we want. Sometimes if we think of larger problems (or more important things to do), the small things we once saw as barriers seem easy to accomplish. When we realize that there are bigger problems in the world than ours, we are able to put our challenges into perspective and move on to a happier, more productive (flow state) life.

The Power Process: Find a Bigger Problem

Most of the time we view problems as barriers. They are a source of inconvenience and annoyance. They get in our way and prevent us from having happy and productive lives. When we see problems in this way, our goal becomes to eliminate problems.

This point of view might be flawed. For one thing, it is impossible to live a life without problems. Besides, they serve a purpose. They are opportunities to participate in life. Problems stimulate us and pull us forward.

Seen from this perspective, the goal becomes not to eliminate problems, but to find problems that are worthy of us. Worthy problems are those that draw on our talents, move us toward our purpose, and increase our skills. The challenge is to tackle those problems that provide the greatest benefits for others and ourselves. Viewed in this way, problems give meaning to our lives.

Problems fill the available space

Problems seem to follow the same law of physics that gases do: They expand to fill whatever space is available. If your only problem is to write a follow-up letter to a job interview, you can spend the entire day thinking about what you're going to say, writing the letter, finding a stamp, going to the post office—and then thinking about all of the things you forgot to say. If, on that same day, you also need to go food shopping, the problem of the letter shrinks to make room for a trip to the grocery store. If you want to buy a car, too, it's amazing how quickly and easily the letter and the grocery shopping tasks are finished. One way to handle little problems is to find bigger ones. Remember that the smaller problems still need to be solved. The goal is to do it with less time and energy.

Bigger problems are plentiful

Bigger problems are not in short supply. Consider world hunger. Every minute of every day, people die because they don't have enough to eat. Also consider nuclear war, which threatens to end life on the planet. Child abuse, environmental pollution, terrorism, human rights violations, drug abuse, street crime, energy shortages, poverty, and wars throughout the world await your attention and involvement. You can make a contribution.

Play full out

Considering bigger problems does not have to be depressing. In fact, it can be energizing—a reason for getting up in the morning. Taking on a huge project can provide a means to channel your passion and purpose.

Some people spend vast amounts of time in activities they consider boring: their jobs, their hobbies, their relationships. They find themselves going through the motions, doing the same walk-on part day after day without passion or intensity. American author Henry David Thoreau described this kind of existence as "lives of quiet desperation."

Playing full out suggests another possibility: We can spend much of our time fully focused and involved. We can experience efficiency and enthusiasm as natural parts of our daily routines. Energy and vitality can accompany most of our activities.

When we take on a bigger problem, we play full out. We do justice to our potentials. We then love what we do and do what we love. We're awake, alert, and engaged. Playing full out means living our lives as if our lives depended on it.

You can make a difference

Perhaps a little voice in your mind is saying, "That's crazy. I can't do anything about global problems" or "Everyone knows that hunger has always been around and always will be, and there is nothing anyone can do about it." These thoughts might prevent you from taking on bigger problems.

Realize that you *can* make a difference. Your thoughts and actions can change the quality of life on the planet.

This is your life. It's your school, your city, your country, and your world. Own it. Inhabit it. Treat it with the same care that you would a prized possession.

One way to find problems that are worthy of your talents and energies is to take on bigger ones. Take responsibility for problems that are bigger than you are sure you can handle. Then notice how your other problems dwindle in importance—or even vanish.

Readings

Readings in this chapter are chosen to highlight some of the most far reaching and controversial topics of present times. Sometimes we become so focused on our own circumstances that we forget about the much larger issues that surround us. While it is easy to insulate ourselves, the following three selections bring to the surface bigger problems that can have a far-reaching impact on each and everyone of us.

Reading One

This reading chronicles the stories of a number of individuals three years after their loved ones were killed in the 9/11 attacks. They discuss how their emotions have changed and share insights into how they feel the event should be remembered.

3 Years after Attacks, Conflicting Emotions

Don Aucoin

On the first anniversary of the Sept. 11, 2001, terrorist attack on the World Trade Center that killed her husband, Cindy McGinty of Foxborough took part in the massive memorial service at ground zero. "I felt a very strong pull to be in New York," she says. "It was the right place to be."

On the second anniversary, she craved solitude rather than solidarity. She and her two sons had to learn to "be this new family that we were," so she took the boys hiking in the Catskill Mountains, far beyond the reach of painful headlines and television footage.

Today McGinty will come full circle. She will be in Boston for a day of mostly private memorial events with hundreds of other New Englanders whose loved ones were brutally torn from them three years ago. It is the right place to be this year as she remembers her late husband, Mike, she says, and the right people to be with, given the almost familial bonds she has forged with numerous widows of 9/11.

But for McGinty and many other relatives of 9/11 victims, this third anniversary also brings with it conflicting emotions. They know that some Americans believe they should "get on with their lives" even as the recent use of 9/11 as a political football in the presidential campaign has made that harder than ever. They still feel a jolt of surprise when they hear of a wedding or a concert scheduled for Sept. 11, and yet while they know it will never be just another day for them a part of them welcomes such signs of a return to normality.

"I struggle with it," acknowledges McGinty. "I don't want people to look at me and pity me, to feel sad when they look at me." In the next breath, though, she expresses anxiety about what she calls "a real danger in forgetting the impact of this, for our nation and for specific families."

Three years ago, there seemed little chance of that. The nation's response in the aftermath of the terrorist attacks which with a death toll of nearly 3,000 were the deadliest ever on US soil represented a rare convergence of public and private mourning. The families of the victims felt nestled in a national embrace. Yet precisely because the attacks were without precedent, there are no clear guidelines for the annual remembrances as the event recedes deeper into the past.

"This isn't your normal way of dying," observes Mike Sweeney of Acton, whose wife, Amy, was a flight attendant on American Airlines Flight 11. She relayed details about the hijackers to an airline supervisor on the ground in Boston, which helped the FBI identify them. "This is a tragic, public, ongoing historical event. It's new ground," Sweeney said.

Consequently, with another year's distance, there is the sense of a nation improvising its long-term responses to the tragedy, uncertain about the proportions that observances ought to assume. Bella M. DePaulo, a social psychologist and visiting professor at the University of California, Santa Barbara, says both the families and the general public nationwide are "torn" in similar ways on this third anniversary. "There is the tug of emotion and empathy that takes you all the way back to ground zero, the yearning to remember and to honor," DePaulo says. "But there is also something immensely gratifying about having the strength and courage to move on, especially from such a brutal horror.

"If you can go on and live your life fully, then they haven't really gotten to you, have they?" she adds. "But then, that just brings you back to your initial sentiment: If you say 'Don't look back,' isn't that disrespectful to the people who lost their lives that day and deserve to be remembered?"

Christie Coombs, whose husband, Jeff, was killed on American Airlines Flight 11, is considered a beacon of strength by the other 9/11 widows with whom she has become close friends. But even Coombs acknowledges that this third anniversary is fraught with emotional complication in a way that the previous two were not.

"A lot of us feel the pressure from society to kind of move on, get on with it," she says in her Abington home, which is filled with pictures of her smiling husband. "I agree we can't live in the moment of Sept. 11, but we can't move on without remembering that it happened."

Toward that end, she is helping put together a book for family members of the victims, filled with photographs and anecdotes about those who died. She plans to read her introduction to the book today at the ceremonies in Boston, and she clearly cherishes her relationships with the other families of 9/11. Still, she acknowledges, "Three years later, you wonder how many more years will we do this, how long will we be gathering together in this way." She gives voice to another worry: "Is the country tired of it? That concerns me."

In recent weeks, the Sept. 11 terrorist attacks have taken center stage in a way some families find dismaying: as a political issue. Speakers at both the Republican and Democratic conventions repeatedly invoked the memory of Sept. 11. Then, a few days ago, Vice President Dick Cheney raised the specter of another terrorist attack in warning against the election of the Democratic nominee, John F. Kerry. Last month, Kerry made headlines when he quickly endorsed the changes in intelligence policy recommended by the 9/11 commission.

"I don't think it should be a political event," says Diann Corcoran of Norwell, whose husband, Jay, died aboard United Airlines Flight 175. "I don't think either campaign should be discussing it."

For some, their anguished questions about what happened to their loved ones were only intensified when they read the recently published "The 9/11

Commission Report: Final Report of the National Commission on Terrorist Attacks Upon the United States."

Sweeney, who read the book, expresses frustration that more security measures have not been implemented. "What changes have actually taken place? [Former CIA director] George Tenet is the only one who has actually lost his job from this," he says.

While there are a number of public vigils and tributes today, the events organized by Massachusetts 9/11 Fund Inc., a nonprofit organization that provides financial support and other services to families, are private with the exception of a flag-lowering and a moment of silence on the State House main lawn at 8:46 a.m. The goal of the other 9/11 Fund events—a speaking program at the Boston Opera House, a lunch at the Ritz-Carlton, a reception for charity cyclists on Boston Common—is not just to remember, but also to recapture a kind of intimacy. In that respect, today's ceremonies may open a new, more muted phase that could establish the template for how 9/11 is commemorated.

Kerry and Romney will be involved in the tributes, but there will be fewer dignitaries than in past years in order to maintain a tight focus on the families. Moreover, a video montage will be shown distilled from tributes to the victims by colleges, churches, and even nursery schools that is designed to show the families their loved ones have not been forgotten, according to Linda Plazonja, executive director of the Massachusetts 9/11 Fund.

Apart from financial worries and concerns about their children, says Plazonja, "their biggest fear was that people would forget, that Americans would move on to another tragedy and this would become a thing of the past. That was terrifying to them, as it would be to anyone who suffered such a loss in such a public way."

They will forever identify with others who suffer such losses. In the past week, the 9/11 families were buffeted anew by reminders of terrorism's horrors when a hostage crisis in Beslan, Russia, ended with hundreds dead, many of them children.

"I can never again look at anything like this as a spectator," Coombs says. "I am immediately drawn in . . . I know what those families are going through."

Beyond that, the approach of the Sept. 11 anniversary brings with it the inevitable torrent of images—the planes crashing into the World Trade Center towers, the wreckage at the Pentagon and in a Pennsylvania field—that bring a crushing pain. "I find I'm not sleeping as well," acknowledges Corcoran. "There's just so many reminders; it's everywhere. And you never know when it's coming out at you. It's out of the blue.

"It's with trepidation that you turn the page of the paper," Corcoran said. "You wake up in the morning and you feel pretty good, and then you can get knocked down and it's Day One all over again."

A source of comfort lies in the fact that so many families have been able to institutionalize the memory of their loved ones in the form of foundations and scholarships. Many of them say they see it as a way to give back to a community that stood by them in their hour of need. Tomorrow the annual Jeff Coombs Memorial Road Race will take place in Abington to raise money for a foundation that provides financial help to local families and organizations. On Friday a golf tournament will take place to raise money for a foundation established in Jay Corcoran's memory that distributes scholarship money to college-bound students in Norwell. On Sept. 19 in Foxborough, a "family fun day" will raise money for a scholarship foundation in the name of Mike McGinty.

And this afternoon, in a ceremony at the Massachusetts State House, Mike Sweeney will join Romney in presenting the Madeline Amy Sweeney Award for Civilian Bravery.

"For at least a small period, it's a little bit of a diversion from the horrific acts that happened on that day," he says.

BOSTON GLOBE [ONLY STAFF-PRODUCED MATERIALS MAY BE USED] by DON AUCOIN. Copyright 2004 by GLOBE NEWSPAPER CO (MA). Reproduced with permission of GLOBE NEWSPAPER CO (MA) in the format Textbook via Copyright Clearance Center.

▶ Reflection Questions

1. Cindy McGinty, whose husband was killed in the World Trade Center, feels there is "a real danger in forgetting the impact of this, for our nation and for specific families." What kinds of danger do you think she means? Do you think she is right to be concerned about this?

2. Another widow, Christie Coombs, says, "A lot of us feel the pressure from society to kind of move on, get on with it." Do you agree that there is a pressure to "get on with" your life after traumatic events happen? Why or why not? What issues do college students face that they may have trouble "moving on" from?

3. During both the 2004 Republican and Democratic conventions, the terrorist attacks became center stage. Some of the families of the victims felt that it should not be a political event. Do you agree? Why or why not? During the 2004 election, fewer than anticipated college students voted. Why? Do you think they were too disappointed with the campaign or were there other reasons college students did not vote?

Reading Two

This reading is a compilation of the stories of a number of individuals in a variety of cities who are homeless. Associated Press reporters spent twenty-four hours meeting people who live on the streets and chronicled their stories.

Day in the Life of Homeless in America

Sharon Cohen

The family sleeps in a single room, its walls bare and windowless, its cracked concrete floor crowded with plastic storage bins and three mattresses: one for dad, one for mom and daughter, one for the three young sons.

Fluorescent lights will flicker on at 6 a.m., to start their new day.

This room in an old red-brick factory-turned-shelter in Chicago is home for the Torres family. They consider themselves lucky to be here. They have a warm place to stay, three meals a day—and each other.

The family is among an estimated 500,000 to 700,000 people who, on any given night in America, lack a real home.

According to some estimates, the homeless population has doubled in the last 20 years. But some experts say more people now fall into that category only because billions of dollars have been spent to build shelters.

Americans are troubled by this issue: An Associated Press poll taken Feb. 11–13 found 53 percent consider homelessness a very serious problem. The survey, conducted by Ipsos-Public Affairs among 1,001 adults, had a sampling error of plus or minus 3 percentage points.

For a snapshot of the nation's homeless, AP reporters and photographers spent 24 hours earlier this month meeting with people who live on the streets and in shelters, following them to jobs or court appearances, talking with those who try to help them.

Here are their stories:

AFTER MIDNIGHT: PORTLAND, MAINE

Scotty Partridge is pacing outside a blue tent pitched among the barren spruce trees on the outskirts of Portland.

"Hobo Jungle" has been his home for nearly a year. Partridge's clothes are frayed, his face windburned and gaunt.

On this 35-degree Fahrenheit (1-degree Celsius) night, most of Portland's homeless are in a shelter, but Partridge prefers a tent furnished with plywood, a radio, a television and a discarded propane heater.

Partridge, 36, once had a good job at a printing company in Chicago, a nice apartment, a woman he was going to marry. But when the relationship soured, he returned to Maine and got hooked on heroin.

On methadone for five years, Partridge survives day to day.

"Every day is so hard . . . ," he says. "You think about, OK, how am I going to eat today and how are my boots going to unthaw . . . Being homeless is a full-time job."

ALMOST DAWN: NEW YORK CITY

John Mitchell rises for work with a siren blaring inside a homeless shelter in Harlem—a signal for residents to line up for twice-a-week drug tests.

A 47-year-old former crack addict, Mitchell says he was in and out of prison and homeless for more than 20 years, robbing people for drug money, digging through trash cans for food.

"I came to the conclusion this time around I learned what that word surrender means," Mitchell says.

Seven months ago, the father of two teens became sober and entered the "Ready Willing & Able" program, run by a non-profit group with support from the city, that provides shelter (10 men to a room), hot meals and a job cleaning the streets that pays up to $7 . . . an hour.

He's also studying at night to be a nurse's aide.

"I gotta keep saying, this is not going to last forever, there's a bigger picture," he says. "It's like riding a bike . . . right now I'm using training wheels. Before I know it, I'll be popping a wheelie."

8:30 A.M.: CHICAGO

A 10-degree Fahrenheit (minus 12-degree Celsius) wind chill whips through the North Side streets of Chicago as 6-year-old Angelina Torres, in her striped wool hat, and her twin, Angel, in his Spiderman gloves, head to kindergarten.

Their mom, Eileen Rivera, leads the way. Her two older sons, Omar, 9, and JJ, 10, have already left for another school—a bus picked them up at 8 a.m. at the Sylvia Center, the shelter where the family has lived for eight months.

As Rivera walks briskly, she notes her twins have stayed in shelters about half their lives. "They just blend right in." She pauses, then adds: "It's sad."

Her husband, Jesus Torres, 43, recently found work driving a forklift, earning $7 . . . an hour. He saves a large part of his earnings. The family is on waiting lists for public and subsidized housing.

Rivera, who has a stress-related illness that has left her bald, tells her children this is just a steppingstone. "Guys," she says, ". . . We have to go through this to get to the shining star."

Rivera knows what that will be: "Your own toilet. Your own tissues. Your own bath. Your own window. Things that are yours. Just yours."

9 A.M.: MIAMI

Retha Ann Cain shuffles her shackled feet into a Miami courtroom.

The 19-year-old was homeless before she was jailed for prostitution. And when her latest 180-day sentence is up in March, she will be homeless again.

Cain has been on and off the streets, in and out of foster care since she was 14. She ran away from Ohio at 17 with a boyfriend and moved to Miami. The two live in a tent.

Cain is in court to face two counts of obstructing traffic to pick up tricks. She has agreed to plead guilty in exchange for credit for time served.

The judge orders Cain to participate in an AIDS education course—Cain says she is HIV-negative—but the young woman isn't interested in a program offering housing and job training.

The judge offers her some free bus tokens.

"Thank you, thank you," Cain says.

"Good luck," the judge replies with a smile.

LUNCH TIME: CINCINNATI

Brent Chasteen slings a backpack over his shoulder and heads out on the streets.

The 42-year-old outreach worker was hired by a business group called Downtown Cincinnati Inc. after the city enacted strict panhandling laws.

Chasteen works his way through downtown and heads to a desolate place near railroad tracks.

"Hey, Wolf!" Chasteen calls into the winter air.

A man emerges from a shiny purple sleeping bag tucked in a cardboard box.

Wolf has been homeless for 10 years.

"Trying to do what other people do—it's a losing battle," he says, sipping a beer.

Chasteen doesn't judge the homeless.

"I know that we may seem to be in separate worlds on the surface," he says, "but many of them share the same kinds of problems that affect me and everybody else."

3:15 P.M.: WEST VIRGINIA

A light snow falls in the mining town of Monongah, West Virginia, as nurse's aide Harleigh Marsh heads home from his job at St. Barbara's Memorial Nursing Home.

Marsh lives at Scott Place, a shelter in nearby Fairmont.

A former sailor, Marsh lives in a dimly lit 14-foot-by-14-foot (4.2-meter-by-4.2-meter) room. After leaving the military in 1979, Marsh tried college, but soon began traveling again, working as a drywall hanger and painter, renting rooms by the week, living from a suitcase.

In Milwaukee, he met a woman and fell in love. They had a son. But she found someone else, leaving him heartbroken. Almost overnight, he was homeless.

He ended up in Scott Place last year; the Veterans Administration provided help for his depression.

Marsh loves his job but after $300 . . . monthly child support payments, he's left with just $140 . . . a week—not enough to visit his 13-year-old boy, William Ray.

"It tears both of us apart," he says.

SUNDOWN: HOLLYWOOD

Nicole Hudson has a roof over her head—for now.

Sitting in Covenant House, a shelter for homeless and runaway teens, she ticks off the places she has lived in her 20 years: eight foster homes, two group homes, two shelters, one transitional apartment. She's also stayed with her mother three times and her grandparents twice.

This is Hudson's fourth stint at Covenant House—she has been kicked out three times for breaking the rules.

She has been on the streets three times in the past year, living on-and-off with 25 other teens in a narrow alley off Hollywood Boulevard.

"What happened to the blue skies, you know, and the sun-shining days when you were little?" she asks in her husky Southern drawl. "It's like the world just crashes when you get older and your mind comes to reality."

LATE EVENING: LAS VEGAS

A few blocks from downtown Las Vegas, Clarence Woods is on his way to buy a pack of cigarettes.

A week ago, he lived on the streets. But work as a day laborer has allowed him to move into a $370-a-month . . . hotel. He doesn't know how long his luck will hold.

The 53-year-old Woods is a father of five but says he's too embarrassed to tell his children where he's living. He says he ended up homeless because he was irresponsible.

Woods says he once owned his own upholstery shop. But he went bankrupt and ended up without a home.

He calls himself a recreational drug user, drinker and gambler.

"It's a real trap," he says, the neon signs flashing behind him, "but it's what Las Vegas is all about."

9 P.M.: SEATTLE (MIDNIGHT EST)

The lights are about to go out at Seattle University where about 100 people live in a homeless "tent city" on asphalt tennis courts.

Among them are Russell Mace and Angela Cope. He says he once ran his own catering and house-painting business in Texas, where he fell in love with Cope. But she returned to Seattle to try to reconcile with her two kids and their father.

Mace, 45, says he turned to the bottle for a time. Then he and Cope, 49, reunited. They lived in cheap hotels until their money ran out.

After the camp goes dark, Mace and Cope walk to their tent, his arm around her back.

On the other coast of America, midnight has just passed and another day for the homeless has just begun.

▶ Reflection Questions

1. The reporters visited nine different cities and spent time with a number of homeless people. What did you notice about the people's reasons for being homeless? Do you think that someone who attends or graduates from college could be homeless? What do you think could lead to this situation?

2. In an Associated Press poll taken in February of 2004, 53 percent of Americans consider homelessness a serious problem. Do you feel it is a serious problem? What can you as a college student do to help?

3. Of the scenarios presented, all have underlying causes that resulted in people living on the streets. Choose one situation and describe how this problem could have a negative impact on society beyond homelessness. What can we, as a society, do?

Reading Three

The stem cell controversy is one of the most emotional issues of our time. Individuals take a stand for stem cell research on the basis of the potential to find cures for life threatening diseases, while others see stem cell research as a moral issue and are opposed. Three separate authors, a neurobiologist, a political scientist, and an ethicist, each provides a unique view on this subject. Also, a professor of biochemistry and cell biology provides an objective view of the issues at stake.

Stem Cells and False Hopes[1]

MAUREEN L. CONDIC, *The Neurobiologist*

We have all witnessed the transforming power of hope—the focus and sustenance hope provides when strength and reason fail to pull us through a difficult situation. Facing tragedy and loss, hope is often the only thing standing between us and the void. Life-threatening illnesses or injuries provide some of the most poignant occasions for hope. We hope that a loved one will survive a critical surgery. We hope that cancer will respond to chemotherapeutic drugs. We hope, often against all odds, that this time, for this one precious and irreplaceable person, death will be thwarted and life will go on.

When medical science offers no legitimate hope for a cure, desperation and grief can drive people to grasp at any straw that might offer hope to them or to their loved ones. For many herbal medicine or other "alternative" therapies become the vehicle for hope when medical science has done all it can do. For others, hope comes from beyond the realm of medicine. Faith often takes up at the limits of hope, to turn the eyes of the desperate to the source of all life, all hope, and all salvation. Facing death with dignity requires us to accept our mortality and find peace beyond the hope possible in this world.

It is precisely the power of hope, the ability of hope to provide solace and motivation in the most desperate situations, that makes the manipulation of hope such an appalling offense. The selling of false hope is a contemptible exploitation. Whatever comfort a false hope temporarily offers, it is far offset by the damage that is caused when the illusion is crushed by reality. Not only do bitterness and resentment replace the optimism a false belief once supported, but for the terminally ill it is often too late to go beyond bitterness and arrive at any kind of peace. To die an angry death, betrayed by hope and cursing those who have lied to you, is a fate few would wish on even their worst enemies.

It is difficult to imagine anyone so hardened by malice that he would intentionally mislead the desperate merely for the pleasure of watching a false hope deflate when it collides with the truth. Yet desperation is a powerful motivator, and the ranks of the desperate have more than once been exploited for the political, social, and economic gain of the unscrupulous. People with nothing to lose, who view a contest as a matter of life or death, tend to make formidable combatants. Marshaling armies of such "desperados" has been a strategy employed to great effect throughout history. No less so today in some fields of medical science.

Patients suffering from incurable medical conditions have been repeatedly used to influence the public and legislative debate over embryonic stem cell research. Setting aside the significant moral objections to experimenting on human embryos, there are very real problems with embryonic stem cell research on purely scientific grounds. As I recently discussed in these pages (*The Basics About Stem Cells,* January), employing embryonic stem cells as a therapeutic treatment for human illness faces the serious challenge of immune rejection by the patient. One of the proposed resolutions to this problem has been to replace the genetic information of the stem cell with that of the patient to generate a copy or "clone" of the patient that could be used as a source of replacement tissue.

In the face of strong public opposition to human cloning, proponents of embryonic stem cell research have advanced a tried-and-true tactic from the realm of product marketing: when people reject a product, repackage it and sell it under a different name. Thus human cloning has been effectively reborn as "somatic cell nuclear transfer" (SCNT), in the hope of selling a failed product under a different brand name to a public that is understandably hesitant to endorse the cloning of people for spare body parts. The contemptible aspect of this particular marketing scheme is the nature of the target audience and the role of false hope in the sales pitch.

I recently had a series of conversations with a woman dying of multiple sclerosis (MS). MS is a particularly cruel and painful disease that progressively robs a person of the ability to walk, to talk, and eventually even to swallow and breathe. The woman, by all measures a bright and well-educated person, was still in the early stages of her illness and was highly motivated to devote every last shred of her energy to promoting the "cure" offered by embryonic stem cell research. In a very real sense, this was to be her life's work, her legacy. The rage and frustration she expressed at those opposed to human cloning was intense.

How, she asked, could people deny her and others in her situation their last, best, and only hope for a cure?

How, indeed. In the face of such an emotional attack, many are driven to accept the imagined "need" for human cloning. The tragic irony, of course, is that the cure so many desperately hope for is based on nothing more than bald assertion. Proponents of embryonic stem cell research and human cloning have enlisted the ranks of the terminally ill not only to lend credibility to their claims, but to provide the valuable emotional trump-card of "How can you deny me a cure?" Those opposed to human cloning can be readily vilified as standing in the way of a cure—a cure that exists only in the hopes of the desperate and the speculations of a small number of scientists.

Perhaps the most distressing aspect of the current turn in the embryonic stem cell debate is that there are few constraints on where emotional exploitation can lead us. A year ago, the American public was asked to accept federal funding of research on human embryonic stem cells, based on the unsupported assertion that such research would cure human disease. Less than one year later, we are now being told that generating human clones is required in order for the true therapeutic potential of embryonic stem cells to be realized. At both junctures, patients with debilitating medical conditions were brought before the public to provide highly emotional testimony regarding their hope for a cure, and many Americans, swayed by compassion, reluctantly stomached their reservations.

What will the next twelve months bring? Will we next be asked to accept the need to "culture" therapeutic clones in artificial wombs for a few months until tissue-specific stem cells can be obtained from growing embryos? Perhaps the cloned embryos will need to be grown even longer, until usable organs for transplant can be "harvested." While these scenarios may seem implausible (and would undoubtedly be dismissed as "preposterous" by embryonic stem cell advocates), the generation of human clones in the laboratory appeared to be equally preposterous one short year ago. The point is simply this: in the absence of credible scientific evidence documenting precisely how embryonic stem cells and cloned human embryos will cure disease, one can assert anything one chooses and all things can be equally justified by hope.

Proponents of embryonic stem cell research and human cloning are well aware that the future of this research cannot be debated solely within the realm of science policy. They have not succeeded in garnering public support on the basis of the scientific evidence, largely because there is no compelling evidence in support of their assertions. Even if strong scientific evidence existed, the equally strong moral objections to this research would undoubtedly persist. Advocates have also not succeeded in defining the matter solely in terms of scientific freedom and the pursuit of knowledge; the history of the last century amply illustrates the need to restrict scientific inquiry in some circumstances. In the face of these failures to recruit the public to their cause, advocates of human cloning and embryonic stem cell research have attempted to recast the issue as one of compassion and hope by marshaling the ranks of the desperate. The strategy appears to be: when you can't win on legitimate grounds, win by any means possible. Such a strategy does not preclude outright deceit and emotional manipulation, all in the name of "hope."

To offer false hope to the desperate as a means of advancing a political, social, or economic agenda is worse than merely cruel, it is objectively evil. Valuable resources are being diverted from other, perhaps more promising, areas of research, and, in the meantime, patients and their families are serving as pawns in a political arena. People facing the prospect of suffering and death deserve better than this. As patients, they deserve the best that science and medicine can offer. As human beings, they deserve honesty. No amount of false hope can alter the fact that after more than twenty years of unrestricted research on animal embryonic stem cells, this field has *failed to yield a single cure for any human illness.*

Embryonic stem cell research and human cloning go to the heart of how we view human life, both at its earliest and its final stages. As is the case for all matters of life and death, this research raises issues that are both painful and profound. Resolution of these issues should certainly *not* be based on unfounded speculation and emotional exploitation of those desperately hoping for a cure.

Stem Cell Controversy[2]

The Political Scientist

BROOKE ELLISON

The ability to view the world through another's eyes is the essence of altruism. When putting their pens to the paper of policy, those who legislate should remove themselves from their own convictions and act for the benefit of the most. This is the basic tenet of democracy, the core belief upon which the United States was founded. However, when looking at the issue of stem cell research, in general, and federally funded research, in specific, our president is inextricably linked to his own, highly conservative, myopic ideology and has failed both to understand the situation of others and hear their voices.

> "The procedure has the potential to affect directly the lives of nearly 100 million people . . . that's more than the populations of New York, California, Texas, and Florida combined!"
>
> **—Brooke Ellison**

In September 1990, when I was 11 years old, I was hit by a car while walking home from my first day of 7th grade. That accident left me paralyzed from my neck down and dependent on a ventilator for every breath I take. As a person with a physical disability, each day is a struggle. Tasks that might seem mundane or taken for granted to others are strenuous challenges for me, sometimes taking long hours to complete instead of mere minutes. With the thought of so much potential on the horizon, a series of hopeful hypotheticals rolls in a perpetual cycle through the minds of those bound by physical challenges. When we place our hopes and visions for our world into the hands of those making collective decisions, we do it with the belief that they will act on behalf of our best interest and not on an isolated viewpoint. To do otherwise is bad policy. To undermine the interests of a majority of citizens is bad policy. To ignore the voices and dash the hopes of those most in need is bad policy. Regarding the issue of current stem cell research legislation, these are bad policies, yet they are being upheld. Every day, millions of disabled people think similar thoughts.

"If I could be freed from the confines of my physical condition, what a miracle it would be." Or, maybe, "If, for a single moment, I could wrap my arms around those I love, what a treasure that would be."

And even, "If, by some chance, President Bush might heed some of my recurrent thoughts and change his stance on stem cell research, what a potentially groundbreaking step it would be."

Based on current legislation, these "ifs" likely won't change into reality. On August 9, 2001, from his ranch in Crawford, Texas, President Bush announced that he would significantly limit federal funds to stem cell research, only agreeing to fund research conducted on stem cell lines already in existence. According to this limitation, federally supported research could be conducted on no more than 78 existing genetic cell lines, although even the most optimistic estimates of viable cells were thought to be far fewer, less than two dozen. To the delight of some and the consternation of others, Mr. Bush indicated that the use of embryonic cells for medical research was a violation of the sanctity of life, analogous to abortion or euthanasia. In the President's own words, "I worry about a culture that devalues life, and believe as your President I have an important obligation to foster and encourage respect for life in America and throughout the world . . . Embryonic stem cell research offers both great promise and great peril. So I have decided we must proceed with great care." Despite millions of testimonies and pleas to the contrary, since that day more than three years ago the opinion of the administration has remained constant and no restrictions have been eased. Despite strides being made in other countries in the field of stem cell research, the U.S. government has remained resolute in its opposition to it.

Therapeutic stem cell research has the potential to provide cures for a considerable number of neurological and degenerative conditions, including Alzheimer's disease, Parkinson's disease, childhood leukemia, heart disease, ALS, several cancers, and spinal cord injuries. The procedure has the potential to affect directly the lives of nearly 100 million people—that's more than one-third of the U.S. population and more than the entire populations of New York, California, Texas, and Florida, combined! Therapeutic stem cell research, however, is sometimes confused with reproductive stem cell procedures, such as genetic engineering, sparking controversy in some political camps. The two types of research differ considerably, though, both in terms of procedure and intent, and represent two diverse ends on a very long, complex spectrum—an understanding that often goes ignored.

Some have argued that using stem cells is just the destruction of one life for the sake of another. To hold such a belief is to view the world in black-and-white terms, thereby ignoring the much more complex gray areas. Yes, it is possible that if a blastocyst, from where stem cells were derived, was to be inserted into a womb and allowed to grow for nine months, there is the potential a life could be born. However, that is not the case for any of the blastocysts that yield stem cells for research. These blastocysts will go unused after *in vitro* fertilization procedures and will never be used to bring about life. These blastocysts, which the President proclaims represent the sanctity of life, will only be kept in freezers at fertility clinics until they have expired, and then they will be discarded. Under current legislation, they are of no use to anybody. To rob the stem cells of their other potential of life, which is to cure diseases or to help regenerate parts of the body, is really to devalue life in another, otherwise avoidable, way.

Others have argued that the work done on stem cells is the same as cloning, and that these cells are essentially promoting the creation of another person. The once almost incomprehensible, futuristic ideas of cloning and "body-doubles" are now considered feasible and fearsome possibilities, and therapeutic stem cell research has been the unwitting victim of the prevalent fears. Orwell's *1984* has somehow come to life in 2004, with the speculations made by some about unintended, science-fiction consequences. But the connection between human reproduction and human therapy is a foggy one at best. The real fear, though, is not the potential of mad scientists reproducing people but the lost potential of sound scientists curing people.

Fourteen years ago, I could have never imagined having to advocate for something that could potentially restore for me the very basic aspects of life and humanity. But, that is something that no one should have to imagine. Science has given medicine more promise than ever before, with the potential to heal and restore people in ways once thought unfathomable. Stem cells, which would otherwise serve no other purpose, hold the promise of life, not just for the newly born but now for the already living, and this opportunity must be seized. The time is now. The time has come when we can change the lives of so many, giving to them the fundamental parts of life and dignity. When he realizes that, maybe President Bush will redefine his right, ethical, and moral conclusion.

The Ethicist

JACK COULEHAN

The first step in analyzing an ethical issue is to get the facts straight. The second step is to clarify the question. Unfortunately, much of the ethical discourse about stem cell research in the United States today skips these steps of the reasoning process and jumps immediately to a bottom-line position, usually couched in impressive terms like *rights, dignity, sacred, person,* and *natural.* This approach tends to create provocative sound bites but makes little or no progress toward responsible public policy. I want to concentrate first on the facts and the issue, which provide a basis for discussion, and then elaborate on the moral territory in which stem cell research belongs.

> *"The strongest moral position is that the embryo is a fully human person. . . . At the opposite pole, an embryo may be considered solely from an instrumental perspective as having essentially no moral standing."*
>
> **—Jack Coulehan**

When we say "stem cells" in this context, what are we speaking about? We are neither talking about bone marrow stem cells, which can differentiate into many different types of blood cells, nor about fetal cells from the umbilical cord, which may be able to differentiate into a wide variety of tissues. There are active research programs in both of these areas, looking into the potential for use in treating disease. One practical result, of course, has been the emergence of bone marrow transplantation. The use of these pluripotential stem cells, which may turn into many different types of cells, is not ethically problematic. Rather, the current controversy surrounds totipotential cells that come only from embryos. These cells eventually differentiate into every organ and tissue in the human body. If that potential could be harnessed, we would be able to use them to regenerate tissue severely damaged by disease; for example, specific types of nerve cells to treat degenerative diseases of the brain. It was in 1998 that researchers at the University of Wisconsin first developed methods of identifying and isolating embryonic stem cells, so the possibility of this type of research has only been around for about six years. In that time it has generated a lot of excitement and some progress, but there have been no practical results.

Thus far, most stem cell research has taken place outside the United States in countries like England, Canada, Belgium, China, Singapore, and Korea. In 2001, President Bush severely compromised our research programs in the United States by limiting federal funding exclusively to projects that utilized already established stem cell lines. At the time the President said there were 66 of these cell lines, but in fact far fewer of them existed, and many of these were unavailable to American scientists. The reason, of course, for the partial ban on federal funding was the Administration's unwillingness to support programs that, in its opinion, encourage abortion.

This raises the question of where stem cell researchers obtain embryos. The specter of aborted fetuses generates a great deal of moral indignation. However, for the most part such fetuses—whether miscarried or electively aborted—could not serve as totipotent stem cell sources, since tissues and organs are already differentiated. In fact, the best source of stem cells is embryos in the blastocyst stage: i.e., clumps of approximately eight or 16 cells. There are hundreds of thousands of such embryos available in this country, created by *in vitro* fertilization (IVF), and frozen, but not implanted, in the woman's uterus. Frozen embryos are maintained for varying periods of time but are eventually destroyed. Thousands are destroyed every year. Such embryos could be utilized for stem cell research.

Another source of embryos for research is cloning. Although we have hundreds of thousands of naturally cloned human beings living among us (identical twins) the concept of artificially inducing the cloning process raises many irrational fears as well as significant moral questions, which require thoughtful consideration. However, stem cell research and cloning are separate issues.

Now we get to the locus of contention—what is the moral status of an embryo in the unimplanted, blastocyst stage? Clearly, we are dealing with an entity unknown in the past which, therefore, does not fit easily into traditional moral categories. The strongest moral position is that the embryo is a fully human person. Hence, it is entitled to all the rights and respect given to babies. This is the consistent position of the Catholic Church, which teaches that personhood begins at conception. At the opposite pole of the moral spectrum an embryo may be considered solely from an instrumental perspective as having essentially no moral standing. This is the view held by Professor Peter Singer, a thoroughgoing utilitarian philosopher who believes that personhood begins only with the onset of fully human consciousness, somewhere around the end of the first year of life.

While positions like these delimit the territory, there is obviously an enormous range of principled positions between the extremes. No one would disagree that a blastocyst contains the genetic machinery necessary to develop into a person; it is at least a potential person. However, most would also acknowledge that, at present, such an embryo lacks any of the characteristic (detectable, at least) attributes of personhood. Hence, it seems reasonable to accord the embryo some respect, as a living entity out of which human dignity eventually develops, yet not to insist that the embryo is somehow a person in itself.

Just how much respect should we bestow the blastocyst, and how does that impact on stem cell research? I suggest three considerations that are important in helping us evaluate the moral status of embryos:

First, embryos produced by IVF techniques, yet remaining outside the uterus, may well be different in their moral status from implanted embryos. The process of development requires complex interaction between mother and fetus. The uterus is not simply a vessel in which the fetus grows, but rather part of a unified fetus-placenta-mother system that ultimately leads to the birth of a new person. Thus, the genetic blueprint is necessary but not sufficient for development of personhood. Frozen embryos, or "fresh" embryos created by IVF, are not "potential persons" to the same extent, or in the same way, as normally or artificially implanted embryos. If that is true, it would be ethical to use externally created embryos for stem cell research but not ethical to induce abortion for the same purpose.

The second consideration has to do with consistency. The Catholic Church has a consistent position that states it is immoral to fertilize eggs (and hence create embryos) outside the woman's body. Therefore, IVF and most other forms of assisted reproduction are intrinsically immoral. If an embryo is formed, it must be considered a person. Consequently, allowing frozen embryos to die—whether they are used for stem cell research or not—is wrong. I don't agree with this analysis, but I admire its consistency. On the other hand, many people who believe that assisted reproduction is good and see no problem with killing extra embryos will argue against using embryonic cells for stem cell research. This is inconsistent and does not hold up under scrutiny.

Finally, some writers have recently argued that the United States needs to get its act together and start funding stem cell research because otherwise we will slip far behind and eventually have to purchase leading-edge treatments (derived from stem cells) from foreign countries. While this is likely to be true, I don't think the argument has moral bite. If countries like England and Canada develop sophisticated new therapies by manipulating stem cells, which we consider an immoral form of research, it is not morally consistent to say that we want to benefit by eating the fruit of that poisoned tree. Of course, the persons urging us to keep up with the Brits do not think stem cell research is unethical, but I can easily imagine many Americans now opposed to such research changing their minds as soon as an effective stem cell treatment for a serious degenerative disease develops.

What lies in the future for embryonic stem cell research? At this point we have no idea. It is very early in the game, which makes it exciting because of all the possibilities. Yet, who knows whether any of them will pan out? One thing is certain. Research employing human blastocysts raises important ethical concerns and ought to be carefully regulated. Thoughtful analysis of the level of respect due to embryos ought to be the first step in developing our national policy.

What Is a Stem Cell and What Is All the Fuss?

PETER GERGEN, *Professor of Biochemistry and Cell Biology Director of the Center for Developmental Genetics, Stony Brook University*

The development of a multicellular organism from a fertilized egg depends on regulating the proliferation of cells during development and their differentiation into cells with different specific functions. So what is a stem cell and how does it fit into developmental control strategies? The central property defining a stem cell is the ability to divide, producing two daughter cells, one of which retains the key parental property of being able to divide again. Stem cells are clearly important during the early proliferative stages of development, but are also found in adults where they help to replace cells that turn over, such as those in blood and skin. Ongoing research is exploring the use of adult stem cells in the treatment of numerous diseases, with one obstacle being the restricted developmental potential of these cells to give rise to different cell types. This obstacle is one reason for the excitement regarding embryonic stem cells, or ES cells.

The most frequently referred to source of ES cells is a small cluster of approximately 100 cells, the inner cell mass in a blastocyst stage. These cells are readily identified and isolated, and can be cultured in an undifferentiated state almost indefinitely. Blastocyst-stage embryos are typically obtained by *in vitro* fertilization, although alternative approaches for generating ES cells from blastocysts, derived by transplantation of nuclei into unfertilized oocytes, are being developed.

An important attribute of ES cells is their ability to generate all of the different cell types in the body, offering enormous potential to treat degenerative diseases.

The first human ES cell lines were described in 1998. However, over the last 20 years there is a large body of research on ES cells from other animals, much of this conducted on mice. Indeed, the ability to culture and manipulate ES cells from the mouse has revolutionized the study of mammalian developmental biology. Genetic manipulation of ES cells has allowed the development of mouse models for a large number of human diseases, and studies are underway to explore the feasibility of treating these diseases with stem cell–based therapies.

So where are we now with respect to research on human stem cells? In August 2001, President Bush announced that federal funds could only be used to support research on the different human ES cell lines already available at that time. As it turns out, only a subset of these government-certified cell lines are useful. This has hampered stem cell research in the United States but has not stopped scientists eager to explore the enormous therapeutic potential. Scientists in Korea recently generated a human ES cell line from a blastocyst created by nuclear transplantation. Scientists in the United States have turned to non-federal sources of support for their research, and most recently California passed a proposition that would provide state funds to support embryonic stem cell research. The federal government has traditionally played a leading role in establishing guidelines followed by the entire scientific community. The current government policy is not constructive and is not being followed. It is time to re-examine our position on stem cell research and make well-informed decisions that are acceptable to the public. A useful Web site for those who would like to learn more about stem cell research is maintained by the International Society for Stem Cell Research at *www.isscr.org.*

[1] Maureen L. Condic, "Stem Cells and False Hopes," *First Things* 125, August/September 2002, pp. 21–22. Reprinted by permission.

[2] "The Stem Cell Controversy," *The Brook,* Vol. 5, No. 2, Winter 2005. Reprinted by permission.

▶ Reflection Questions

1. According to Condic, embryonic stem cells provide false hope. Do you agree? Explain your answer. Should college students be concerned about taking a stand on this issue? Explain.

2. One of the writers, Brooke Ellison, has a disability. Is her perspective on stem cell research a result of her physical state? Is this right? Can you think of an example where a college student would take a stand on something because of her or his own circumstances? Give an example.

3. These readings provide three unique perspectives on stem cell research. In college, courses are sometimes offered that are called interdisciplinary. That is, they look at a subject from a variety of disciplines. What is the value in this approach? Explain.

Writing Assignment

audience: Your fellow students

purpose: To persuade college students that community service or service learning is an important part of a college education

length: Minimum of three typed pages, double-spaced

Write a persuasive essay to convince your reader, using examples from the three readings and your own experience, that a way to prepare young adults for the real world is to teach them the larger problems and issues faced in society and the happiness they will find when they are part of the solution.

Journal Entries: DISCOVERY AND INTENTION STATEMENTS

Ask yourself if you think you will be ready to face the real world at graduation time. Describe what you think the first three years after graduation will be like for you. Is it what you want? If not, is there anything you could do now to change it?

How do these readings relate to the Power Process "find a bigger problem"? What have you learned about yourself by reading these selections? Have the readings made you think about what your life could be like given the possibility of some change of events that affects you? What are some of the tools that you will need to succeed in college on the basis of the readings? Resilience, for example? Can you think of some specific examples of situations where you might use these tools? Write one or two sentences about what you have learned and what you intend to do as a result of these readings, what you will do to make it work, and what you risk if you don't do what you intend to do.

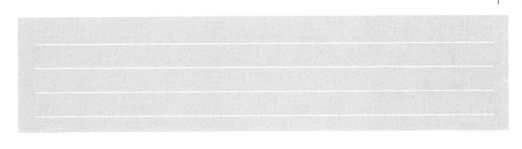

 ## Mastering Vocabulary

List five words that were new to you (more or less if necessary). For each, include which reading you found the word in, the definition, and where you got the definition from, as well as a time or place you might use the word again.

1.

2.

3.

4.

5.

 ## Additional Activities

1. The teacher will divide the class into two groups, one in support of stem cell research and the other against it. The teacher will randomly assign students to take a position, not necessarily the one they support. Groups will make a list of reasons why their position is the right one and be prepared to defend their reasons in a debate.

2. Visit your college community service center and find out what volunteer opportunities there are for students. Class members should agree to participate in a community service event, either in pairs or as a class. When the event is over, report back about your experiences.

Online Study Center **Improve Your Grade**
Visit the Online Study Center for resources and exercises to accompany this text
http://college.hmco.com/pic/msreader1e

CHAPTER EIGHT

Employ Your Word

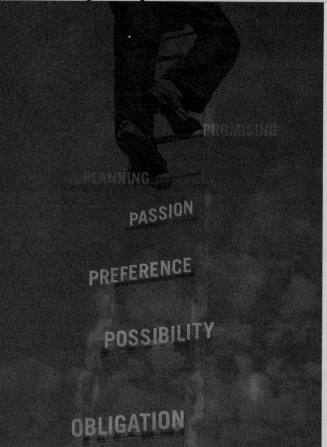

PROMISING

PLANNING

PASSION

PREFERENCE

POSSIBILITY

OBLIGATION

When someone gives their word, they make a promise that we believe they will keep. Wars have been stopped when individuals have given their word, as well as business deals closed and friendships cemented. However, sometimes what we say can be heard differently, depending on the hearer's interpretation. Remember back to Chickering's work in Chapter One? He suggests that one of the skills the workers of the twenty-first century will need is communication skills that include "an eloquence in expressing them [one's opinions and judgments] and a force in urging them." While what we say is important, how we say it and how it is perceived is critical.

The Power Process: Employ Your Word

When you speak and give your word, you are creating—literally. Your speaking brings life to your values. In large part, others know who you are by the words you speak and the agreements you make. You can learn who you are by observing which commitments you choose to make and which ones you choose to avoid.

Your word makes things happen. Circumstances, events, and attitudes fall into place. The resources needed to accomplish whatever was promised become available. When you give your word, all this comes about.

The person you are right now is, for the most part, a result of the choices and agreements you've made in your life up to this point. Your future is determined largely by the choices and agreements you will make from this point on. By making and keeping agreements, you employ your word to create your future.

The world works by agreement

There are over six billion people on planet Earth. We live on different continents and in different nations, and communicate in different languages. We have diverse political ideologies and subscribe to various social and moral codes.

This complex planetary network is held together by people keeping their word. Agreements minimize confusion, prevent social turmoil, and keep order. Projects are finished, goods are exchanged, and treaties are made. People, organizations, and nations know what to expect when agreements are kept. When people keep their word, the world works. Agreements are the foundation of many things that we often take for granted. Language, our basic tool of communication, works only because we agree about the meanings of words. A pencil is a pencil only because everyone agrees to call a thin, wood-covered column of graphite a pencil. We could just as easily call them ziddles. Then you might hear someone say, "Do you have an extra ziddle? I forgot mine."

Money exists only by agreement. If we leave a $100 Monopoly bill (play money) on a park bench next to a real $100 bill (backed by the U.S. Treasury), one is more likely to disappear than the other. The only important difference between the two pieces of paper is that everyone agrees that one can be exchanged for goods and services and the other cannot. Shopkeepers will sell merchandise for the "real" $100 bill because they trust a continuing agreement.

Relationships work by agreement

Relationships are built on agreements. They begin with our most intimate personal contacts and move through all levels of families, organizations, communities, and nations.

When we break a promise to be faithful to a spouse, to help a friend move to a new apartment, or to pay a bill on time, relationships are strained and the consequences can be painful. When we keep our word, relationships are more likely to be satisfying and harmonious. Expectations of trust and accountability develop. Others are more likely to keep their promises to us.

Perhaps our most important relationship is the one we have with ourselves. Trusting ourselves to keep our word is enlivening. As we experience success, our self-confidence increases.

When we commit to complete a class assignment and then keep our word, our understanding of the subject improves. So does our grade. We experience satisfaction and success. If we break our word, we create a gap in our learning, a lower grade, and possibly negative feelings.

Ways to make and keep agreements

Being cautious about making agreements can improve the quality of our lives. Making only those promises that we fully intend to keep improves the likelihood of reaching our goals. We can ask ourselves what level of commitment we have to a particular promise.

At the same time, if we are willing to take risks, we can open new doors and increase our possibilities for success. The only way to ensure that we keep all of our agreements is either to make none or to make only those that are absolutely guaranteed. In either case, we are probably cheating ourselves. Some of the most powerful promises we can make are those that we have no idea how to keep. We can stretch ourselves and set goals that are both high and realistic. If we break an agreement, we can choose to be gentle with ourselves. We can be courageous, quickly admit our mistake to the people involved, and consider ways to deal with the consequences.

Examining our agreements can improve our effectiveness. Perhaps we took on too much—or too little. Perhaps we did not use all the resources that were available to us—or we used too many. Perhaps we did not fully understand what we were promising. When we learn from both our mistakes and our successes, we can become more effective at employing our word.

Move up the ladder of powerful speaking

The words used to talk about whether or not something will happen fall into several different levels. We can think of each level as one rung on a ladder—the ladder of powerful speaking. As we move up the ladder, our speaking becomes more effective.

Obligation. The lowest rung on the ladder is *obligation*. Words used at this level include *I should, he ought to, someone better, they need to, I must,* and *I had to.* Speaking this way implies that people and circumstances other than ourselves are in control of our lives. When we live at the level of obligation, we often feel passive and helpless to change anything.

Note: When we move to the next rung, we leave behind obligation and advance to self-responsibility. All of the rungs work together to reinforce this characteristic.

Possibility. The next rung up is *possibility*. At this level, we examine new options. We play with new ideas, possible solutions, and alternative courses of action. As we do, we learn that we can make choices that dramatically affect the quality of our lives. We are not the victims of circumstance. Phrases that signal this level include *I might, I could, I'll consider, I hope to,* and *maybe.*

Preference. From possibility we can move up to *preference*. Here we begin the process of choice. The words *I prefer* signal that we're moving toward one set of possibilities over another, perhaps setting the stage for eventual action.

Passion. Above preference is a rung called *passion*. Again, certain words signal this level: *I want to, I'm really excited to do that, I can't wait.* Possibility and passion are both exciting places to be. Even at these levels, though, we're still far from action. Many of us want to achieve lots of things and have no specific plan for doing so.

Planning. Action comes with the next rung—*planning*. When people use phrases such as *I intend to, my goal is to, I plan to,* and *I'll try like mad to,* they're at the level of planning. The intention statements you write in this book are examples of planning.

Promising. The highest rung on the ladder is *promising*. This is where the power of your word really comes into play. At this level, it's common to use phrases such as these: *I will, I promise to, I am committed, you can count on it.* This is where we bridge from possibility and planning to action. Promising brings with it all of the rewards of employing your word.

Readings

Readings in this chapter are all related to the power and use of words. Is e-mail having an impact on the way we write? Certainly it has an impact on the medium we use to convey thoughts. We write letters less and e-mail more. But has this quick and easy way of exchanging words made us less capable communicators? Perhaps we communicate more often, but are we more effective in the way we communicate?

Reading One

The author of this reading, Sam Dillon, a former college professor and now the head of an online school for business writing, receives e-mails everyday from managers and executives looking for ways to help their employees become better writers. In fact, in a recent study by the National Commission on Writing it was reported that even the top companies spend billions of dollars annually on remedial writing training.

What Corporate America Can't Build: A Sentence

Sam Dillon

Bloomington, Ill.—R. Craig Hogan, a former university professor who heads an online school for business writing here, received an anguished e-mail message recently from a prospective student.

"i need help," said the message, which was devoid of punctuation. "i am writing a essay on writing i work for this company and my boss want me to help improve the workers writing skills can yall help me with some information thank you."

Hundreds of inquiries from managers and executives seeking to improve their own or their workers' writing pop into Dr. Hogan's computer in-basket each month, he says, describing a number that has surged as e-mail has replaced the phone for much workplace communication. Millions of employees must write more frequently on the job than previously. And many are making a hash of it.

"E-mail is a party to which English teachers have not been invited," Dr. Hogan said. "It has companies tearing their hair out."

A recent survey of 120 American corporations reached a similar conclusion. The study, by the National Commission on Writing, a panel established by the College Board, concluded that a third of employees in the nation's blue-chip companies wrote poorly and that businesses were spending as much as $3.1 billion annually on remedial training.

The problem shows up not only in e-mail but also in reports and other texts, the commission said.

"It's not that companies want to hire Tolstoy," said Susan Traiman, a director at the Business Roundtable, an association of leading chief executives whose corporations were surveyed in the study. "But they need people who can write clearly, and many employees and applicants fall short of that standard."

Millions of inscrutable e-mail messages are clogging corporate computers by setting off requests for clarification, and many of the requests, in turn, are also chaotically written, resulting in whole cycles of confusion.

Here is one from a systems analyst to her supervisor at a high-tech corporation based in Palo Alto, Calif.: "I updated the Status report for the four discrepancies Lennie forward us via e-mail (they in Barry file) . . . to make sure my logic was correct It seems we provide Murray with incorrect information . . . However after verifying controls on JBL—JBL has the indicator as B ????—I wanted to make sure with the recent changes—I processed today—before Murray make the changes again on the mainframe to 'C'."

The incoherence of that message persuaded the analyst's employers that she needed remedial training.

"The more electronic and global we get, the less important the spoken word has become, and in e-mail clarity is critical," said Sean Phillips, recruitment director at another Silicon Valley corporation, Applera, a supplier of equipment for life science research, where most employees have advanced degrees. "Considering how highly educated our people are, many can't write clearly in their day-to-day work."

Some $2.9 billion of the $3.1 billion the National Commission on Writing estimates that corporations spend each year on remedial training goes to help current employees, with the rest spent on new hires. The corporations surveyed were in the mining, construction, manufacturing, transportation, finance, insurance, real estate and service industries, but not in wholesale, retail, agriculture, forestry or fishing, the commission said. Nor did the estimate include spending by government agencies to improve the writing of public servants.

An entire educational industry has developed to offer remedial writing instruction to adults, with hundreds of public and private universities, for-profit schools and freelance teachers offering evening classes as well as workshops, video and online courses in business and technical writing.

Kathy Keenan, a onetime legal proofreader who teaches business writing at the University of California Extension, Santa Cruz, said she sought to dissuade students from sending business messages in the crude shorthand they learned to tap out on their pagers as teenagers.

"hI KATHY i am sending u the assignment again," one student wrote to her recently. "i had sent you the assignment earlier but i didnt get a respond. If u get this assgnment could u please respond . thanking u for ur cooperation."

Most of her students are midcareer professionals in high-tech industries, Ms. Keenan said.

The Sharonview Federal Credit Union in Charlotte, N.C., asked about 15 employees to take a remedial writing course. Angela Tate, a mortgage processor, said the course eventually bolstered her confidence in composing e-mail, which has replaced much work she previously did by phone, but it was a daunting experience, since she had been out of school for years. "It was a challenge all the way through," Ms. Tate said.

Even C.E.O.'s need writing help, said Roger S. Peterson, a freelance writer in Rocklin, Calif., who frequently coaches executives. "Many of these guys write in inflated language that desperately needs a laxative," Mr. Peterson said, and not a few are defensive. "They're in denial, and who's going to argue with the boss?"

But some realize their shortcomings and pay Mr. Peterson to help them improve. Don Morrison, a onetime auditor at Deloitte & Touche who has built a successful consulting business, is among them.

"I was too wordy," Mr. Morrison said. "I liked long, convoluted passages rather than simple four-word sentences. And I had a predilection for underlining words and throwing in multiple exclamation points. Finally Roger threatened to rip the exclamation key off my keyboard."

Exclamation points were an issue when Linda Landis Andrews, who teaches at the University of Illinois at Chicago, led a workshop in May for midcareer executives at an automotive corporation based in the Midwest. Their exasperated supervisor had insisted that the men improve their writing.

"I get a memo from them and cannot figure out what they're trying to say," the supervisor wrote Ms. Andrews.

When at her request the executives produced letters they had written to a supplier who had failed to deliver parts on time, she was horrified to see that tone-deaf writing had turned a minor business snarl into a corporate confrontation moving toward litigation.

"They had allowed a hostile tone to creep into the letters," she said. "They didn't seem to understand that those letters were just toxic."

"People think that throwing multiple exclamation points into a business letter will make their point forcefully," Ms. Andrews said. "I tell them they're allowed two exclamation points in their whole life."

Not everyone agrees. Kaitlin Duck Sherwood of San Francisco, author of a popular how-to manual on effective e-mail, argued in an interview that exclamation points could help convey intonation, thereby avoiding confusion in some e-mail.

"If you want to indicate stronger emphasis use all capital letters and toss in some extra exclamation points," Ms. Sherwood advises in her guide, available at www.webfoot.com, where she offers a vivid example.

">Should I boost the power on the thrombo?

"NO!!!! If you turn it up to eleven, you'll overheat the motors, and IT MIGHT EXPLODE!!"

Dr. Hogan, who founded his online Business Writing Center a decade ago after years of teaching composition at Illinois State University here, says that the use of multiple exclamation points and other nonstandard punctuation like the :-) symbol are fine for personal e-mail but that companies have erred by allowing experimental writing devices to flood into business writing.

He scrolled through his computer, calling up examples of incoherent correspondence sent to him by prospective students.

"E-mails—that are received from Jim and I are not either getting open or not being responded to," the purchasing manager at a construction company in Virginia wrote in one memorandum that Dr. Hogan called to his screen. "I wanted to let everyone know that when Jim and I are sending out e-mails (example- who is to be picking up parcels) I am wanting for who ever the e-mail goes to to respond back to the e-mail. Its important that Jim and I knows that the person, intended, had read the e-mail. This gives an acknowledgment that the task is being completed. I am asking for a simple little 2 sec. Note that says "ok", "I got it", or Alright."

The construction company's human resources director forwarded the memorandum to Dr. Hogan while enrolling the purchasing manager in a writing course.

"E-mail has just erupted like a weed, and instead of considering what to say when they write, people now just let thoughts drool out onto the screen," Dr. Hogan said. "It has companies at their wits' end."

"What Corporate America Can't Build: A Sentence" by Sam Dillon, the *New York Times*, 7 December 2004. Copyright © 2004 by The New York Times Company. Reprinted with permission.

▶ Reflection Questions

1. This reading reports that even CEOs need help with writing. Do you think that first-year students need help with writing? Why or why not? What are some of the resources first-year students have to help with writing? Think about both on-campus and off-campus (online) supports. Give examples.

2. Take one of the examples that Dillon uses to illustrate ineffective communication. Do you agree with his criticisms? Is the younger generation more accepting of this kind of communication? Give an example of an acceptable message and then rewrite it in a way that very subtly crosses the line. In your opinion, what kinds of words and writing styles cross the line from acceptable to unacceptable?

3. Do you agree with the quote "E-mail has just erupted like a weed, and instead of considering what to say when they write, people just let thoughts drool out onto the screen"? Why or why not? Do you think you will use e-mail in your intended career? If you know what field you plan to work in, give an example. If you are not yet sure of your major, compare a job in a field where one will need to use e-mail extensively versus a job in a field where one will not.

Reading Two

In this reading, McQuain discusses the importance of clearly communicating what we mean. He suggests that we should express what we mean honestly, including using strong words when we should and less inflated words when we should. He describes a segment of Dwight Eisenhower's State of the Union Address in 1960 where Eisenhower said: "We live in a sea of semantic disorder in which old labels no longer faithfully describe. Police states are called people's democracies. Armed conquest of free people is called liberation."

Honest Words: Low-Impact Language
Jeffrey McQuain

Euphemism, the ultimate form of meekspeak, once had an important function. When a writer or speaker wished to avoid offending or insulting, a euphemistic term would be substituted. Today, though, euphemism is everywhere, bloating the language with dishonest words.

"His response has a credibility gap" avoids *lie,* and "Catch a classic episode of the television series tonight" avoids *rerun.* Similarly, *Department of Kinetic Wellness* is what a high school in Wisconsin calls its physical education program, and a trailer park is now glorified as a *mobile home resort.* The subject of English in many schools is no longer *English;* instead, it has become *language arts.* Even the simple *library* has been stretched, becoming a *media resource center.*

The use of inflated language is not the honest mistake of choosing the wrong word. When a guest on a radio talk show spoke of his youth and a lasting "childish dream of visiting Australia," he misspoke, substituting *childish* ("foolish") for *childhood* (a word that points back to the user's younger days). Euphemism, however, is deliberate and often dishonest.

This generation may be witnessing the passing away of honest language. In a crowded grocery store, a perplexed customer stops the manager next to the fruits and vegetables. "What's the difference," the customer asks, "between a yam and a sweet potato?" The manager pauses to think and finally answers, "Eight cents a pound."

Truth lurks in that old joke about the difference in naming, and that truth is based on the power of euphemism. Nothing is sold *used* anymore; even old wrecks of cars have taken the high road to being labeled *preowned.* If the new name suggests a higher quality, all the better, says the seller. Even *honest* implies something less than honest; restaurants now offer "soup made fresh from honest ingredients."

This Humpty Dumpty approach to language—a word means just what the user chooses—also requires a gullible audience, willing to accept whatever meaning the speaker or writer assigns to a word. (The same audience has probably been fooled by the comment "The word *gullible* isn't in the dictionary.") Without that implicit acceptance of a twisted meaning, the new term remains meaningless. Compared with words used for their true meanings, euphemism always forfeits its power.

EXPRESS TERMS HONESTLY

The twentieth century has been an age of euphemism. In 1929, the writer Paul Richard commented, "The vagabond, when rich, is called a tourist." Soon the floodgate opened.

When Dwight Eisenhower gave his State of the Union Address in 1960, he questioned the new way of words: "We live . . . in a sea of semantic disorder in which old labels no longer faithfully describe," the president said. "Police states are called 'people's democracies.' Armed conquest of free people is called 'liberation.'"

Politicians no longer want to raise taxes; instead, health care is to be paid for by *premiums.* Even the taxpayer is no longer so called. Check the fine print in the bulletins of the Internal Revenue Service, in which taxpayers are now referred to as "valued customers." That term implies voluntary business, but trying not to do business with the IRS is a crime.

Historically, some euphemisms have proved more useful than others. The delicacy of discussing death has given way to *passed away* or even the confusing *gone.* Less helpful was the Victorian era's use of *piano limbs* to avoid mentioning *legs,* just as *cashmere perspirer* is no improvement on the actual *sweater.* No other euphemism, however, can touch the mistaken impression created by *buy the farm;* that euphemism for *die,* as in "He just bought the farm," can be misunderstood, suggesting the recently deceased is still alive and dealing in real estate.

STRENGTHEN WEAK TERMS

Lucille Ball knew the humor in avoiding certain words. In an episode of *I Love Lucy,* she banters with her husband about using coercion to get her own way; he calls it blackmail. "Oh, let's not call it that," she responds. He repeats that it is still blackmail. "I know," Lucy agrees, "but let's not *call* it that."

Hiding behind euphemism is a sure way to make readers and listeners upset with the word user. Dishonest language appears so frequently that candid words become refreshing. Two years ago, the media celebrated a Virginia judge who reversed an earlier decision, adding the straightforward statement "I was *wrong.*" That adjective carried more blunt force than *incorrect* or *mistaken,* strengthened by its shortness.

Many weak euphemisms have shorter, stronger counterparts. *Layoffs* or cutting the work force should not be hidden as *downsizing* or *rightsizing,* and shrinking the number of workers is definitely not *miniaturizing.* Losing a job is not pleasant, no matter the name given to the process, and such weakness in word usage may lead the audience to wonder what else in the message is meant to remain hidden or unclear.

Sometimes writers and speakers twist the message on purpose. The use of hyperbole—deliberate overstatement—is found in any scheme labeled "Get rich quick!" Writers choose hyperbole for comic effect; when Shirley Jackson wrote of the humor in rearing four children, she used inflated terms to call those misadventures *Life Among the Savages* and *Raising Demons.*

Advertisers are especially adept at putting the hype into hyperbole. Overstatement can leave an audience skeptical, however, when every product is *new and improved* and *recommended most.* Similarly, the language is inflated when each passing rain shower is labeled "one of the worst storms in years"; even if the storm is severe, "a severe storm" does not need to be stretched into hyperbole—unless, of course, there are facts to back up the stronger statement.

The reverse of hyperbole is meiosis, also known as understatement. When the British first referred to the Atlantic Ocean as "the Pond," there was force in understating. Now, though, meiosis leans toward the dishonest ("Some assembly required") if not the outright lie ("The check is in the mail"). Be vigilant in finding terms that do not mislead.

FLATTEN INFLATED TERMS

Inflation seems to have taken over the language. Not every success is a *monster.* Not every performer is a *superstar,* nor every model a *supermodel.* Even the *information superhighway* has an inflated name. Advertisers give *an incredible discount* or try to lure customers with *a fabulous offer,* asking consumers to believe a discount that is not believable or accept an offer that should appear only in fables.

The simple *diet* has been unnecessarily stretched to *food program* and recently widened to *personal weight management.* A crime once known as a *felony* tries to masquerade today as a *felonious criminal incident.* In sheer force, a single word almost always outweighs a euphemistic phrase, but not when the word is inflated: Burger King has raised the person who takes the order and makes change from a *cashier* to an *expeditor.*

One sure way to flatten inflated terms is to remember the roots of words, the basis for their current meanings. *Astonishing* has become the usual synonym for *surprising;* the adjective *astonishing* comes from the Latin *tonere,* meaning "to thunder," and the accurate user of *astonishing* should feel the effect of being "thunderstruck."

Not every offer is *once in a lifetime,* nor every discount *out of this world.* Putting too much weight into modifiers for everyday words may inflate the meaning to the bursting point. Try instead to find exact nouns and verbs that require few modifiers to clarify the meaning.

In 1994, the federal government finally dropped its poorest designation of workers: *essential employees.* During winter storms in past years, Washington shut down except for the defense and safety workers who were considered crucial to the city's maintenance. Each winter the call went out for *essential employees,* an inflated term with the insulting implication that the majority of government workers are not essential. A better term was needed, and the government's choice was finally apt: *emergency workers.*

Inflate the values of words, and risk miscommunicating the message. *Euphemism* comes from the Greek roots for "good speaking," but the best speaking makes the message clear and honest. Insist on true meaning as much as possible, and audiences will come to trust the message as well as the messenger.

The ultimate word on euphemisms should be that the normal word almost always outpowers the formal word. Take *ultimate*, which may be replaced by *final*, which may be replaced by *last*. Knowing when to be formal and when to be forceful can help any writer or speaker overcome the urge to blur or inflate.

Watch the wording in the following sentences. Each example of euphemism may lead to humor or at least obscured language. Being specific is the surest way to eliminate (or *end*) the use of euphemism.

DEFLATING LANGUAGE

"The gentleman robbing the bank escaped the police." (Ignore the urge to elevate every man to *gentleman* or every woman to *lady;* often, as in this case, the result sounds ridiculous.)

"The field is not to be populated." (Computer users and form writers have come to expect this wordy version of "Leave the space blank.")

"Throughout the guitar concert, chords were digitally operated." (The review means to say "chords were *fingered.*")

"I'm an insect psychologist, a holistic pest-control technician." (This exterminator was having fun with the term *exterminator,* just as housewives have become *domestic engineers* and janitors are *sanitation engineers.*)

"We refer to those second showings as *encore performances.*" (A *rerun* by any other name, including *classic episode,* still looks the same.)

"The government is planning to introduce a new revenue enhancement." (This announcement normally follows a political promise of "no new taxes.")

"Incidental casualties have not yet been assessed." (Behind this military jargon is the reality of *innocent victims.*)

"During his career as a criminal, he burglarized hundreds of houses." (Burglary does not qualify as a *career;* try *years* or *time.*)

"We will be softening our prices 25 percent." (*Softening* is *lowering;* when prices go back up, will they be *hardening.*)

"His entrepreneurial endeavor will come to fruition in the next month or so." (A *new business* will soon be opening.)

"The medical booklet suggests that you consult your provider of care if you have questions." (This medical authority used to be called a *doctor.*)

"Next month we expect to be rightsizing our work force." (Employees should be prepared for the company's *downsizing,* another euphemism for *layoffs.*)

"The music store offers the assistance of customer sales counselors." (A *clerk* will try to help.)

"Headquarters are expected to be fully operational next month." (This inflation means *ready* or *working.*)

"For further recipes, please consult with our food service specialist." (Consider this phrase a meekspeak version of *cook.*)

▶ Reflection Questions

1. Do you think it's a good idea to use euphemisms? Give an example where you think it is appropriate to use one and explain why.

2. During your first year of college you will be writing for a variety of purposes that include both your classes and out-of-class activities. Give an example of an out-of-class activity where one might use inflated words for emphasis.

3. In 1994, the federal government dropped the term *essential workers* and replaced it with *emergency workers*. What do you see as the difference in these terms? Do you think this change was worth the time and money that was probably invested in making the switch?

Reading Three

In this reading, Vanderkam points out that many college students don't have the necessary writing skills to produce coherent essays or clear résumés. She believes that students simply have not written enough, do not have the necessary grammatical skills, haven't received the feedback they need, and often don't rewrite essays. She believes that schools have failed students.

Writing a Wrong: Too Many Students Can't Put Pen—or Pencil—to Paper

Laura Vanderkam

Ariel Horn is reaping praise these days for her first novel, *Help Wanted, Desperately*. But the writing feedback she remembers most wasn't a review. It was a letter, "B+" specifically, on a paper her junior year in high school.

"I was indignant!" she says. "How could my teacher not recognize my literary genius?"

Perhaps, the teacher noted, it was because her genius lay buried beneath grammatical woes. Horn rewrote the essay—and to this day cannot write in the passive voice.

"I have flashbacks of that B+ paper," she says.

Horn now teaches English in a Manhattan public school. Her students, too, revise papers multiple times as Horn advises their grammar and style. With 100-plus students, "I am personally in grading hell," she says. But her charges do learn to write.

Unfortunately, studies suggest that they're part of a small, lucky crew. As high school seniors race to meet December college-application deadlines, most face the oft-required "personal statement" with understandable dread. Only a quarter of America's 12th-graders, the 2002 National Assessment of Educational Progress found, can write tolerable essays. Only about 2% create the kind of zesty prose that makes reading worthwhile.

The well-financed among the rest hire editing services such as Essay Edge or Kaplan and zoom to the top of the college admissions pile. Meanwhile, schools that fail to teach writing face few consequences. For three years, the federal No Child Left Behind Act (NCLB) has held schools to strict reading and arithmetic standards. But the law is strangely quiet about the third "R" of the trio.

Education Secretary Rod Paige, who ushered NCLB into the schools, resigned Nov. 15. President Bush wants his new Education secretary, Margaret Spellings, to expand NCLB's math and reading testing in high schools.

Why stop at two of three R's? Holding schools accountable for teaching kids to write will both level the college playing field and give students a job skill they deserve.

A recent survey of corporate America by the National Commission on Writing found clear prose is a résumé must. "In most cases, writing ability could be your ticket in . . . or it could be your ticket out," one human resources (HR) director notes. Yet, "people's writing skills are not where they need to be," another says. Cover letters sag with needless words, fuzzy logic and grammatical mistakes. Ask college admissions counselors about application essays, and they list the same sins.

This is simple cause and effect. Grown-up Johnny can't write because young Johnny writes little beyond short book reports or haiku—and he rarely revises his work.

"The way we learn to write is to write—and to make errors—and to correct them," says Marilyn Whirry, a former National Teacher of the Year, who taught writing in California for three decades. Like Horn, young writers need teachers who circle weak verbs and the passive voice. But if a teacher has 100 students, a mere five minutes per paper per week is eight hours of Saturday work. A second draft doubles the load.

So even good teachers rarely bother. The results show. One national writing exam prompt asked 11th-graders to concoct a newspaper article on a haunted house. Almost half flunked; half gave "adequate" responses. That sounds OK until you read part of an "adequate" sample: "Man builds strange house to scare ghosts. He says that he did it to confuse the ghosts. But why may we ask would he want to spend 10 years building a house."

Flat. Poorly punctuated. Unlikely—in an admissions essay or job cover letter—to merit a second read.

Getting into college is tough enough without the handicap of poor writing skills. The essay-editing industry grows roughly 20% a year because, in a world where SAT prep classes coach board scores to oblivion and grade inflation runs rampant, colleges believe essays allow a glimpse of the real applicant.

The percentage of schools where essays carry "considerable importance" in admissions has grown from 14% in 1993 to 23% in 2003, and 37% among schools that admit fewer than 50% of applicants. Editors note the shoddiness of the essays they see; a few hundred dollars spent on prose polishing is the best admissions investment families can make.

But not everyone has the cash. We pay taxes to support schools, so schools should teach kids to write their own essays. And as the HR directors note, writing is a skill that workers need and too few of them have. NCLB reforms can help schools improve writing with two carrot-and-stick steps:

- Require schools to boost volume. Since writing is learned by writing, as Marilyn Whirry says, all subjects should require papers. History, science and health all benefit from the intensity writing requires.

  So, incidentally, do English classes. Too many English teachers give tests—"What color was Hester Prynne's 'A'?"—rather than assign papers requiring original ideas.

  They've got an excuse. The standards movement covers reading comprehension, not thesis statements. But as the SAT expands this spring to cover essay writing, states can test this skill—and make schools face the same consequences for failure as they do when kids can't read.

- Pay to make grading fly. Students learn grammar, mechanics and grace when teachers demand—and correct—three or more drafts of each paper. NCLB can cool teachers' "grading hell" by giving schools grants to outsource grading—not to India, but to freelance writers or grad students looking for cash.

  Whirry placed an ad in her town's paper seeking folks with college English degrees. She trained her new graders, then supervised the process. She saved time and could still assign 30 essays a year.

Not every classroom can be like Horn's, where students learn grammar by day and hear the teacher read her fiction at Barnes & Noble by night. But all students deserve the tools to make their ideas understood. As one HR director told the National Commission on Writing, "Applicants who provide poorly written letters likely wouldn't get an interview."

Schools fail students headed to college and the job market when they let poor writing slide.

"Writing a Wrong," by Laura Vanderkam, *USA Today,* December 1, 2004. Reprinted by permission of the author.

▶ Reflection Questions

1. How do you think schools can help students develop better writing skills? Should writing be required in most high school classes, not only English? Why or why not?

2. What does Marilyn Whirry mean when she says "The way we learn to write is to write—and to make errors and correct them"? Do you agree with this statement? Why or why not?

3. How would you assess your writing? Do you believe you are a good writer? Can you write a coherent essay or clear résumé? How do you know? (Do not base your answer on the grades you have received on papers, but give specific examples.)

Writing Assignment

audience: Your professor

purpose: To write an essay using examples of "meekspeak" and inflated words to describe an experience you had during your first semester in college

length: A five-paragraph essay typed and double-spaced (Make two copies so that other members of the class can read your example.)

For this assignment, choose a time when you were describing how difficult you thought the test was you took in a class. You could begin by saying it was "a challenging test." You might also report that this was "the hardest test you ever took" (maybe it was?) or that you studied "most of the night" when in fact you went to bed at 2 A.M. Every time you use an example of "meekspeak" or an inflated word, **bold** it. Essays will be shared with another class member for peer review.

Journal Entries: DISCOVERY AND INTENTION STATEMENTS

Think of a time when you were writing to someone or writing a paper when you did not feel confident about your message. What did you do? Did you just send it or turn it in? How did you feel after you did that? Can you think of any campus resources that you might use to help you? Would you use them? Why or why not?

How do these readings relate to the Power Process "employ your word"? What are some of the tools that you will need to succeed in college based on the readings? Sometimes when we respond quickly to an e-mail, especially when we are upset about something, what we think we said is perceived very differently by the receiver. Can you think of some specific example of a situation where this happened to you? If it has never happened, think of a situation where it might. Consider how impulsive behaviors can cause communication breakdowns. Write one or two sentences about what you have learned and what you intend to do as a result of these readings, what you will do to make it work, and what you risk if you don't do what you intend to do.

Mastering Vocabulary

List five words that were new to you (more or less if necessary). For each, include which reading you found the word in, the definition, and where you got the definition from, as well as a time or place you might use the word again.

1.

2.

3.

4.

5.

 # Additional Activities

1. Look at the e-mail you sent this week and find an example that illustrates what Dillon describes in the first reading. What could you do to make your message more effective?

2. Look in the local newspaper to find advertisements that use inflated words like "once in a lifetime" or "lowest prices of the season." Cut these ads out and bring them to class to discuss the impact on the consumer. Do you think there might be a relationship between these advertisements and the level of education of the consumer?

3. Define *meekspeak* and give the reasons it was used in the past and now. Find an example of "meekspeak" and show it to three other people. Are your interpretations the same?

Online Study Center   **Improve Your Grade**
Visit the Online Study Center for resources and exercises to accompany this text
http://college.hmco.com/pic/msreader1e

CHAPTER NINE

Choose Your Conversations and Your Community

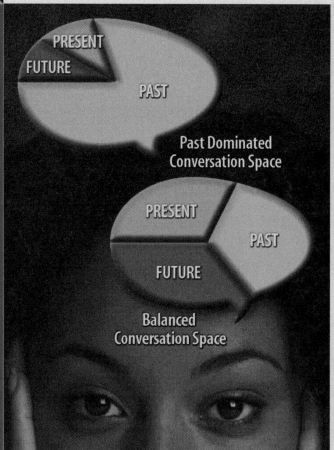

PRESENT
FUTURE
PAST

Past Dominated
Conversation Space

PRESENT
PAST
FUTURE

Balanced
Conversation Space

Conversations we have with others expand our experiences. Presumably, in each conversation we have, we have an opportunity to learn something new. Unfortunately, what we learn may not always be something positive, since conversations are influenced by whomever we are talking to. College is a wonderful time to expand whom we have conversations with. Perhaps your hometown was small, or maybe you were with the same students all throughout high school. No matter your circumstances, your conversations and the topics discussed are always limited by whom you know. College is the time to expand your conversations and maximize what you learn from them.

The Power Process: Choose Your Conversations and Your Community

Conversations can exist in many forms. One involves people talking out loud to each other. At other times, the conversation takes place inside our own heads, and we call it thinking. We are even having a conversation when we read a magazine or a book, watch television or a movie, or write a letter or a report. These observations have three implications that wind their way through every aspect of our lives.

Conversations shape our lives

One is that conversations exercise incredible power over what we think, feel, and do. We become our conversations. They shape our attitudes, our decisions, our opinions, our emotions, and our actions. Each of these is primarily the result of what we say over and over again, to ourselves and to others. If you want clues as to what a person will be like tomorrow, listen to what she's talking about today.

Conversation is constant

This leads to a second discovery. Given that conversations are so powerful, it's amazing that few people act on this fact. Most of us swim in a constant sea of conversations, almost none of which we carefully and thoughtfully choose.

Consider how this works. It begins when we pick up the morning paper. The articles on the front page invite us to a conversation about current events. Often the headlines speak of war, famine, unemployment figures, and other species of disaster. The advertisements start up a conversation about fantastic products for us to buy. They talk about hundreds of ways for us to part with our money.

That's not all. If we flip on the radio or television or if we surf the Web, millions of other conversations await us. Thanks to modern digital technology, many of these conversations take place in CD-quality sound, high-resolution images, and living color twenty-four hours each day.

Something happens when we tune in to conversation in any of its forms. We give someone else permission to dramatically influence our thoughts—the conversation in our heads. When we watch a movie, scenes from that movie become the images in our minds. When we read a book, passages from that book become the voice in our heads. It's possible to let this happen dozens of times each day without realizing it.

You have a choice

The real power of this process lies in a third discovery: We can choose our conversations. Certain conversations create real value for us. They give us fuel for reaching our goals. Others distract us from what we want. They might even create lasting unhappiness and frustration.

We can choose more of the conversations that exhilarate and sustain us. Sometimes we can't control the outward circumstances of our lives. Yet no matter what happens, we can retain the right to choose our conversations.

Suppose that you meet with an instructor to ask about some guidelines for writing a term paper. She launches into a tirade about your writing skills and lack of preparation for higher education. This presents you with several options. One is to talk about what a jerk the instructor is and give up on the idea of learning to write well. Another option is to refocus the conversation on what you can do to improve your writing skills, such as working with a writing tutor or taking a basic composition class. These two sets of conversations will have vastly different consequences for your success in school.

The conversations you have are dramatically influenced by the people you associate with. If you want to change your attitudes about almost anything—prejudice, politics, religion, humor—choose your conversations by choosing your community. Spend time with people who speak about and live consistently with the attitudes you value. Use conversations to change habits. Use conversations to create new options in your life.

A big part of this Power Process is choosing *not* to participate in certain conversations. Sometimes we find ourselves in conversations that are not empowering—gripe sessions, gossip, and the like. That's a time for us to switch the conversation channel. It can be as simple as changing the topic, politely offering a new point of view, or excusing ourselves and walking away.

Some conversations are about antagonism. Instead of resolving conflict, they fan the flames of prejudice, half-truths, and misunderstanding. We can begin taking charge of these conversations by noticing where they start and choosing ways to change them.

Go for balance

One immediate way to take charge of any conversation is to notice its *time frame*—whether the conversation dwells on the past, the present, or the future.

Conversations about the past can be fun and valuable. When we focus exclusively on the past, however, we can end up rehashing the same incidents over and over again. Our future could become little more than a minor variation of what has already occurred in our lives.

Conversations with a focus on the future can also be empowering. A problem arises if these conversations focus on worst-case scenarios about what could go wrong next week, next month, or next year. Having too many of these conversations can add a baseline of worry and fear to our lives.

As an alternative, we can choose to have constructive conversations about the present as well as the past and future. Conversations about the past can dwell on what we learn from our experiences. Conversations about the present can focus on what we currently love about our lives and on ways to solve problems. Instead of worrying about the future, we can use our planning skills to set goals that we feel passionately about and consider ways to prevent potential problems.

In looking for ways to balance our conversations, we can also select among four categories of *topics:* things, other people, ourselves, and relationships. Most conversations fall into one of these categories.

Many people talk about things (cars, houses, trips, football games, weather) or gossip about others (politicians, actors, neighbors, kids, coworkers) far more than they talk about anything else. To create more balance in your conversations, remember the other two categories of topics. Talk about yourself—your heartfelt desires, fears, and joys—and about ways to create more loving relationships as well.

Conversations promote success

Excelling in higher education means allowing plenty of time for conversations that start in class and continue in your reading and your notes. Extend those conversations by visiting with your instructors during their office hours, talking to classmates, and forming study groups.

Right now you're holding a conversation about student success. This conversation has a big red cover that features the words *Becoming a Master Student.* Its chapters invite you to twelve subconversations that can make a real difference in what you get in exchange for your hard-earned tuition money.

When we choose our conversations, we discover a tool of unsurpassed power. This tool has the capacity to remake our thoughts—and thus our lives. It's as simple as choosing the next article you read or the next topic you discuss with a friend.

Begin applying this Power Process today. Start choosing your conversations and watch what happens.

Readings

Readings in this chapter are about conversations you may have with people that you would not have communicated with in the past. The readings suggest topics one might engage in on a college campus and include what it means to communicate and display civility on campus. There is a reading about students with learning disabilities (the invisible disability) as well as a selection on females in college. Women are the majority of the college population and are enrolling in fields such as science and mathematics that were once male-dominated areas.

Reading One

The college professor Mike Adams is concerned about the growing lack of civility and respect on college campuses. He shares his class policies regarding cell phones and tardiness. In addition, he gives some suggestions about people to interview and provides the questions if students ever have to write a paper on civility for his class.

Welcome to Civility 101

Mike S. Adams

January 5, 2004

Dear Students:

Welcome back! I hope you had a good Christmas break (or Kwanzaa break, or whatever you celebrate). Mine was great but now it's time to get back to work as we kick off a new semester. Those of you who have had my classes before need to pay close attention to this memo because I am changing some of my class policies this semester. Specifically, I am changing the way that I deal with those who interrupt class by either walking in late or by allowing their cell phones to ring during a lecture.

At the end of last semester, I decided that something had to be done about this diminishing level of respect shown by students towards their professors and their fellow classmates. This decision came shortly after I sat in on another professor's class. While I was listening to a 75-minute lecture, the students interrupted the professor at least 58 times before I lost count.

First, a student came in class three minutes late. Then another student came in 15 minutes late. Then another student came in 25 minutes late. Then the first cell phone went off. Then the second cell phone went off. The other 53 interruptions were variations of "what was that again?" and "could you repeat that?" A raised hand accompanied none of these 53 interruptions from daydreaming students. They just shouted at the professor to get his attention. And they didn't seem to care whether he was in the middle of a sentence. Interestingly, most of these students were in their third year of college.

I haven't ever had a major problem with the hand raising issue. I just don't answer students' questions if they don't raise their hand. But the cell phone and tardiness problems have exploded over the last five years or so. Most of my liberal colleagues have just allowed these problems to get worse. No matter how bad it gets, these PhDs just can't seem to find a solution. Actually, that isn't fair. They could find a solution if they wanted to, but they just don't like imposing their own truths upon their students, who may live according to a different set of truths. And, of course, being disrupted by late students with cell phones gives them something to whine about during department meetings.

As most of you know, I take a different approach to these problems. First, I shut the door at the beginning of each class period. Then, if a student walks in late, he (it usually is a male, no offense to tardy feminists) gets three points deducted from his final average. If his cell-phone rings (no offense to co-dependent feminists), I deduct three points from his final average per ring. And if she (sorry guys, it is usually a female) actually answers the call, she fails the course. And, last semester, I actually started deducting points from the students' average if they (regarding gender, this is a closer call—no pun intended) are merely in possession of a cell phone. But, unfortunately, last semester, four different students let their cell phones (which were hidden in their pockets) go off in class. All four were one-ringers. I also had one student in each class who decided to repeatedly come to class late.

In light of the on-going problems with tardiness and cell phones, I am going to modify my class policies this semester. I am not going to follow the advice of my anti-war colleagues who think that we need to talk to tardy cell phone people in order to find out why they hate us. Instead, I am going to let them do most of the talking. The specifics of my new policy follow:

If your cell phone goes off in class, or if you are late to class, you must write a 2500-word paper (minimum) entitled "The Death of Civility at the Postmodern University." In this paper, you will be asked to write about the decline of civility in our public universities in recent decades. Please note that if you are late more than once, or if your cell phone goes off on more than one occasion, your paper must be a minimum of 5000 words. If you have three separate transgressions, you automatically fail the course. Finally, the paper must be of "A" quality in order for you to stay in the course. You will receive no other credit for completing this project, except, of course, for its positive impact upon your character.

Since you have probably never written on this subject, and since the paper is fairly long, I have listed a couple of suggestions to help you get started and to help you fulfill the minimum word requirement. These suggestions are not exhaustive, nor are they mandated, but I think they will be helpful.

SUGGESTION #1

Interview a person who was alive during World War II. Ask them the following questions:

1. How often did students walk into class late when you were in school?
2. How many of your failures in school were the result of a lack of "nurturing" by your teachers?
3. Did your teachers spend a lot of time boosting your self-esteem and soothing your inner child, even when you failed to adhere to the rules of the classroom?
4. Did any of your teachers ever suggest that punctuality was an antiquated Western notion with racist, sexist, and classist overtones?
5. Did students ever get up and leave in the middle of a lecture if they had to go to the bathroom, without asking the permission of the teacher?
6. Did students ever take long potty breaks in the middle of exams, without asking the permission of the teacher?
7. Did students ever get up and leave class just because they were bored?
8. Did you ever appeal a test score in front of the entire class or help other students do the same? If so, did you predicate your complaint with "hey Dr. Ummm," or "dude, you ripped me off."
9. Did you ever interrupt a professor to ask whether what he was saying was "important" or whether you "had to know it for the next test?"
10. Did people actually manage to finish school without having a cell phone with them at all times?

SUGGESTION #2

Interview an employee at the Office of Campus Diversity or any professor currently teaching in the social sciences or humanities. Ask them the following questions:

1. Is it possible that the diversity movement, with its emphasis on moral relativism, causes students to dismiss the rules a professor establishes with regard to appropriate class conduct?
2. If it is good to refrain from judging other people, doesn't that mean that we should stop expelling people for plagiarism?
3. Isn't the statement "it is good to refrain from judging other people" itself judgmental?
4. Is it possible that liberal professors who teach that people are not responsible for their own behavior unwittingly encourage their students to engage in anti-social behavior such as compulsive tardiness?
5. Is cheating wrong just because a professor says it is wrong?
6. If a student claims that cheating is acceptable in his/her culture, is he/she exempt from punishment for cheating?
7. Can a student be given credit for an answer that the professor deems to be wrong, just because the student "feels" it is right?

8. What if everyone decided to come to class late every day?

9. If tardiness becomes even more prevalent than it is today, can we just write "whenever, man" under the designation for class meeting time in the course-scheduling catalogue?

10. When professors come to class late, does that in any way encourage their students to do the same thing? Does that undermine the professor's moral authority?

In closing, let me say that I hope you don't put yourself in the position of having to write a civility paper this semester. If you do, I would advise you to follow the first suggestion and interview a person who was alive during World War II. I don't mean to stereotype, but these people tend to be very helpful and patient.

Unfortunately, you may find the second suggestion to be less fruitful. University professors and administrators tend to be less patient and less accessible. After all, they're usually busy constructing a Utopian society. They seldom have time to talk about civility.

"Welcome to Civility 101" by Mike S. Adams, January 5, 2004. Reprinted by permission of the author.

▶ Reflection Questions

1. What did you learn about civility from this essay?

2. Do you agree with Professor Adams's approach in closing the door when class begins, so that if a student is tardy, he can identify the student and deduct points from his grade? What is your response to this as the person who may be late? What is your response as one of the students in the class which has been disrupted by students who come in late? Would you change anything about his policy, and if so, why? Do you feel Professor Adams is choosing his conversation carefully with his students? Why or why not?

3. When students are late or their cell phone goes off in class, Professor Adams requires them to write a paper related to civility. He gives the students some suggestions for interviewing people who were alive during World War II. Why do you think he suggests this? Is it a good idea?

Reading Two

Diversity on campus now encompasses a fast-growing group of college students—students with learning disabilities. However, as Thomas Wolanin, a higher education policy expert says, "It's not like someone who is in a wheelchair or is blind, where you are immediately aware of the disability. There is a kind of extra burden of proof or extra suspicion that greets students with learning disabilities." Students who require any kind of extra support may need to have conversations with roommates, professors, and the like to share their strengths and challenges with these individuals in order to succeed in college.

"Invisible" Disability Now Visible on Campus
Back to School

Bill Schackner

Days after enrolling as a college freshman, David Carson had to admit to a stranger that he couldn't spell the name of the school he was attending.

An employee watching him struggle to write out a check couldn't believe he needed her help to spell "Indiana," "University" and "Pennsylvania."

"Just write IUP!" she snapped, flashing a look so cutting he remembers it to this day.

"I felt very small," says Carson, who took to carrying a prepared list of the spellings he'd need to survive each day. "I thought I was dumb."

Turns out he had a learning disability affecting his spelling, one that drove him from IUP and two other schools but one he overcame in time to graduate from La Roche College in 1992 with a near-perfect grade average of 3.91. Now a college recruiter who speaks to those with similar disabilities, Carson is watching as this latest group of once-excluded students becomes increasingly visible on America's college campuses.

He knows their growing ranks mean more will ultimately succeed. But he also knows many will struggle with self-doubt and embarrassment as he once did, or simply give up.

About one in 25 college students is learning disabled, up sharply from the 1980s, as more students who have been diagnosed with such disorders set their sights beyond high school, according to a June report by the Washington, D.C.–based Institute for Higher Education Policy. The most common among this group of disabilities is dyslexia, a difficulty acquiring and using language that often translates into poor spelling, writing or reading.

Nationwide, students with learning disabilities are the fastest-growing segment of all disabled students in college and are part of what some say is the newest wave of campus diversity. Just as laws brought more working-class students, racial minorities and women onto campuses, disabled students are gaining access they were once denied.

But unlike other disabilities, those that involve learning are "invisible," experts say. Some argue that, once on campus, the biggest obstacle these students face is skepticism as to whether they are using special classroom accommodations as a crutch or, worse, want to game the system.

"It's not like someone who is in a wheelchair or is blind where you are immediately aware of the disability," said Thomas Wolanin, a higher education policy expert and co-author of the Institute's report. "There is this kind of extra burden of proof or extra suspicion that greets students with learning disabilities."

Is it fair that someone with normal intelligence but an impaired ability to write sentences gets permission to deliver essays orally instead of on paper? Are professors obliged to adjust their teaching style because one student processes information differently from the rest of the class?

"That's the debate. Are we giving them an advantage or are we just leveling the playing field?" said Eileen Henry, who works with learning disabled students at Muskingum College, a small Ohio campus known nationally for its work in the field. "I happen to believe we are leveling the playing field and I'm still not sure the Americans with Disabilities Act actually does that.

"I have heard other teachers say things like, 'I'm not going to change my teaching style just for them. They have to adapt to what I do.'"

Judging by sheer volume of programs, colleges and universities are doing more than ever to accommodate—and in some cases actively recruit—these students. A 500-page guidebook published by Thomson-Peterson's profiles 1,100 campuses that offer help, ranging from tutors to special software to substituting a class most at odds with a disability.

"I see more and more campuses making a serious commitment," said Lydia Block, an educational consultant in Columbus, Ohio.

But others argue that even as these programs proliferate, the quality of help varies widely. And what limited information exists on the subject indicates these students are significantly more likely to drop out.

Forty-six percent of them did compared with 33 percent of students without a disability, according to one study by the U.S. Department of Education.

"These kids tend to go from college to college," insists Trea Graham of Mt. Lebanon, an advocate, consultant and mother of a learning disabled son. "They almost always go to more than one school because they aren't successful."

Under law, certain classroom accommodations are available, including extra time to take tests, books on tape and help with note-taking, but only if a student with a documented disability identifies himself as such and seeks help.

Many do so and benefit from it.

Graham's son, David, is one of them. He earned a chemistry degree last year from Muskingum, where students pay up to $4,850 a year extra for specialized tutoring and other assistance.

Graham, 23, who was diagnosed in junior high school with a written expression disorder, struggles to translate thoughts into written sentences. When he tried, he said, "I would make six sentences into one incredibly long sentence" without punctuation.

Getting permission to take essay exams on a computer rather than in his own handwriting "allowed me to go back and put in the punctuation and divide up the sentences," Graham said.

Also helpful was the extra time he received to finish exams and the option of taking them away from class in a room with less noise and distraction.

Encouragement from professors and others buoyed him, too. It was different from what he remembered about high school, where he said getting classroom accommodations sometimes meant being treated "like you were a pain . . . or you were retarded."

At Muskingum, said Graham, "They were used to dealing with stuff like this. It wasn't a big deal."

The problem, say some advocates, is that such experiences are far from universal.

Ian Swayne, 20, of Franklin Park, was so turned off by his early college experiences he wants to enroll this winter at Vermont's Landmark College, a school that charges up to $43,000 but is renowned for working exclusively with attention disorders and learning disabilities like the dyslexia Swayne was diagnosed with in 10th grade.

Swayne said he didn't appreciate being berated by one instructor for copying a term off a classmate's worksheet. It didn't make sense to search the textbook for the term, he contends, because his disability makes it impossible to scan pages of text at any reasonable speed.

But the instructor wasn't buying his explanation.

"Her thing was, she thought I was cheating," he said. "She patronized me by saying her 6-year-old was able to look stuff up."

Sometimes, say campus administrators, the real problem is a student's own reluctance to seek help. Intent on escaping labels placed on them in high school, some will shun the very assistance that can be the difference between thriving and flunking out.

"It's not unusual for me to talk to a freshman who says, 'I don't want the accommodation. I want to do it on my own. I want to be like everyone else,'" said Larry Powell, who works with learning disabled students at Carnegie Mellon University.

Knowing they are flirting with disaster, especially on a campus with such a punishing workload, Powell gives the same advice over and over. "It's best to arm yourself," he tells them. "Take the accommodation."

At Carnegie Mellon, where there are about 125 learning disabled students, Powell said professors are respectful. But sometimes a parent's ultimate opinion of his operation comes down to simply how well the child did.

And often, that depends on how well the family or the high school prepared that student for a world where they suddenly are responsible under the law to secure whatever special assistance they require.

"I've had students who come in here and can't tell me what their diagnosis is," said Muskingum's Henry.

"When I ask them how they think it influences their life, they look to their parents to answer the question. They haven't even thought of it."

In speeches he gives to college-bound students with learning disabilities, Carson, of Upper St. Clair, emphasizes the need to be one's own advocate. He has self-published a 100-page survival guide for them that borrows heavily from his own tortuous diploma hunt, which stretched from 1975 to 1992.

Articulate in conversation, he uses complex thoughts that flow easily from one to the next. But not so on paper. His written expression disability reduces those ideas to brief, halting sentences that seem almost childlike.

"Everybody says to me, just write the way you talk. But it doesn't work like that," said Carson, 47, now an Allied Health recruiter at the Community College of Allegheny County. "I wish that it did."

But in a point he makes over and over to students, Carson has come to believe those words and sentences don't reflect the ideas behind them.

"I can't spell at all, I read very slowly, I write like a fifth-grader and I am very smart," he says in a typical opening to audiences. "And so are you."

▶ Reflection Questions

1. In this reading Schackner reports that sometimes campus administrators say the biggest challenge for a student with a learning disability is the student's own reluctance to seek help. Why do you think this may be true? What suggestions do you have for a student with a learning disability?

2. What is your campus's commitment to supporting students with disabilities? While you may not think you have a need for disability services, suppose you broke your leg and couldn't easily get around campus. How might campus support services for students with disabilities help you?

3. Could you predict any difficulties between roommates if one did have a learning disability and did not share it with her roommate? What kind of problems might you find?

4. If students with disabilities are permitted extra time on an exam and allowed to take the exam on a computer, should all students be given the same right? Is it a right for everyone? Why or why not?

Reading Three

Would you like to have a conversation with Harvard's former president Lawrence H. Summers about his comments that biological differences may prevent women from performing well in science and engineering? This article is the American Association of University Professors' (AAUP's) response to President Summers's suggestion that innate differences between the genders may be the reason why fewer women than men seek careers in math and sciences. See if you agree with the AAUP or with President Summers.

For the Record

The AAUP's Committee on Women Responds to Lawrence Summers

In January 2005, Harvard University president Lawrence Summers suggested at a scholarly meeting attended by many accomplished women scientists that innate differences between the genders may be one reason that fewer women than men pursue careers in science and mathematics. At its spring 2005 meeting, the AAUP's Committee on Women in the Academic Profession drafted the following response to his widely publicized comments.

The ongoing debate over Lawrence Summers's January 14 remarks indicates how fraught a topic gender equity in the academy—and specifically in the sciences—continues to be. The Association's Committee on Women in the Academic Profession would like to take this opportunity to respond. While we agree with Dr. Summers that women continue to be underrepresented in these fields, we disagree with his uninformed speculation about why this is the case. Our response is based on a number of recent studies, including a 2002 report of the National Science Foundation titled *Women, Minorities, and Persons with Disabilities in Science and Engineering*, and the work of University of California, Berkeley, researchers Mary Ann Mason and Marc Goulden on academic careers and family formation.

The research shows that although there has been an increase in the number of women who hold graduate degrees in science and engineering, there are still significant institutional barriers to success for women scientists, including insufficient lab space, salaries that lag behind those of male colleagues, and the difficulty of balancing work and family. In our assessment, these and other roadblocks, including gender bias and discrimination, are the primary reasons for the underrepresentation of women in the sciences and engineering. Summers misses the point that bias plays a part in decisions with respect to women faculty—continuing discrimination, continuing lack of academic support, and continuing insensitivity to work and family conflicts.

The data from the AAUP's annual survey of faculty compensation and tenure status indicate that women in all disciplines are underrepresented at doctoral universities and are also less likely to achieve senior faculty status. Women also suffer from continuing disadvantages in salary; overall, full-time women faculty earn approximately 80 percent of what men earn. In addition, other data show that women are more likely to hold part-time or non-tenure-track faculty positions across all types of institutions.

Further, the AAUP's research indicates that work and family conflicts play a role in the underrepresentation of women in science and engineering—perhaps more so than in other disciplines. Women constitute fewer than 20 percent of science and engineering faculty in four-year colleges and universities (for more information, see the Web site of the National Science Foundation's ADVANCE program). As Mason and Goulden's research has shown, tenured women in science are less likely than other tenured women to have children, suggesting women in academic science perceive that they must choose either family or career. In November 2001, the AAUP adopted its "Statement of Principles on Family Responsibilities and Academic Work" which addresses the dilemma faced by junior faculty members whose years of probationary service coincide with a time in their lives during which they might become new parents. The AAUP statement contends that "the goal of every institution should be to create an academic community in which all members are treated equitably, families are supported, and family-care concerns are regarded as legitimate and important," and it suggests policies such as stopping the tenure clock and paid family leave that could be instituted to address the difficulty of balancing family and career.

Reprinted with permission from the July/August 2005 issue of *Academe*, the magazine of the American Association of University Professors.

▶ Reflection Questions

1. Although more women than men attend college and proportionally more women graduate, why do *you* think there are fewer women in the math and science areas?

2. Given the fact that women are graduating in record numbers, they still do not hold positions as high as men in most companies and their salaries lag behind. What are some of the reasons for this? How do you feel about it?

3. What suggestions for women would you have about choosing a college major? Would you tell them that the sky is the limit for their future career? Think about what careers are more likely to pay women the same as their male counterparts. Be prepared to support your answer.

◆ Writing Assignment _____

audience: College administrators

purpose: To share your concerns with college administrators about one of the three topics noted below

length: Minimum of three typed pages, double-spaced

College is a time and place where differences of opinions and concerns can be shared freely and, if done appropriately, with no negative consequences. In this writing assignment you have a choice. You can share your concerns with the college administration on the need for a uniform college cell phone policy, the need for colleges to work closely with businesses recruiting college graduates so that females get the same salaries as males, or the need for only students with disabilities to be allowed untimed testing and use of a computer for tests.

Journal Entries: DISCOVERY AND INTENTION STATEMENTS

How do these readings relate to the Power Process "choosing your conversations and your community"? Think about a time when you wish you had had a conversation with someone and a time when you do not. What was your reason for not communicating with that person? What, if anything, do you wish you had told that person, and what was the result of not sharing your thoughts or concerns?

What are some of the tools that you will need to succeed in college on the basis of the readings? Can you think of some specific examples of situations where you might use these tools? Refer to Chickering's suggestions (see chapter one, pg.28) that in the future, workers need to be able to see multiple sides of an issue to be successful. Write one or two sentences about what you have learned and what you intend to do as a result of these readings, what you will do to make it work, and what you risk if you do not do what you intend to do.

Mastering Vocabulary

List five words that were new to you (more or less if necessary). For each, include which reading you found the word in, the definition, and where you got the definition from, as well as a time or place you might use the word again.

1.

2.

3.

4.

5.

 ## Additional Activities

1. Suppose you were a faculty member and were concerned about students arriving late to class and having cell phones go off in class. How would you handle these situations? Develop a policy that you will share with the class. You could simply have a conversation with the class, but be prepared to state what you might do if this conversation did not get the results you wanted.

2. Develop a college recruiting brochure for prospective majors in one of the sciences. Aim for recruitment of both males and females for the major.

3. Explore your college's Office for Students with Disabilities. What services are provided? Are there costs involved? How do students get testing if they think they may have a disability? How are disabilities documented? Report back to the class.

Online Study Center **Improve Your Grade**
Visit the Online Study Center for resources and exercises to accompany this text
http://college.hmco.com/pic/msreader1e

CHAPTER TEN

Risk Being a Fool

Have you ever not tried something because you thought you would make a fool of yourself? Sometimes this fear of failure gets in the way of trying something new. If we never try anything new, then we can never succeed at new things. A student voice, Steve Tran, said in the Power Process that he was always afraid of doing new things, so he didn't take risks for fear of what people might think of him. This kind of thinking makes us powerless to grow. Tran, like you, can learn to overcome this fear.

The Power Process: Risk Being a Fool

A powerful person has the courage to take risks. And taking risks means being willing to fail sometimes—even to be a fool. This idea can work for you because you already are a fool.

Don't be upset. All of us are fools at one time or another. There are no exceptions. If you doubt it, think back to that stupid thing you did just a few days ago. You know the one—Yes *that* one. It was embarrassing and you tried to hide it. You pretended you weren't a fool. This happens to everyone.

People who insist that they have never been fools are perhaps the biggest fools of all. We are all fallible human beings. Most of us, however, spend too much time and energy trying to hide our foolhood. No one is really tricked by this—not even ourselves. And whenever we pretend not to be something we're not, we miss part of life.

For example, many of us never dance because we don't want to risk looking ridiculous. We're not wrong. We probably would look ridiculous. That's the secret of risking being a fool.

It's OK to look ridiculous while dancing. It's all right to sound silly when singing to your kids. Sometimes it's OK to be absurd. It comes with taking risks.

Taking risks is not being foolhardy

Sometimes it's not OK to be absurd. This Power Process comes with a warning label: Taking risks does *not* mean escaping responsibility for our actions. "Risk being a fool" is not a suggestion to get drunk at a party and make a fool of yourself. It is not a suggestion to act the fool by disrupting class. It is not a suggestion to be foolhardy or to "fool around."

"Risk being a fool" means recognizing that foolishness—along with dignity, courage, cowardice, grace, clumsiness, and other qualities—is a human characteristic. We all share it. You might as well risk being a fool because you already are one, and nothing in the world can change that. Why not enjoy it once in a while? Consider the case of the person who won't dance because he's afraid he'll look foolish. This same person will spend an afternoon tripping over his feet on a basketball court. If you say that his jump shot from the top of the key looks like a circus accident, he might even agree.

"So what?" he might say. "I'm no Michael Jordan." He's right. On the basketball court, he is willing to risk looking like a fool in order to enjoy the game.

He is no Fred Astaire, either. For some reason, that bothers him. The result is that he misses the fun of dancing. (Dancing badly is as much fun as shooting baskets badly—and maybe a lot more fun.)

There's one sure-fire way to avoid any risk of being a fool, and that's to avoid life. The writer who never finishes a book will never have to worry about getting negative reviews. The center fielder who sits out every game is safe from making any errors. And the comedian who never performs in front of an audience is certain to avoid telling jokes that fall flat. The possibility of succeeding at any venture increases when we're comfortable with making mistakes—that is, with the risk of being a fool.

Look at courage in a new way

Again, remember the warning label. This Power Process does not suggest that the way to be happy in life is to do things badly. Courage involves the willingness to face danger and risk failure. Mediocrity is not the goal. The point is that mastery in most activities calls for the willingness to do something new, to fail, to make corrections, to fail again, and so on. On the way to becoming a good writer, be willing to be a bad writer.

Consider these revised clichés: Anything worth doing is worth doing badly at first. Practice makes improvement. If at first you don't fail, try again.

Most artists and athletes have learned the secret of being foolish. Comedians are especially well versed in this art. All of us know how it feels to tell a joke and get complete silence. We truly look and feel like fools. Professional comedians risk feeling that way for a living. Being funny is not enough for success in the comedy business. A comedian must have the courage to face failure.

Courage is an old-fashioned word for an old-fashioned virtue. Traditionally, people have reserved that word for illustrious acts of exceptional people—the campaigns of generals and the missions of heroes.

This concept of courage is fine. At the same time, it can be limiting and can prevent us from seeing courage in everyday actions. Courage is the kindergartner who, with heart pounding, waves good-bye to his parents and boards the bus for his first day of school. Courage is the forty-year-old who registers for college courses after being away from the classroom for twenty years.

For a student, the willingness to take risks means the willingness to experiment with new skills, to achieve personal growth, and sometimes to fail. The rewards of risk taking include expanded creativity, more satisfying self-expression, and more joy.

An experiment for you

Here's an experiment you can conduct to experience the joys of risk taking. The next time you take a risk and end up doing something silly or stupid, allow yourself to be totally aware of your reaction. Don't deny it. Don't cover it up. Notice everything about the feeling, including the physical sensations and thoughts that come with it. Acknowledge the foolishness. Be exactly who you are. Explore all of the emotions, images, and sensations surrounding your experience.

Also remember that we can act independently of our feelings. Courage is not the absence of fear but the willingness to take risks even when we feel fear. We can be keenly homesick and still register for classes. We can tremble at the thought of speaking in public yet still walk up to the microphone.

When we fully experience it, the fear of taking risks loses its power. Then we have the freedom to expand and grow.

Readings

Readings in this chapter were chosen to help you think about your options and the fact that when you make a decision, sometimes you have to take a risk. Risk is not without challenge, so when we take a risk, the unknown can be very stressful. But, without thinking about the "what ifs" and the possibilities in life, we may look back and wish that we had the chance to do things over.

Reading One

In this selection, Schwartz encourages us to think about the purpose of college. Is the purpose of college to train students to be prepared for a job right out of college? Is the purpose of education to prepare them for what Schwartz calls "50 years of self-fulfillment"? In fact, Schwartz tells us that most students want both. Why wouldn't they? Sometimes students are scared or pressured by someone or even pressure themselves to select a major that assures them they will get a good job. Maybe this major is not the major they want. Or maybe they avoid taking courses in areas they are not comfortable with. Choosing a major, selecting courses, and deciding what you, a student, want out of college can be risky.

The Higher Purpose

Steven Schwartz

The goal of university education is to help build a fairer, more just society, says Steven Schwartz.

Twenty-eight years ago, the US educator Harlan Cleveland had this to say about the conflicting views of higher education:

"The outsiders want the students trained for their first job out of university, and the academics inside the system want the student educated for 50 years of self-fulfilment. The trouble is that the students want both. The ancient collision between each student's short-term and long-term goals, between 'training' and 'education', between 'vocational' and 'general,' between honing the mind and nourishing the soul, divides the professional educators, divides the outside critics and supporters, and divides the students, too."

We still have no consensus on the purpose of higher education. This should not be surprising. After all, the "collision" of values is "ancient" indeed. Writing in the 16th century, Francis Bacon insisted that knowledge should be practical and "not be a courtesan, for pleasure." More recently, John Cardinal Newman took the opposite view. "Useful knowledge," he said, is a "deal of trash." Consensus on the purposes of higher education remains a long way off.

Today, most religion-based universities can say with certainty why they exist. Their job is to teach students the values that their religion believes to be the basis of good moral character. But the decline in religion and the widespread acceptance of moral relativism, even idiot nihilism, has made it impossible for British secular universities to provide this prescriptive type of education.

Abandoning their moral purposes has led universities to stress their utilitarian nature—get a degree and get a better job. Universities and their representative bodies routinely trumpet their economic impact. We have put so much emphasis on this aspect of our activities that the government now believes that universities exist mainly to bolster the economy.

A sound economy is, of course, a necessary means to achieve our social goals. But first we need an agreed set of social goals. Otherwise, we are a nation of means without ends. If their contribution to the economy provides the means, what are the ends that universities should be striving to achieve? The answer is greater social justice. Universities contribute to a just society in two ways: by producing graduates who improve social life and by promoting social mobility.

Let's begin with graduates who make Britain a better place to live. The presence in society of a corps of competent persons is a powerful force for improvement. Lawyers can advance the cause of formal justice, while doctors promote health. Teachers prepare the next generation, while scientists make discoveries that reverberate throughout the world.

University education can also exert important indirect effects.

Universities offer counseling, art exhibitions, music and drama performances, consultation on public and private issues, medical, scientific and social research and many other public services. Students learn the importance of public service from their university's example.

Through interaction with academics and their own peers, students learn about freedom of expression, tolerance and responsible citizenship.

Graduates transmit these values to other people who did not attend university.

And then there is social mobility. If higher education can be made available to students from diverse backgrounds, it can become an instrument for progress toward egalitarian objectives. Although more women and minority-group members have been to university in recent years, social equity has thus far proved to be an elusive goal. The government is trying to increase the number of people exposed to higher education. Some academics believe that the target will lower standards. Their opponents argue that current university selectivity favors a social elite.

Yet both arguments miss the key point. Widening participation does not just mean more people from diverse backgrounds in university. It is also a way of creating a more inclusive society. Participation in higher education means exposure to liberal social attitudes about the value of individuals.

Students learn to appreciate other cultures and times. They are exposed to art and music and the habit of lifelong learning. And, of course, there are the economic outcomes already mentioned. By providing avenues for social mobility, universities make it possible for students from deprived backgrounds not only to move up to better jobs but also to participate more fully in society.

By encouraging students from all backgrounds to come to university, universities can do more than almost any other institution to improve social mobility and justice. Here then is at least one moral purpose of higher education that we can all sign up to—making Britain a more open, more just and fairer place to live.

"The Higher Purpose" by Steven Schwartz, from *The Times Higher Education Supplement*, May 16, 2003. © Times Supplements Limited, 1996. Reprinted by permission.

▶ Reflection Questions

1. In Chapters One and Two, there are also readings that allude to the purpose of higher education. On the basis of those readings and this one, what do you think the purpose of higher education is?

2. Do you agree with the author that an important part of college should be "self-understanding or self-knowledge as well as knowledge of other cultures"? Does your college's mission statement explicitly or implicitly support knowledge of self as described here? Explain.

3. Should colleges require courses that expose students to diverse cultures and ways of thinking? Are there risks involved in requiring such courses? Are there risks in not requiring such courses? In both cases, what are they?

Reading Two

Sometimes the pressure to succeed or do well may supersede the desire to do what is right. Think about some of the recent scandals in business. For example, think about the CEO of Enron and about Martha Stewart. We might hypothesize that they never intended to do something that was unethical. Perhaps the fear of losing money or the fear of failure helped them to justify what they were doing. Maybe they thought that they would not hurt anyone. Sometimes when students resort to cheating, they may do so because they feel they must do well. They may also feel as though they are really not hurting anyone.

How to Fight College Cheating

Lawrence M. Hinman

Recent studies have shown that a steadily growing number of students cheat or plagiarize in college—and the data from high schools suggest that this number will continue to rise. A study by Don McCabe of Rutgers University showed that 74 percent of high school students admitted to one or more instances of serious cheating on tests. Even more disturbing is the way that many students define cheating and plagiarism. For example, they believe that cutting and pasting a few sentences from various Web sources without attribution is not plagiarism.

Before the Web, students certainly plagiarized—but they had to plan ahead to do so. Fraternities and sororities often had files of term papers, and some high-tech term-paper firms could fax papers to students. Overall, however, plagiarism required forethought.

Online term-paper sites changed all that. Overnight, students could order a term paper, print it out and have it ready for class in the morning—and still get a good night's sleep. All they needed was a charge card and an Internet connection.

One response to the increase in cheating has been to fight technology with more technology. Plagiarism-checking sites provide a service to screen student papers. They offer a color-coded report on papers and the original sources from which the students might have copied. Colleges qualify for volume discounts, which encourages professors to submit whole classes' worth of papers—the academic equivalent of mandatory urine testing for athletes.

The technological battle between term-paper mills and anti-plagiarism services will undoubtedly continue to escalate, with each side constructing more elaborate countermeasures to outwit the other. The cost of both plagiarism and its detection will also undoubtedly continue to spiral.

But there is another way. Our first and most important line of defense against academic dishonesty is simply good teaching. Cheating and plagiarism often arise in a vacuum created by routine, lack of interest and overwork. Professors who give the same assignment every semester, fail to guide students in the development of their projects and have little interest in what the students have to say contribute to the academic environment in which much cheating and plagiarism occurs.

Consider, by way of contrast, professors who know their students and who give assignments that require regular, continuing interaction with them about their projects—and who require students to produce work that is a meaningful development of their own interests. These professors create an environment in which cheating and plagiarism are far less likely to occur. In this context, any plagiarism would usually be immediately evident to the professor, who would see it as inconsistent with the rest of the student's work. A strong, meaningful curriculum taught by committed professors is the first and most important defense against academic dishonesty.

The second remedy is to encourage the development of integrity in our students. A sense of responsibility about one's intellectual development would preclude cheating and plagiarizing as inconsistent with one's identity. It is precisely this sense of individual integrity that schools with honor codes seek to promote.

Third, we must encourage our students to perceive the dishonesty of their classmates as something that causes harm to the many students who play by the rules. The argument that cheaters hurt only themselves is false. Cheaters do hurt other people, and they do so to help themselves. Students cheat because it works. They get better grades and more advantages with less effort. Honest students lose grades, scholarships, recommendations and admission to advanced programs. Honest students must create enough peer pressure to dissuade potential cheaters. Ultimately, students must be willing to step forward and confront those who engage in academic dishonesty.

Addressing these issues is not a luxury that can be postponed until a more convenient time. It is a short step from dishonesty in schools and colleges to dishonesty in business. It is doubtful that students who fail to develop habits of integrity and honesty while still in an academic setting are likely to do so once they are out in the "real" world. Nor is it likely that adults will stand up against the dishonesty of others, particularly fellow workers and superiors, if they do not develop the habit of doing so while still in school.

"How to Fight College Cheating" by Lawrence M. Hinman, *Washington Post*, September 2, 2004. Reprinted by permission of the author.

▶ Reflection Questions

1. What do you think is the primary reason students resort to cheating? Do you think anyone gets hurt if they cheat?

2. Plagiarism is a form of cheating that has become easier because of the Internet. That kind of plagiarism may seem clear. If you work with another student and you both turn in the same paper is this plagiarism? Are there differences between plagiarizing from the Internet or from working with another student, and if so, should these actions be treated differently in terms of consequences? Find your

college policy on cheating or plagiarism. Is it explained to you in any class? If it is not, does that mean that if you cheat or plagiarize, you should not be punished, or is it assumed that we should all know and exercise ethical behavior?

3. What are the risks involved with stepping forward and confronting those who are not honest in school (i.e., cheating or plagiarizing)? Would you confront someone about this and risk the consequences? What might the consequences be?

4. Have your ever known anyone who was not completely honest when filing their taxes? Why do you think that someone who you think normally displays extremely ethical behavior might think cheating on taxes is acceptable?

Reading Three

Scholars who have studied this particular work of Robert Frost have debated its meaning. Some argue that it is about a universal lesson in life: to be an individual and take risks. However, the line "for the passing there had worn them both about the same" implies that both paths have been equally traveled. Is it possible that each person can derive their own meaning about making choices and taking risks from this poem? Read and think about how this might apply to you.

The Road Not Taken

Robert Frost

Two roads diverged in a yellow wood,
And sorry I could not travel both
And be one traveler, long I stood
And looked down one as far as I could
To where it bent in the undergrowth;

Then took the other, as just as fair,
And having perhaps the better claim,
Because it was grassy and wanted wear;
Though as for that the passing there
Had worn them really about the same,

And both that morning equally lay
In leaves no step had trodden black.
Oh, I kept the first for another day!
Yet knowing how way leads on to way,
I doubted if I should ever come back.

I shall be telling this with a sigh
Somewhere ages and ages hence:
Two roads diverged in a wood, and I—
I took the one less traveled by,
And that has made all the difference.

"The Road Not Taken" from *THE POETRY OF ROBERT FROST* edited by Edward Connery Lathem. Copyright 1969 by Henry Holt and Company. Reprinted by permission of Henry Holt and Company, LLC.

▶ Reflection Questions

1. Sometimes taking a risk might mean taking the road less traveled, like Frost. Can you think of an example in college when you chose to do something different from what everyone else was doing? What was this, and how did other students respond to your action?

2. What is your interpretation of the lines "Two roads diverged in a wood, and I—I took the one less traveled by, and that has made all of the difference"? Did Frost risk "being a fool"?

3. What do you think that Frost was thinking as he was making his choice about which path to take?

◀ Writing Assignment _____

audience: A new college student considering a major

purpose: To persuade them to think about how they might need to take risks and courses that they never thought they would like or do well in to help them choose a major and a career that they will enjoy

length: Minimum of three typed pages, double-spaced

Prior to this writing assignment, ask at least ten people who are in the work force (you can ask campus employees, family members, and friends) if they had it to do over, would they have chosen the same major or the same career. Ask them if they had avoided any particular courses or majors, that now, looking back, they wish that they had not. For example, it's possible that someone decided not to go into nursing because they were fearful they could not pass the math courses. Or someone never took a course in philosophy because it seemed to be so abstract, but later felt that the kind of logic learned in such a course would be valuable later in life. Once you have some background information, write to prospective students about the kinds of issues that they should consider when choosing a major. Give them suggestions on how they might be able to be successful in a major where they are concerned about some courses that need to be taken. Suggest possible work experiences like internships. When you give specific advice, include the name and place of a particular service on your campus that would be helpful.

Journal Entries: DISCOVERY AND INTENTION STATEMENTS

In this journal entry write about how you see yourself in five years, taking the major you have chosen or think you will choose. Continue this journal entry by describing the job you have always dreamed of. How would this affect your life in the future—for instance, five years from now? What are you thinking as you write this entry? Are you afraid to take a risk? Why or why not? Maybe you are lucky enough to be in the major that you have always dreamed of.

How do these readings relate to the Power Process? How does ethical decision making relate to what you will need to succeed in college and beyond? Can you think of some specific examples of situations where you might make decisions that are not popular but the right thing to do? Can you think about why you might take a job that you don't really like? Write one or two sentences about what you have learned and what you intend to do as a result of these readings, what you will do to make it work, and what you risk if you don't do what you intend to do.

Mastering Vocabulary

List five words that were new to you (more or less if necessary). For each, include which reading you found the word in, the definition, and where you got the definition from, as well as a time or place you might use the word again.

1.

2.

3.

4.

5.

 ## Additional Activities

1. Learn more about Robert Frost at www.frostfriends.org. Find out what prompted him to write this poem. Was there something in his life that encouraged him to take risks and risk "being a fool"?

2. Look at www.turnitin.com or http://college.hmco.com/english/plagiarism_prevention. Both are online tools that detect plagiarism. Does your school use such a tool? What are the pros and cons for using a system such as these? Consider setting up a class debate based on one or both of these tools.

3. Each member of the class will report something that they did to take a risk and share how they felt. For example, a student may have joined a club that they were hesitant to join, and it turned out to be a positive experience.

Online Study Center   **Improve Your Grade**
Visit the Online Study Center for resources and exercises to accompany this text
http://college.hmco.com/pic/msreader1e

CHAPTER ELEVEN

Surrender

Sometimes things happen in life that we have no control over. Perhaps there is a death in our family. Since death is an inevitable part of the life cycle, there is nothing we can do to prevent it. Nonetheless it has an impact on us. Sometimes there are things that we do that we want to change and can't on our own. The readings in this chapter vary from a young woman's struggle with her weight, to how to stop procrastinating (and yes, sometimes we need to ask for help for things such as these), and finally to the amount of debt college students can incur. Sometimes we may have to surrender and ask for help.

The Power Process: Surrender

Life can be magnificent and satisfying. It can also be devastating.

Sometimes there is too much pain or confusion. Problems can be too big and too numerous. Life can bring us to our knees in a pitiful, helpless, and hopeless state. A broken relationship with a loved one, a sudden diagnosis of cancer, total frustration with a child's behavior problem, or even the prospect of several long years of school are situations that can leave us feeling overwhelmed—powerless.

In these troubling situations, the first thing we can do is to admit that we don't have the resources to handle the problem. No matter how hard we try and no matter what skills we bring to bear, some problems remain out of our control. When this is the case, we can tell the truth: "It's too big and too mean. I can't handle it."

Releasing control, receiving help

Desperately struggling to control a problem can easily result in the problem's controlling you. Surrender is letting go of being the master in order to avoid becoming the slave.

Once you have acknowledged your lack of control, all that remains is to surrender. Many traditions make note of this. Western religions speak of surrendering to God. Hindus say surrender to the Self. Members of Alcoholics Anonymous talk about turning their lives over to a Higher Power. Agnostics might suggest surrendering to the ultimate source of power. Others might speak of following their intuition, their inner guide, or their conscience. William James wrote about surrender as a part of the conversion experience.

In any case, surrender means being receptive to help. Once we admit that we're at the end of our rope, we open ourselves up to receiving help. We learn that we don't have to go it alone. We find out that other people have faced similar problems and survived. We give up our old habits of thinking and behaving as if we have to be in control of everything. We stop acting as general manager of the universe. We surrender. And that creates a space for something new in our lives.

Surrender works

Surrender works for life's major barriers as well as for its insignificant hassles.

You might say, as you struggle to remember someone's name, "It's on the tip of my tongue." Then you surrender. You give up trying and say, "Oh well, it will come to me later." Then the name pops into your mind.

An alcoholic admits that he just can't control his drinking. This becomes the key that allows him to seek treatment.

A person with multiple sclerosis admits that she's gradually losing the ability to walk. She tells others about this fact. Now the people around her can understand, be supportive, and explore ways to help.

A man is devastated when his girlfriend abandons him. He is a "basket case," unable to work for days. Instead of struggling against this fact, he simply admits the full extent of his pain. In that moment, he is able to trust. He trusts that help will come and that one day he will be OK again. He trusts in his ability to learn and to create a new life. He trusts that new opportunities for love will come his way.

After trying unsuccessfully for years to have a baby, a couple finally surrenders and considers adoption. The woman then conceives in a few months.

After finding out she has terminal cancer, a woman shifts between panic and depression. Nothing seems to console her. Finally, she accepts the truth and stops fighting her tragedy. She surrenders. Now at peace, she invests her remaining years in meaningful moments with the people she loves.

A writer is tackling the first chapter of his novel, feeling totally in control. He has painstakingly outlined the whole plot, recording each character's actions on individual 3×5 cards. Three sentences into his first draft, he finds that he's spending most of his time shuffling cards instead of putting words on paper. Finally, he puts the cards aside, forgets about the outline, and just tells the story. The words start to flow effortlessly, and he loses himself in the act of writing.

In each of these cases, the people involved learned the power of surrendering.

What surrender is not

Surrender is not resignation. It is not a suggestion to quit and do nothing about your problems. You have many skills and resources. Use them. You can apply all of your energy to handling a situation and surrender at the same time. Surrender includes doing whatever you can in a positive, trusting spirit. Giving up is fatalistic and accomplishes nothing. So let go, keep going, and know that the true source of control lies beyond you.

This Power Process says, in effect, don't fight the current. Imagine a person rafting down a flowing river with a rapid current. She's likely to do fine if she surrenders control and lets the raft flow with the current. After all, the current always goes around the rocks. If she tries to fight the current, she could end up in an argument with a rock about where the current is going—and lose.

Detachment helps us surrender

Watching yourself with detachment can help your ability to surrender. Pretend that you are floating away from your body, and then watch what's going on from a distance.

Objectively witness the drama of your life unfolding as if you were watching a play. When you see yourself as part of a much broader perspective, surrender seems obvious and natural.

"Surrender" might seem inconsistent with the Power Process: "I create it all." An old parable says that the Garden of Truth, the grand place everyone wants to enter, is guarded by two monsters—Fear and Paradox. Most of us can see how fear keeps us from getting what we want. The role of paradox might not be as clear.

The word *paradox* refers to a seemingly contradictory statement that might nonetheless be true. It is our difficulty in holding seemingly contradictory thoughts that sometimes keeps us out of the Garden of Truth. If we suspend the sovereignty of logic, we might discover that ideas that seem contradictory can actually coexist. With application, we can see that both "Surrender" and "I create it all" are valuable tools.

Readings

Readings in this chapter address circumstances in our lives that seem to be beyond our control. In "The Fat Girl," Louise views herself as fat and appears to see no way out. In the selection on procrastination, the reader learns that there may be underlying reasons for procrastination and sometimes we have to "surrender" and ask for help to overcome it. The final reading is about debt and how young Americans, particularity those in and recently out of college, may need to "surrender"—if only to surrender their credit cards.

Reading One

Louise appeared to be doomed to a life of being overweight. From the time she was a young girl, she was told, beginning with comments from her mother, that in order to get a husband or boyfriend (her mother's words), she had better watch her weight. She was surrounded by people that she believed never had to think about food. Louise became a closet eater, later lost weight, only to regain it.

The Fat Girl

Andre Dubus

Her name was Louise. Once when she was sixteen a boy kissed her at a barbecue; he was drunk and he jammed his tongue into her mouth and ran his hands up and down her hips. Her father kissed her often. He was thin and kind and she could see in his eyes when he looked at her the lights of love and pity.

It started when Louise was nine. You must start watching what you eat, her mother would say. I can see you have my metabolism. Louise also had her mother's pale blonde hair. Her mother was slim and pretty, carried herself erectly, and ate very little. The two of them would eat bare lunches, while her older brother ate sandwiches and potato chips, and then her mother would sit smoking while Louise eyed the bread box, the pantry, the refrigerator. Wasn't that good, her mother would say. In five years you'll be in high school and if you're fat the boys won't like you; they won't ask you out. Boys were as far away as five years, and she would go to her room and wait for nearly an hour until she knew her mother was no longer thinking of her, then she would creep into the kitchen and, listening to her mother talking on the phone, or her footsteps upstairs, she would open the bread box, the pantry, the jar of peanut butter. She would put the sandwich under her shirt and go outside or to the bathroom to eat it.

Her father was a lawyer and made a lot of money and came home looking pale and happy. Martinis put color back in his face, and at dinner he talked to his wife and two children. Oh give her a potato, he would say to Louise's mother. She's a growing girl. Her mother's voice then became tense: If she has a potato she shouldn't have dessert. She should have both, her father would say, and he would reach over and touch Louise's cheek or hand or arm.

In high school she had two girl friends and at night and on weekends they rode in a car or went to movies. In movies she was fascinated by fat actresses. She wondered why they were fat. She knew why she was fat: she was fat because she was Louise. Because God had made her that way. Because she wasn't like her friends Joan and Marjorie, who drank milk shakes after school and were all bones and tight skin. But what about those actresses, with their talents, with their broad and profound faces? Did they eat as heedlessly as Bishop Humphries and his wife who sometimes came to dinner and, as Louise's mother said, gorged between amenities? Or did they try to lose weight, did they go about hungry and angry and thinking of food? She thought of them eating lean meats and salads with friends, and then going home and building strange large sandwiches with French bread. But mostly she believed they did not go through these failures; they were fat because they chose to be. And she was certain of something else too: she could see it in their faces: they did not eat secretly. Which she did: her creeping to the kitchen when she was nine became, in high school, a ritual of deceit and pleasure. She was a furtive eater of sweets. Even her two friends did not know her secret.

Joan was thin, gangling, and flat-chested; she was attractive enough and all she needed was someone to take a second look at her face, but the school was large and there were pretty girls in every classroom and walking all the corridors, so no one ever needed to take a second look at Joan. Marjorie was thin too, an intense, heavy-smoking girl with brittle laughter. She was very intelligent, and with boys she was shy because she knew she made them uncomfortable, and because she was smarter than they were and so could not understand or could not believe the levels they lived on. She was to have a nervous breakdown before earning her Ph.D. in philosophy at the University of California, where she met and married a physicist and discovered within herself an untrammeled passion: she made love with her husband on the couch, the carpet, in the bathtub, and on the washing machine. By that time much had happened to her and she never thought of Louise. Joan would finally stop growing and begin moving with grace and confidence. In college she would have two lovers and then several more during the six years she spent in Boston before marrying a middle-aged editor who had two sons in their early teens, who drank too much, who was tenderly, boyishly grateful for her love, and whose wife had been killed while rock-climbing in New Hampshire with her lover. She would not think of Louise either, except in an earlier time, when lovers were still new to her and she was ecstatically surprised each time one of them loved her and, sometimes at night, lying in a man's arms, she would tell how in high school no one dated her, she had been thin and plain (she would still believe that: that she had been plain; it had never been true) and so had been forced into the weekend and night-time company of a neurotic smart girl and a shy fat girl. She would say this with self-pity exaggerated by Scotch and her need to be more deeply loved by the man who held her.

She never eats, Joan and Marjorie said of Louise. They ate lunch with her at school, watched her refusing potatoes, ravioli, fried fish. Sometimes she got through the cafeteria line with only a salad. That is how they would remember her: a girl whose hapless body was destined to be fat. No one saw the sandwiches she made and took to her room when she came home from school. No one saw the store of Milky Ways, Butterfingers, Almond Joys, and Hersheys far back on her closet shelf, behind the stuffed animals of her childhood. She was not a hypocrite. When she was out of the house she truly believed she was dieting; she forgot about the candy, as a man speaking into his office Dictaphone may forget the lewd photographs hidden in an old shoe in his closet. At other times, away from home, she thought of the waiting candy with near lust. One night driving home from a movie, Marjorie said: "You're lucky you don't smoke; it's incredible what I go through to hide it from my parents." Louise turned to her a smile which was elusive and mysterious; she yearned to be home in bed, eating chocolate in the dark. She did not need to smoke; she already had a vice that was insular and destructive.

She brought it with her to college. She thought she would leave it behind. A move from one place to another, a new room without the haunted closet shelf, would do for her what she could not do for herself. She packed her large dresses and went. For two weeks she was busy with registration, with shyness, with classes; then she began to feel at home. Her room was no longer like a motel. Its walls had stopped watching her, she felt they were her friends, and she gave them her secret. Away from her mother, she did not have to be as elaborate; she kept the candy in her drawer now.

The school was in Massachusetts, a girls' school. When she chose it, when she and her father and mother talked about it in the evenings, everyone so carefully avoided the word boys that sometimes the conversations seemed to be about nothing but boys. There are no boys there, the neuter words said; you will not have to contend with that. In her father's eyes were pity and encouragement; in her mother's was disappointment, and her voice was crisp. They spoke of courses, of small classes where Louise would get more attention. She imagined herself in those small classes; she saw herself as a teacher would see her, as the other girls would; she would get no attention.

The girls at the school were from wealthy families, but most of them wore the uniform of another class: blue jeans and work shirts, and many wore overalls. Louise bought some overalls, washed them until the dark blue faded, and wore them to classes. In the cafeteria she ate as she had in high school, not to lose weight nor even to sustain her lie, but because eating lightly in public had become as habitual as good manners. Everyone had to take gym, and in the locker room with the other girls, and wearing shorts on the volleyball and badminton courts, she hated her body. She liked her body most when she was unaware of it: in bed at night, as sleep gently took her out of her day, out of herself. And she liked parts of her body. She liked her brown eyes and sometimes looked at them in the mirror: they were not shallow eyes, she thought; they were indeed windows of a tender soul, a good heart. She liked her lips and nose, and her chin, finely shaped between her wide and sagging cheeks. Most of all she liked her long pale blonde hair, she liked washing and drying it and lying naked on her bed, smelling of shampoo, and feeling the soft hair at her neck and shoulders and back.

Her friend at college was Carrie, who was thin and wore thick glasses and often at night she cried in Louise's room. She did not know why she was crying. She was crying, she said, because she was unhappy. She could say no more. Louise said she was unhappy too, and Carrie moved in with her. One night Carrie talked for hours, sadly and bitterly, about her parents and what they did to each other. When she finished she hugged Louise and they went to bed. Then in the dark Carrie spoke across the room: "Louise? I just wanted to tell you. One night last week I woke up and smelled chocolate. You were eating chocolate, in your bed. I wish you'd eat it in front of me, Louise, whenever you feel like it."

Stiffened in her bed, Louise could think of nothing to say. In the silence she was afraid Carrie would think she was asleep and would tell her again in the morning or tomorrow night. Finally she said Okay. Then after a moment she told Carrie if she ever wanted any she could feel free to help herself; the candy was in the top drawer. Then she said thank you.

They were roommates for four years and in the summers they exchanged letters. Each fall they greeted with embraces, laughter, tears, and moved into their old room, which had been stripped and cleaned for them for the summer. Neither girl enjoyed summer. Carrie did not like being at home because her parents did not love each other. Louise lived in a small city in Louisiana. She did not like summer because she had lost touch with Joan and Marjorie; they saw each other, but it was not the same. She liked being with her father but with no one else. The flicker of disappointment in her mother's eyes at the airport was a vanguard of the army of relatives and acquaintances who awaited her: they would see her on the streets, in stores, at the country club, in her home, and in theirs; in the first moments of greeting, their eyes would tell her she was still fat Louise, who had been fat as long as they could remember, who had gone to college and returned as fat as ever. Then their eyes dismissed her, and she longed for school and Carrie, and she wrote letters to her friend. But that saddened her too. It wasn't simply that Carrie was her only friend, and when they finished college they might never see each other again. It was that her existence in the world was so divided; it had begun when she was a child creeping to the kitchen; now that division was much sharper, and her friendship with Carrie seemed disproportionate and perilous. The world she was destined to live in had nothing to do with the intimate nights in their room at school.

In the summer before their senior year, Carrie fell in love. She wrote to Louise about him, but she did not write much, and this hurt Louise more than if Carrie had shown the joy her writing tried to conceal. That fall they returned to their room; they were still close and warm, Carrie still needed Louise's ears and heart at night as she spoke of her parents and her recurring malaise whose source the two friends never discovered. But on most week-ends Carrie left, and caught a bus to Boston where her boyfriend studied music. During the week she often spoke hesitantly of sex; she was not sure if she liked it. But Louise, eating candy and listening, did not know whether Carrie was telling the truth or whether, as in her letters of the past summer, Carrie was keeping from her those delights she may never experience.

Then one Sunday night when Carrie had just returned from Boston and was unpacking her overnight bag, she looked at Louise and said: "I was thinking about you. On the bus coming home tonight." Looking at Carrie's concerned, determined face, Louise prepared herself for humiliation. "I was thinking about when we graduate. What you're going to do. What's to become of you. I want you to be loved the way I love you. Louise, if I help you, really help you, will you go on a diet?"

Louise entered a period of her life she would remember always, the way some people remember having endured poverty. Her diet did not begin the next day. Carrie told her to eat on Monday as though it were the last day of her life. So for the first time since grammar school Louise went into a school cafeteria and ate everything she wanted. At breakfast and lunch and dinner she glanced around the table to see if the other girls noticed the food on her tray. They did not. She felt there was a lesson in this, but it lay beyond her grasp. That night in their room she ate the four remaining candy bars. During the day Carrie rented a small refrigerator, bought an electric skillet, an electric broiler, and bathroom scales.

On Tuesday morning Louise stood on the scales, and Carrie wrote in her notebook: *October 14: 184 lbs*. Then she made Louise a cup of black coffee and scrambled one egg and sat with her while she ate. When Carrie went to the dining room for breakfast, Louise walked about the campus for thirty minutes. That was part of the plan. The campus was pretty, on its lawns grew at least one of every tree native to New England, and in the warm morning sun Louise felt a new hope. At noon they met in their room, and Carrie broiled her a piece of hamburger and served it with lettuce. Then while Carrie ate in the dining room Louise walked again. She was weak with hunger and she felt queasy. During her afternoon classes she was nervous and tense, and she chewed her pencil and tapped her heels on the floor and tightened her calves. When she returned to her room late that afternoon, she was so glad to see Carrie that she embraced her; she had felt she could not bear another minute of hunger, but now with Carrie she knew she could make it at least through tonight. Then she would sleep and face tomorrow when it came. Carrie broiled her a steak and served it with lettuce. Louise studied while Carrie ate dinner, then they went for a walk.

That was her ritual and her diet for the rest of the year, Carrie alternating fish and chicken breasts with the steaks for dinner, and every day was nearly as bad as the first. In the evenings she was irritable. In all her life she had never been afflicted by ill temper and she looked upon it now as a demon which, along with hunger, was taking possession of her soul. Often she spoke sharply to Carrie. One night during their after-dinner walk Carrie talked sadly of night, of how darkness made her more aware of herself, and at night she did not know why she was in college, why she studied, why she was walking the earth with other people. They were standing on a wooden foot bridge, looking down at a dark pond. Carrie kept talking; perhaps soon she would cry. Suddenly Louise said: "I'm sick of lettuce. I never want to see a piece of lettuce for the rest of my life. I hate it. We shouldn't even buy it, it's immoral."

Carrie was quiet. Louise glanced at her, and the pain and irritation in Carrie's face soothed her. Then she was ashamed. Before she could say she was sorry, Carrie turned to her and said gently: "I know. I know how terrible it is."

Carrie did all the shopping, telling Louise she knew how hard it was to go into a supermarket when you were hungry. And Louise was always hungry. She drank diet soft drinks and started smoking Carrie's cigarettes, learned to enjoy inhaling, thought of cancer and emphysema but they were as far away as those boys her mother had talked about when she was nine. By Thanksgiving she was smoking over a pack a day and her weight in Carrie's notebook was one hundred and sixty-two pounds. Carrie was afraid if Louise went home at Thanksgiving she would lapse from the diet, so Louise spent the vacation with Carrie, in Philadelphia. Carrie wrote her family about the diet, and told Louise that she had. On the plane to Philadelphia, Louise said: "I feel like a bedwetter. When I was a little girl I had a friend who used to come spend the night and Mother would put a rubber sheet on the bed and we all pretended there wasn't a rubber sheet and that she hadn't wet the bed. Even me, and I slept with her." At Thanksgiving dinner she lowered her eyes as Carrie's father put two slices of white meat on her plate and passed it to her over the bowls of steaming food.

When she went home at Christmas she weighed a hundred and fifty-five pounds; at the airport her mother marveled. Her father laughed and hugged her and said: "But now there's less of you to love." He was troubled by her smoking but only mentioned it once; he told her she was beautiful and, as always, his eyes bathed her with love. During the long vacation her mother cooked for her as Carrie had, and Louise returned to school weighing a hundred and forty-six pounds.

Flying north on the plane she warmly recalled the surprised and congratulatory eyes of her relatives and acquaintances. She had not seen Joan or Marjorie. She thought of returning home in May, weighing the hundred and fifteen pounds which Carrie had in October set as their goal. Looking toward the stoic days ahead, she felt strong. She thought of those hungry days of fall and early winter (and now: she was hungry now: with almost a frown, almost a brusque shake of the head, she refused peanuts from the stewardess): those first weeks of the diet when she was the pawn of an irascibility which still, conditioned to her ritual as she was, could at any moment take command of her. She thought of the nights of trying to sleep while her stomach growled. She thought of her addiction to cigarettes. She thought of the people at school: not one teacher, not one girl, had spoken to her about her loss of weight, not even about her absence from meals. And without warning her spirit collapsed. She did not feel strong, she did not feel she was committed to and within reach of achieving a valuable goal. She felt that somehow she had lost more than pounds of fat; that some time during her dieting she had lost herself too. She tried to remember what it had felt like to be Louise before she had started living on meat and fish, as an unhappy adult may look sadly in the memory of childhood for lost virtues and hopes. She looked down at the earth far below, and it seemed to her that her soul, like her body aboard the plane, was in some rootless flight. She neither knew its destination nor where it had departed from; it was on some passage she could not even define.

During the next few weeks she lost weight more slowly and once for eight days Carrie's daily recording stayed at a hundred and thirty-six. Louise woke in the morning thinking of one hundred and thirty-six and then she stood on the scales and they echoed her. She became obsessed with that number, and there wasn't a day when she didn't say it aloud, and through the days and nights the number stayed in her mind, and if a teacher had spoken those digits in a classroom she would have opened her mouth to speak. What if that's me, she said to Carrie. I meant what if a hundred and thirty-six is my real weight and I just can't lose anymore. Walking hand-in-hand with her despair was a longing for this to be true, and that longing angered her and wearied her, and every day she was gloomy. On the ninth day she weighed a hundred and thirty-five and a half pounds. She was not relieved; she thought bitterly of the months ahead, the shedding of the last twenty and a half pounds.

On Easter Sunday, which she spent at Carrie's, she weighed one hundred and twenty pounds, and she ate one slice of glazed pineapple with her ham and lettuce. She did not enjoy it: she felt she was being friendly with a recalcitrant enemy who had once tried to destroy her. Carrie's parents were laudative. She liked them and she wished they would touch sometimes, and look at each other when they spoke. She guessed they would divorce when Carrie left home, and she vowed that her own marriage would be one of affection and tenderness. She could think about that now: marriage. At school she had read in a Boston paper that this summer the cicadas would come out of their seventeen year hibernation on Cape Cod, for a month they would mate and then die, leaving their young to burrow into the ground where they would stay for seventeen years. That's me, she had said to Carrie. Only my hibernation lasted twenty-one years.

Often her mother asked in letters and on the phone about the diet, but Louise answered vaguely. When she flew home in late May she weighed a hundred and thirteen pounds, and at the airport her mother cried and hugged her and said again and again: You're so *beautiful*. Her father blushed and bought her a martini. For days her relatives and acquaintances congratulated her, and the applause in their eyes lasted the entire summer, and she loved their eyes, and swam in the country club pool, the first time she had done this since she was a child.

She lived at home and ate the way her mother did and every morning she weighed herself on the scales in her bathroom. Her mother liked to take her shopping and buy her dresses and they put her old ones in the Goodwill box at the shopping center; Louise thought of them existing on the body of a poor woman whose cheap meals kept her fat. Louise's mother had a photographer come to the house, and Louise posed on the couch and standing beneath a live oak and sitting in a wicker lawn chair next to an azalea bush. The new clothes and the photographer made her feel she was going to another country or becoming a citizen of a new one. In the fall she took a job of no consequence, to give herself something to do.

Also in the fall a young lawyer joined her father's firm, he came one night to dinner, and they started seeing each other. He was the first man outside her family to kiss her since the barbecue when she was sixteen. Louise celebrated Thanksgiving not with rice dressing and candied sweet potatoes and mince meat and pumpkin pies, but by giving Richard her virginity which she realized, at the very last moment of its existence, she had embarked on giving him over thirteen months ago, on that Tuesday in October when Carrie had made her a cup of black coffee and scrambled one egg. She wrote this to Carrie, who replied happily by return mail. She also, through glance and smile and innuendo, tried to tell her mother too. But finally she controlled that impulse, because Richard felt guilty about making love with the daughter of his partner and friend. In the spring they married. The wedding was a large one, in the Episcopal church, and Carrie flew from Boston to be maid of honor. Her parents had recently separated and she was living with the musician and was still victim of her unpredictable malaise. It overcame her on the night before the wedding, so Louise was up with her until past three and woke next morning from sleep so heavy that she did not want to leave it.

Richard was a lean, tall, energetic man with the metabolism of a pencil sharpener. Louise fed him everything he wanted. He liked Italian food and she got recipes from her mother and watched him eating spaghetti with the sauce she had only tasted, and ravioli and lasagna, while she ate antipasto with her chianti. He made a lot of money and borrowed more and they bought a house whose lawn sloped down to the shore of a lake; they had a wharf and a boathouse, and Richard bought a boat and they took friends waterskiing. Richard bought her a car and they spent his vacations in Mexico, Canada, the Bahamas, and in the fifth year of their marriage they went to Europe and, according to their plan, she conceived a child in Paris. On the plane back, as she looked out the window and beyond the sparkling sea and saw her country, she felt that it was waiting for her, as her home by the lake was, and her parents, and her good friends who rode in the boat and waterskied; she thought of the accumulated warmth and pelf of her marriage, and how by slimming her body she had bought into the pleasures of the nation. She felt cunning, and she smiled to herself, and took Richard's hand.

But these moments of triumph were sparse. On most days she went about her routine of leisure with a sense of certainty about herself that came merely from not thinking. But there were times, with her friends, or with Richard, or alone in the house, when she was suddenly assaulted by the feeling that she had taken the wrong train and arrived at a place where no one knew her, and where she ought not to be. Often, in bed with Richard, she talked of being fat: "I was the one who started the friendship with Carrie, I chose her, I started the conversations. When I understood that she was my friend I understood something else: I had chosen her for the same reason I'd chosen Joan and Marjorie. They were all thin. I was always thinking about what people saw when they looked at me and I didn't want them to see two fat girls. When I was alone I didn't mind being fat but then I'd have to leave the house again and then I didn't want to look like me. But at home I didn't mind except when I was getting dressed to go out of the house and when Mother looked at me. But I stopped looking at her when she looked at me. And in college I felt good with Carrie; there weren't any boys and I didn't have any other friends and so when I wasn't with Carrie I thought about her and I tried to ignore the other people around me, I tried to make them not exist. A lot of the time I could do that. It was strange, and I felt like a spy."

If Richard was bored by her repetitions he pretended not to be. But she knew the story meant very little to him. She could have been telling him of a childhood illness, or wearing braces, or a broken heart at sixteen. He could not see her as she was when she was fat. She felt as though she were trying to tell a foreign lover about her life in the United States, and if only she could command the language he would know and love all of her and she would feel complete. Some of the acquaintances of her childhood were her friends now, and even they did not seem to remember her when she was fat.

Now her body was growing again, and when she put on a maternity dress for the first time she shivered with fear. Richard did not smoke and he asked her, in a voice just short of demand, to stop during her pregnancy. She did. She ate carrots and celery instead of smoking, and at cocktail parties she tried to eat nothing, but after her first drink she ate nuts and cheese and crackers and dips. Always at these parties Richard had talked with his friends and she had rarely spoken to him until they drove home. But now when he noticed her at the hors d' oeuvres table he crossed the room and, smiling, led her back to his group. His smile and his hand on her arm told her he was doing his clumsy, husbandly best to help her through a time of female mystery.

She was gaining weight but she told herself it was only the baby, and would leave with its birth. But at others times she knew quite clearly that she was losing the discipline she had fought so hard to gain during her last year with Carrie. She was hungry now as she had been in college, and she ate between meals and after dinner and tried to eat only carrots and celery, but she grew to hate them, and her desire for sweets was as vicious as it had been long ago. At home she ate bread and jam and when she shopped for groceries she bought a candy bar and ate it driving home and put the wrapper in her purse and then in the garbage can under the sink. Her cheeks had filled out, there was loose flesh under her chin, her arms and legs were plump, and her mother was concerned. So was Richard. One night when she brought pie and milk to the living room where they were watching television, he said: "You already had a piece. At dinner."

She did not look at him.

"You're gaining weight. It's not all water, either. It's fat. It'll be summer-time. You'll want to get into your bathing suit."

The pie was cherry. She looked at it as her fork cut through it; she speared the piece and rubbed it in the red juice on the plate before lifting it to her mouth.

"You never used to eat pie," he said. "I just think you ought to watch it a bit. It's going to be tough on you this summer."

In her seventh month, with a delight reminiscent of climbing the stairs to Richard's apartment before they were married, she returned to her world of secret gratification. She began hiding candy in her underwear drawer. She ate it during the day and at night while Richard slept, and at breakfast she was distracted, waiting for him to leave.

She gave birth to a son, brought him home, and nursed both him and her appetites. During this time of celibacy she enjoyed her body through her son's mouth; while he suckled she stroked his small head and back. She was hiding candy but she did not conceal her other indulgences; she was smoking again but still she ate between meals, and at dinner she ate what Richard did, and coldly he watched her, he grew petulant, and when the date marking the end of their celibacy came they let it pass. Often in the afternoons her mother visited and scolded her and Louise sat looking at the baby and said nothing until finally, to end it, she promised to diet. When her mother and father came for dinners, her father kissed her and held the baby and her mother said nothing about Louise's body, and her voice was tense. Returning from work in the evenings Richard looked at a soiled plate and glass on the table beside her chair as if detecting traces of infidelity, and at every dinner they fought.

"Look at you," he said. "Lasagna, for God's sake. When are you going to start? It's not simply that you haven't lost any weight. You're gaining. I can see it. I can feel it when you get in bed. Pretty soon you'll weigh more than I do and I'll be sleeping on a trampoline."

"You never touch me anymore."

"I don't want to touch you. Why should I? Have you looked at yourself?"

"You're cruel," she said. "I never knew how cruel you were."

She ate, watching him. He did not look at her. Glaring at his plate, he worked with fork and knife like a hurried man at a lunch counter.

"I bet you didn't either," she said.

That night when he was asleep she took a Milky Way to the bathroom. For a while she stood eating in the dark, then she turned on the light. Chewing, she looked at herself in the mirror; she looked at her eyes and hair. Then she stood on the scales and looking at the numbers between her feet, one hundred and sixty-two; she remembered when she had weighed a hundred and thirty-six pounds for eight days. Her memory of those eight days was fond and amusing, as though she were recalling an Easter egg hunt when she was six. She stepped off the scales and pushed them under the lavatory and did not stand on them again.

It was summer and she bought loose dresses and when Richard took friends out on the boat she did not wear a bathing suit or shorts; her friends gave her mischievous glances, and Richard did not look at her. She stopped riding on the boat. She told them she wanted to stay with the baby, and she sat inside holding him until she heard the boat leave the wharf. Then she took him to the front lawn and walked with him in the shade of the trees and talked to him about the blue jays and mockingbirds and cardinals she saw on their branches. Sometimes she stopped and watched the boat out on the lake and the friend skiing behind it.

Every day Richard quarreled, and because his rage went no further than her weight and shape, she felt excluded from it, and she remained calm within layers of flesh and spirit, and watched his frustration, his impotence. He truly believed they were arguing about her weight. She knew better: she knew that beneath the argument lay the question of who Richard was. She thought of him smiling at the wheel of his boat, and long ago courting his slender girl, the daughter of his partner and friend. She thought of Carrie telling her of smelling chocolate in the dark and, after that, watching her eat it night after night. She smiled at Richard, teasing his anger.

He is angry now. He stands in the center of the living room, raging at her, and he wakes the baby. Beneath Richard's voice she hears the soft crying, feels it in her heart, and quietly she rises from her chair and goes upstairs to the child's room and takes him from the crib. She brings him to the living room and sits holding him in her lap, pressing him gently against the folds of fat at her waist. Now Richard is pleading with her. Louise thinks tenderly of Carrie broiling meat and fish in their room, and walking with her in the evenings. She wonders if Carrie still has the malaise. Perhaps she will come for a visit. In Louise's arms now the boy sleeps.

"I'll help you," Richard says. "I'll eat the same things you eat."

But his face does not approach the compassion and determination and love she had seen in Carrie's during what she now recognizes as the worst year of her life. She can remember nothing about that year except hunger, and the meals in her room. She is hungry now. When she puts the boy to bed she will get a candy bar from her room. She will eat it here, in front of Richard. This room will be hers soon. She considers the possibilities: all these rooms and the lawn where she can do whatever she wishes. She knows he will leave soon. It has been in his eyes all summer. She stands, using one hand to pull herself out of the chair. She carries the boy to his crib, feels him against her large breasts, feels that his sleeping body touches her soul. With a surge of vindication and relief she holds him. Then she kisses his forehead and places him in the crib. She goes to the bedroom and in the dark takes a bar of candy from her drawer. Slowly she descends the stairs. She knows Richard is waiting but she feels his departure so happily that, when she enters the living room, unwrapping the candy, she is surprised to see him standing there.

From *Adultery and Other Choices* by Andre Dubus. Reprinted by permission of David R. Godine, Publisher, Inc. Copyright © 1977 by Andre Dubus.

▶ Reflection Questions

1. Carrie, Louise's friend, found out that she was eating in bed. She told her, "I wish you'd eat in front of me, Louise, whenever you feel like it." It was not until four years later that Louise enlisted Carrie's support to lose weight. At what point in her life should Louise have asked for support? How? Why do you think she did not? What do you think led her to finally ask?

2. Louise liked her body when she was asleep. She liked parts of her body, especially her brown eyes: "They were not shallow eyes, she thought; they were indeed windows of a tender soul, a good heart." Have you ever thought what it was like to be different? Did you ever think about people who were different in ways other than their physical appearance? Have you ever been in a situation where you were the minority? What was the situation and how did you feel?

3. What is your impression of Louise's husband, Richard? Do you think he should have been more supportive? Do you think he loved Louise only when she was thin, or do you think there was more to the reason he was probably going to leave her than that she had gotten fat? Do you see situations like this in college?

Reading Two

How is it that some people always seem to be organized and get everything done? They appear to be able to accomplish a multitude of things without looking stressed. Maybe their secret is that they simply don't procrastinate. As the Nike slogan goes, "Just do it," instead of talking about doing it. This reading provides insight into the whys behind procrastination and suggestions for overcoming it. Sometimes one has to surrender and admit that they may need some help.

How to Get Unstuck Now!

Dr. Gail Saltz

David looks miserable as he tells me that, once again, he has to pay a late penalty for failing to turn in his taxes on time. He feels angry and guilty that this delay will now cost him the money he was saving for the family vacation. His family and friends have been calling him lazy for years. It seems to him that the harder he tries to "get it right," the worse his procrastinating gets. "It's ruining my relationships and holding me back at work," he says. "Why am I doing this?"

Maria, on the other hand, had always gotten things done on time—until she was up for a promotion. Suddenly, this very conscientious woman was late with her assignments. She knew that she was screwing up her chances for advancement yet was baffled as to why she kept doing it.

WHO PROCRASTINATES?

David is one of the 20 percent of Americans considered "chronic procrastinators." Maria, like the majority of us, is an occasional procrastinator whose repeated delays take place in a particular realm.

Almost everyone procrastinates some of the time. The results can range from annoyance to misery—for both the person doing it and those affected by it. Research has shown that procrastinators tend to feel extremely stressed, resulting in more insomnia, colds and stomachaches than nonprocrastinators suffer. In one survey of 300 college students who confessed to being procrastinators, nearly half said they would rather donate blood than write an assigned paper, almost a third said they would rather visit the dentist; and more than one in five said they would rather pick up trash on campus.

Both men and women suffer from anxiety as a result of procrastination. Interestingly, women suffer from guilt as well—nearly twice as often as men.

WHY WE PROCRASTINATE

Too often procrastinators receive the advice from professionals or others to just "quit it." Would that it were really that simple! The idea that procrastinators are simply lazy is a myth, and their behavior rarely is changed by just deciding to stop. Laziness might respond to giving yourself a good kick in the pants. Procrastination doesn't.

Unlike laziness, procrastination is caused by fears—the result of emotional stories that each of us carries around inside us. Understanding the reasons why *you* procrastinate ultimately can change your behavior and your life. To do that, think about what it means to you to get things done and about the stuff you're putting off. See which of the following stories resonates with you:

"I'm so afraid of failing that I would rather not try than to try but fail."

Fear of failure probably is the most common story. If that's you, you may be a perfectionist who feels that doing a "just OK" task is mortifying. These types

Are You a Chronic Procrastinator?

Besides the obvious "I always put work off till the last minute" and "I'm always late to wherever I'm going"...

_____ Do you often avoid decisions?

_____ Do you make big plans but then never carry them out?

_____ Do you avoid trying something new?

_____ Are you staying in your job despite being unhappy for fear of making a move?

_____ Do you tend to get sick when you have a task you don't want to do?

_____ When you don't get something done, do you blame others for it?

_____ Do you tend to make so many fun plans that it leaves you with no time to do your work?

_____ Do you avoid arguments?

If you habitually put things off and also answered "yes" to two or more of these questions, you may be a chronic procrastinator. See the box on the next page for tips on breaking the pattern.

---

also believe that they need to please others in order to be accepted. In the extreme, they may believe that they are only lovable and worthwhile if their performance is outstanding.

"I'm afraid to be successful because people will envy me or see me as a threat, and then I'll lose them."

Fear of success can lead to procrastination as well. You may imagine that if you succeed, you'll then be expected to be wildly successful *all* the time, or that you'll become a workaholic, or even that on some level you'll feel you are not deserving of success. All are common reasons for procrastination.

"I need to be defiant, or they will rule me and win."

This too is a common story. If it's yours, you may believe that all of life is a battle for control. Perhaps you grew up in a home with an authoritarian parent who was extremely controlling. Sometimes people with this story respond to the whole world as if it were that parent and seek to passive-aggressively control that world by procrastinating.

"This task holds no interest for me unless it is so last-minute as to be perilous and thrilling."

People who say this to themselves generally are chronic procrastinators who, unlike the others, do not appear anxious. They are the thrill-seeking, risk-taking drama lovers. If you are such a procrastinator, you may feel that the daily grind is boring, and boredom is terrifying. Waiting until the last moment lets thrill-seeking procrastinators shake things up by creating their own crisis.

UNDERSTANDING YOUR OWN STORY

Figuring out what your fears are is an important first step. So is taking notice of which situations tend to trigger your procrastinating. Is it work, your love

Tackle It Now

- **Prioritize tasks.** If everything seems like a priority, you'll feel overwhelmed and get none of it done. And if nothing seems important, nothing will get done. Create a "to do" list ranking tasks in order of priority. Marking a specific number of hours to work and to play on your calendar also helps.
- **Question your beliefs.** Do you tell yourself that you work better under pressure? Prove it. Do one task at the last minute and one ahead. Test other myths, such as "I don't have the ability" and "It has to be done perfectly."
- **Control your impulsiveness.** Most procrastinators jump from one task to the next and never finish anything. Make yourself complete one task before moving on to another.
- **Old habits die hard.** Don't expect it to change overnight. If you change one thing a week, you are making progress, and that progress will show you that more change is possible.

life, friends, your body or money? The specific arena of life in which you procrastinate is a clue as to where you feel most conflicted and afraid. That's likely to be the arena that is most important to you at this time.

David, the chronically late tax-filer, came to understand that he was afraid of failing. He imagined messing up his taxes, failing at his job and even disappointing his loved ones. So he avoided doing many things in order to spare himself the chance of failure. Eventually, he came to see that he had damaged them all by procrastinating. This understanding helped him to change his behaviors.

Maria tapped into her knowledge that her success threatened her competitive husband. Once she understood that, she was able to catch herself delaying her work and to forge ahead. She also was able to discuss the issue with her husband, who ultimately became more supportive.

BREAK THE PATTERN

These steps can help you (or someone you know) break the pattern of procrastination:

1. **Articulate what you get out of procrastinating.** (Examples: "I avoid risking failure"; "I can't stand to not have fun.") This is what keeps you locked in.
2. **Consider the problems your procrastination creates vs. what you think you get out of it.** (Example: "I like being a victim, but that means I never get ahead in life.")
3. **Start small.** Do the least-noxious task to get yourself rolling. Remind yourself along the way—or enlist someone else to remind you—that the actual cost of *not* doing it is greater than the imagined fear of getting it done. (See the "Tackle It Now" box for more ideas.)
4. **Help a procrastinator.** Living or working with a procrastinator can be exasperating. It's easier to be objective about someone else's state of mind than your own. Plus, *you* aren't being bogged down by anxiety or fear. But rather than blame the procrastinator in your life—which merely perpetuates the

cycle of anxiety and delay—describe the story you see him or her acting out. Offer to help break the cycle.

"How to Get Unstuck Now!" by Dr. Gail Saltz, *Parade,* March 20, 2005. © 2005 Dr. Gail Saltz. All rights reserved. Reprinted by permission of *Parade* and the author.

▶ Reflection Questions

1. Saltz suggests a number of explanations about why people procrastinate. Have you ever put off anything? Do any of these explanations describe your behavior? A list of behaviors is included that are supposed to answer the question "Are you a chronic procrastinator?" Look at the list. Does this describe you?

2. Has the author left out any behaviors that you think might explain procrastination in college students? If so, what are they? Do you think the suggestions she offers for overcoming these behaviors would work for everyone? Why or why not?

3. Near the end of the reading there are suggestions on how to address procrastination. The box heading reads "Tackle It Now." Do you think these would work for everyone? If not, what else do you think the author should include in this list? Do you have any additional suggestions? What strategies work for you or what do you think might work for you, and why?

Reading Three

Every day we are barraged with advertisements for the latest in clothing, cosmetics, music, electronics, travel, cars, and gadgets. Often, there is a beautiful young model (male or female) using the item and smiling. In addition, when the mail comes, there is inevitably an envelope stamped with "Low interest rates" or "Easy credit" in an attempt to get us to sign up for another credit card. Madison Avenue knows exactly what they are doing. They are targeting unsuspecting individuals, often college students, who want to have it all, and often find themselves surrounded by possessions, but don't have any money—and end up deep in debt.

How to Avoid the Dread of Debt

Melissa Johnson

Like many students, Corey McDaniel is no stranger to debt. The first year he was in college, the communication studies junior applied for a CitiBank Visa card through an application offered by creditors at Jones' Diner.

"I bought random stuff," McDaniel said. "I bought food, clothes, shoes and 22-inch rims for my F150."

During his sophomore year, McDaniel acquired a second credit card. His debt now totals $3,300.

"I'm working on paying it off," McDaniel said. "I should be through before I graduate."

Though on the high end of the debt scale, McDaniel is not alone.

According to the Nellie Mae student loan agency, 78 percent of undergraduate students had credit cards in 2000, and the average undergrad had $1,843 in credit card debt.

Theatre senior Jennifer Garza is an example of the 22 percent who "just say no" to credit cards.

"I don't like the pressure of having to pay something off," Garza said. "I mean, you charge it up, and you miss payments and your credit starts to go bad. Before you know it, you owe $6,000."

Scholarship and financial aid counselor Aimee Nieto sees students every day who are struggling with credit card debt. She said there are numerous reasons why the problem is so wide-spread among college students.

"For a lot of students, the maturity level isn't there," Nieto said. "Students don't understand that the $20 meal they eat today will become an $80 meal in three years."

Nieto also explained that a student's financial situation is not designed to handle credit.

"Credit is for people with a constant source of income. Most college students don't have that, and they have no means to repay the debt they incur," Nieto said.

Though Nieto said the rising cost of education doesn't have a direct effect on student debt because most students don't charge their tuition; when students' award packages are taken up entirely by tuition and supplies, they often turn to credit cards to cover discretionary spending.

"(Students) are taken in by the materialistic society they live in," Nieto said. "They want to buy purses and get fake nails, and they have to have the newest cell phone. Creditors make it enticing. They say 'fill this out, and I'll give you a T-shirt or a Frisbee.'"

Marketing senior Greg Garner proved Nieto's theory correct. While sitting in line at the Office of Student Financial Aid, Garner explained that he got his first and only credit card as a freshman in college because of a free T-shirt giveaway in The Quad.

"I think I was short on clothes that day," Garner said. "But somehow I qualified for a Visa card. I pretty much spent $500 on gasoline, a cell phone and beer."

Though Garner cut up the card after he reached its limit, he said he has not paid the bill and estimates it is now at $800.

Chloe Carson, an administrative assistant in charge of solicitation requests at Campus Activities and Student Organizations, said credit card solicitation on campus has been banned for three years.

"Before (the policy change), like all other solicitation requests, the company had to be sponsored by a student organization," Carson said.

The student organization, in turn, would receive a percentage of profits or merchandise in exchange for its sponsorship. Carson said student organizations would receive upward of $300 for sponsoring credit card companies. Texas State did not receive any profit.

Though Carson said recent solicitation activities on campus are not sponsored by the university and are in violation of university policy, the solicitors still persist. During the past academic school year, Texas State students have been handed fliers advertising a free lunch at Alvin Ord's Sandwich Shop. The paper ad says to bring a Texas State student ID to receive a free sandwich. The fliers fail to mention lunch is compliments of CitiBank.

When students come to Alvin Ord's to redeem the coupon, they are greeted by representatives from the company who offer, among other financial services, credit cards to undergrads.

To get a free sandwich, students have to apply for a Citi Platinum Select Card for College Students. They also have to allow a digital picture to be taken of their student ID.

The Citi Platinum Select Card attracts applicants with a zero percent APR introductory rate and no minimum income or co-signer requirement, but after six months, the standard variable for purchases and balance transfers climbs to 14.74 percent, and for cash advances, the standard variable APR increases to 19.99 percent, according to the CitiBank Web Site.

When asked to comment on the Alvin Ord's/Citibank campaign, Citigroup's Office of Financial Education Public Affairs Representative Elizabeth Fogarty said the situation was a result of "third-party vendors." When asked to elaborate, Fogarty said CitiBank hires third-party workers who represent the company but are not actual employees.

Paul Martin, manager of Alvin Ord's, said CitiBank approached the shop with the promotion idea.

"Citi contacted us," Martin said. "They buy the sandwiches, so we aren't out anything."

Martin said the promotion has been good for business and garnered many repeat customers.

"It exposes us to the community and allows us to get the word out about our sandwiches," Martin said. "People try them and are like 'hey, these are pretty good,' and then they come back for more."

On average, Martin said he feels college students are as aware of money management as the rest of the population, if not more.

"I don't know that college students are any more or less aware than anyone else," Martin said. "I think they may even be more knowledgeable about interest rates and credit cards because they have so much practice with them."

When asked whether Alvin Ord's had clearance to pass out fliers on campus, Martin said that the majority of the advertising was done by Citibank and that he has not personally made contact with the CASO office.

Martin said he was not aware that this form of solicitation violated campus policy.

In response to questions about CitiBank's violation of university policy, Fogarty declined to comment, saying she would need to speak to the college division and call back at a later time.

In later e-mail correspondence, Fogarty wrote, "Citi has strict guidelines that third-party vendors are expected to follow, which include adhering to all campus guidelines. As far as promotional premiums, they are a standard business practice. They are a way to thank students for their potential future business."

Despite the prevalence of credit card marketing campaigns aimed at young adults, students at Texas State have options when it comes to avoiding creditors and reconciling debt. One step is for students to ask the registrar's office to withhold their names and addresses from credit agencies. A list of student and faculty directory information can [be purchased by] anyone for $60, said Steve Bazan at the Texas State Office of the Registrar.

Experts also suggest students obtain a copy of their credit report every year to make sure the information is correct and to guard against identity theft. According to the Federal Trade Commission Web site, a recent amendment to the federal Fair Credit Reporting Act requires each of the three nationwide consumer-reporting companies to provide a free credit report, upon request, once every 12 months. Reports can be obtained starting June 1, 2005.

Regarding illegal campus solicitation, Carson recommends that students report such activities to the CASO office or the University Police Department.

Senior psychologist at the Texas State Counseling Center Scott Janke said student debt is a topic that sometimes comes up in counseling sessions. Janke said the center can assist students with the anxiety associated with credit card bills, but the center does not have financial advisors on staff. If credit card spending is a student's primary concern, he or she is usually referred to the Consumer Credit Counseling Service in San Marcos or the Office of Student Financial Aid.

The Office of Student Financial Aid offers an online loan/debt management seminar. The interactive 35-minute course discusses eight financial topics, including Spending Strategies, Types of Credit and You and Selecting Credit Cards.

Attorney Marilee Kainer at the Office of the Attorney for Students said legal counsel for debt issues is available by appointment. The office's Web site also offers links to area credit counseling services.

Janke said that though these resources may be adequate for some students, they may not offer solutions for all.

"There are some students who are in horrendous debt situations, and they need professional financial advice."

"How to Avoid the Dread of Debt," by Melissa Johnson, *The University Star,* April 27, 2005. Reprinted by permission.

▶ Reflection Questions

1. Have you ever experienced buyer's remorse? What this means is you bought something on impulse, later to regret it. What did you do? Did you return the item? Was it too late? Did you ever do it again?

2. Do you think there should be laws against credit card companies soliciting college students to get credit cards? Why or why not?

3. What suggestions would you give college students to avoid debt? At what point should they surrender and seek help? Who would you go to if you needed help?

Writing Assignment

audience: Fellow college students

purpose: To persuade college students that sometimes we all have to surrender and seek help

length: Minimum of three typed pages, double-spaced

Using any of the topics in the readings for this chapter, write an essay that convinces students that we all have times in our lives when we need to say, "I need help." We need to recognize our problems and challenges and seek support. In this writing assignment, use examples from the readings as well as from your own experiences.

▶ Journal Entries: DISCOVERY AND INTENTION STATEMENTS

Write about a time when you made fun of someone about something that person had no control over. Examples might include someone who was fat, had old clothes, drove an old car, or had bad skin. Why did you do it? Looking back on it, how do you feel?

How do these readings relate to the Power Process of "surrender"? What are some of the tools that you will need to succeed in college on the basis of these readings? Can you think of some specific examples of situations where you have to admit to something you need to do in order to be successful? What do you think are some of the most common behaviors that first-year students need to change? What tools could you develop to make the necessary change and how might you use these tools? Write one or two sentences about what you have learned and what you intend to do as a result of these readings, what you will do to make it work, and what you risk if you don't do what you intend to do.

Mastering Vocabulary

List five words that were new to you (more or less if necessary). For each, include which reading you found the word in, the definition, and where you got the definition from, as well as a time or place you might use the word again.

1.

2.

3.

4.

5.

Additional Activities

1. Eating disorders are rampant on college campuses. See what services your college has for students who struggle with an eating disorder.

2. Prepare a budget for yourself for the semester. Bring it to class and share it with a partner. Are there similarities or differences between your plans? What are they?

3. As a class, brainstorm about what college students spend money on. When you have a list, divide it into what is needed and what is just wanted.

4. During this next week, observe your own behavior and identify a time when you procrastinated. Can you figure out why? At the next class, share this with a partner and ask for support (maybe in an email or at a lunch meeting during the week) to try to avoid procrastination during the week.

Online Study Center   **Improve Your Grade**
Visit the Online Study Center for resources and exercises to accompany this text
http://college.hmco.com/pic/msreader1e

CHAPTER TWELVE

Be It

In this final chapter, you have the chance to think about all that you have learned through the readings, writings, reflections, and experiences from this book and throughout your first semester in college. This is the time for you to make some choices and to decide who you want to be. While there are some things in life that you cannot control, you can control your responses. The bottom line is that you control your life and have the choice to determine your path. Think about it. You have the chance to "be it"!

The Power Process: Be It

All of the techniques in this book are enhanced by this Power Process. To tap into its full benefits, consider that most of our choices in life fall into three categories. We can

- Increase our material wealth (what we have)
- Improve our skills (what we do)
- Develop our "being" (who we are).

Many people devote their entire lifetime to the first two categories. They act as if they are "human havings" instead of human beings. For them, the quality of life hinges on what they have. They devote most of their waking hours to getting more—more clothes, more cars, more relationships, more degrees, more trophies. "Human havings" define themselves by looking at the circumstances in their lives—what they have.

Some people escape this materialist trap by adding another dimension to their identities. In addition to living as "human havings," they also live as "human doings." They thrive on working hard and doing everything well. They define themselves by how efficiently they do their jobs, how effectively they raise their children, and how actively they participate in clubs and organizations. Their thoughts are constantly about methods, techniques, and skills.

Look beyond having and doing

In addition to focusing on what we have and what we do, we can also focus on our being. While it is impossible to live our lives without having things and doing things, this Power Process suggests that we balance our experience by giving lots of attention to who we are—an aspect of our lives that goes beyond having and doing. Call it soul, passion, purpose, or values. Call it *being*. This word describes how we see ourselves—our deepest commitments, the ground from which our actions spring.

The realm of being is profound and subtle. It is also difficult to capture in words, though philosophers have tried for centuries. Christian theologian Paul Tillich described this realm when he defined faith as "ultimate commitment" and the "ground of being." In the New Testament, Jesus talked about being when he asked his followers to love God with all of their heart, soul, and mind. An ancient Hindu text also touches on being: "You are what your deep, driving desire is."

If all this seems far removed from taking notes or answering test questions, read on. Consider an example of how "Be it" can assist in career choices. In a letter to his father, a young man wrote:

We just went to see the Dance Theatre of Harlem. It was great! After the last number, I decided that I want to dance more than anything. I have a great passion to do it, more than anything else I can think or dream of. Dancing is what will make me happy and feel like I can leave this earth when my time comes. It is what I must do. I think that if I never fulfill this passion, I will never feel complete or satisfied with what I have done with my life.

In his heart, this man *is* a dancer now, even before his formal training is complete. From his passion, desire, commitment, and self-image (his *being*) comes his willingness to take classes and rehearse (*doing*). And from his doing he might eventually *have* a job with a professional dance company.

Picture the result as you begin

The example of the dancer illustrates that once you have a clear picture of what you want to *be*, the things you *do* and *have* fall more naturally into place.

The idea is this: Getting where you want to be by what you do or by what you have is like swimming against the current. Have → do → be is a tough journey. It's much easier to go in the other direction: be → do → have.

Usually, we work against nature by trying to have something or do something before being it. That's hard. All of your deeds (what you do) might not get you where you want to be. Getting all of the right things (what you have) might not get you there either.

Take the person who values athletics and wants to master tennis. He buys an expensive racket and a stylish tennis wardrobe. Yet he still can't return a serve. Merely having the right things doesn't deliver what he values.

Suppose that this person takes a year's worth of tennis lessons. Week after week, he practices doing everything "right." Still, his game doesn't quite make it.

What goes wrong is hard to detect. "He lost the match even though he played a good game," people say. "Something seemed to be wrong. His technique was fine, but each swing was just a little off." Perhaps the source of his problem is that he cannot see himself as ever mastering the game. What he has and what he does are at war with his mental picture of himself.

You can see this happen in other areas of life. Two people tell the same joke in what seems to be the same way. Yet one person brings a smile, while the other person has you laughing so hard your muscles hurt. The difference in how they do the joke is imperceptible. When the successful comedian tells a joke, he does it from his experience of already being funny.

To have and do what you want, be it. Picture the result as you begin. If you can first visualize where you want to be, if you can go there in your imagination, if you can be it today, you set yourself up to succeed.

Be a master student now

Now relate this Power Process to succeeding in school. All of the techniques in this book can be worthless if you operate with the idea that you are an ineffective student. You might do almost everything this book suggests and still never achieve the success in school that you desire.

For example, if you believe that you are stupid in math, you are likely to fail at math. If you believe that you are not skilled at remembering, all of the memory techniques in the world might not improve your recall. Generally, we don't outperform our self-concept.

If you value success in school, picture yourself as a master student right now. Through higher education you are gaining knowledge and skills that reflect and reinforce this view of yourself.

This principle works in other areas of life. For example, if you value a fulfilling career, picture yourself as already being on a path to a job you love. Use affirmations and visualizations to plant this idea firmly in your mind. Change the way you see yourself, and watch your actions and results shift as if by magic.

While you're at it, remember that "Be it" is not positive thinking or mental cheerleading. This Power Process works well when you take a First Step—when you tell the truth about your current abilities. The very act of accepting who you are and what you can do right now unleashes a powerful force for personal change.

In summary, flow with the natural current of be → do → have. Then watch your circumstances change.

If you want it, be it.

Readings

The readings in this final chapter were selected to help you make choices. As the final Power Process points out, the selections we make in life tend to fall into three categories: We can increase our wealth, improve our skills, and develop our being. While many of the previous readings stressed the importance of the quality of life and the contributions that we make, we also need to lead productive lives in careers where we can earn a living.

Of course the ultimate goal is to work in a job where we can earn money to support our lifestyles and continue to improve our skills, but foremost to live a quality life filled with respect for ourselves and others and a sense of responsibility to give back to others.

Reading One

Declaring a major is a critical thinking exercise that you have been preparing for your whole life. As the title of this reading suggests, when you choose a major, you need to try to be conscious of whether you are choosing the major because you think you will make lots of money or because it is something you really will enjoy doing. Take special note of the young woman in this reading who questions whether she made the right choice of a major in college *after* she graduated. Will you do the same?

Choosing a College Major: For Love or for the Money?

David Koeppel

Like countless other college students, Susannah Lloyd-Jones struggled with her choice of major. Finally, in her junior year at Loyola University in Chicago, she picked sociology, a decision that "opened my mind and introduced me to other cultures," she said. More than two years after graduation, though, Ms. Lloyd-Jones, now a 24-year-old paralegal from Maplewood, N.J., occasionally wonders if she made the right decision. "It might have been easier if I had been a business major," she said, "because that's where the money is."

Ms. Lloyd-Jones says if she had it to do over, she would probably still study sociology but take more business classes and work some internships. She said students feel tremendous pressure over the choice of a major, which could be an important career decision, when many are just beginning to understand themselves.

Many students and career counselors say the pressure to choose the "right" major is more intense than ever because of factors like rising tuition costs and the uncertain economy. Parents and students today often consider college more an investment than a time of academic and personal exploration. Some students say they are education consumers seeking the best return on that investment, which is often financed with a student loan.

The annual cost of a four-year public college averages $11,354, a 7.8 increase from 2003–4, according to the College Board; a four-year private college averages $27,516, a 5.6 percent increase.

In their recently published "College Majors Handbook With Real Career Paths and Payoffs" (Jist Publishing), three economists from Northeastern University in Boston try to quantify just how much students with a variety of majors can expect to earn in their careers. The authors concluded that choosing a major was more crucial to future financial success than the college attended.

One of the authors, Paul E. Harrington, an economist and associate director at the Center for Labor Market Studies at Northeastern, said that, on average, humanities and education majors fared far worse financially than students in business or engineering.

In 2002, workers with degrees in chemical engineering and accounting were on the high end, earning an average of $75,579 and $63,486, respectively. On the low end, philosophy majors made an average of $42,865 and elementary education graduates $38,746.

Mr. Harrington said the research was not intended to dissuade sociology majors from following their passions. Instead, he hopes the information will help students prepare carefully when choosing a major. He recommends that students contemplating majors in the liberal arts or humanities also take some business-oriented courses. A philosophy major, Mr. Harrington said, should probably get some real-world internship experience.

"The world is a more unforgiving place than it used to be, and investment costs are too high for four years of drift," he said. "If a student doesn't take the right sequence of math courses in high school, they can lose out on the best jobs."

But some people worry that choosing a career based primarily on economic factors can lead students to make poor choices. Jieun Chai, a 2000 Stanford University graduate, for instance, deeply regrets not majoring in Asian languages.

"I'm so angry at myself for giving in to peer pressure, parental pressure and societal pressure," Ms. Chai wrote on her Web journal. "Why are you taking only language classes? Think about your career in consulting, engineering, medicine or law."

Alysha Cryer, who was Ms. Lloyd-Jones's roommate at Loyola, withstood pressure from classmates and family members who urged her to attend law school or study business.

Ms. Cryer said that sticking with sociology was the most satisfying, if not financially rewarding, decision she could have made.

After graduating in 2002, she took a public relations and marketing job at a nonprofit organization in Chicago called Little Brothers, a group that matches volunteers with elderly clients. Her starting salary was $24,000, barely enough to survive in Chicago. In 2003, she moved to Manhattan to work for Catalyst, a nonprofit research and advisory organization. "With education so expensive, many in my generation are mired in debt," Ms. Cryer said. "Some people choose to sacrifice personal happiness to make money."

Peter Vogt, a career counselor in Minneapolis and the moderator on the Career Planning for College Students message board at Monster.com, a Web site for job seekers, says many of his 20-something clients think they have squandered their college years on the wrong studies.

"They think they only have one chance and that they've blown it," Mr. Vogt said. "'I should have picked X instead of Y. I should have taken the unpaid internship instead of working at T.G.I. Friday's to pay for tuition.'"

He tells graduates they should think of themselves not as psychology or sociology majors, but as workers with marketable skills like research, writing and communications.

A danger in the Northeastern economists' research, he said, is that it adds to the "mythology" that only dollar figures are important in choosing a field of study, and it does not account for differences in personality, aptitude, interest and values. Mr. Vogt considers the pressures facing current students far greater than those of generations past.

Trudy Steinfeld, director of career services at New York University, tells students that majors should be less about preparing for one career and more about preparing for many options, and probably several careers, over a lifetime. She agrees with the Northeastern data showing that finance, accounting and technology degrees will lead to higher salaries. But she says she also sees liberal arts majors who become equally successful.

"College should be about stretching yourself and discovering who you are and what you want," Ms. Steinfeld said. "Schools should not become factories. There are hundreds of majors out there, and it's almost always a mistake to base the decision on money alone."

Ms. Steinfeld agrees, though, that students can run into overwhelming pressure from many sources.

Parents paying even a portion of college costs may wonder if a major in philosophy will pay the bills. And if their children change majors, it could extend college from 8 semesters to 9 or 10, at an additional cost.

Nevertheless, Priscilla Molina, 18, an N.Y.U. sophomore, is taking her time choosing a major. Many of her friends are pursuing business careers, but that, she said, will not affect her decision: She is fascinated by international relations and is leaning toward anthropology.

"I want to pick a path that I'm interested in, one that opens my mind," she said. "You're only in college once. I don't want to regret why I didn't major in something I enjoy."

"Choosing a College Major: For Love or for the Money?" by David Koeppel, *the New York Times*, December 5, 2004. Copyright © 2004 by The New York Times Co. Reprinted with permission.

▶Reflection Questions

1. How do you define marketable skills? Consider the courses you are currently taking, whether or not they are specifically related to your major. Define the marketable skills you are learning in each of these courses, and relate them to your intended career.

2. What is your intended major? Describe why you chose this major. Identify potential career options that you intend to investigate or pursue. What internship opportunities could you research to learn more about your career?

3. This reading suggests that sometimes students are under pressure to choose a major. Have you experienced any of these types of pressures? What suggestions do you have for students who must respond to these pressures?

Reading Two

This reading further elaborates the concept that college graduates are not ready for the real world. Levine suggests that the problems stem from students who were overscheduled from an early age, overprotected by parents, not challenged in high school, and primarily interested in activities that give them praise and provide fun. As a result they are unprepared to venture out into the world. Levine suggests that colleges have a huge role in preparing young adults for the future.

College Graduates Aren't Ready for the Real World

Mel Levine

We are witnessing a pandemic of what I call "worklife unreadiness," and colleges face a daunting challenge in immunizing students against it.

Swarms of start-up adults, mostly in their 20s, lack the traction needed to engage the work side of their lives. Some can't make up their minds where to go and what to do, while others find themselves stranded along a career trail about which they are grievously naïve and for which they lack broad preparation. Whether they spent their undergraduate or graduate years focused on a discrete pursuit—say, engineering, law, or medicine—or whether their college education was unbound from any stated career intentions, many are unprepared to choose an appropriate form of work and manage their first job experience

In conducting interviews for my new book, *Ready or Not, Here Life Comes,* I heard repeatedly from employers that their current crop of novice employees appear unable to delay gratification and think long term. They have trouble starting at the bottom rung of a career ladder and handling the unexciting detail, the grunt work, and the political setbacks they have to bear. In fact, many contemporary college and graduate students fail to identify at all with the world of adults.

A variety of unforeseen hazards can cause an unsuccessful crossover from higher education to the workplace. Start-up adults may often not even sense that they are failing to show initiative or otherwise please their superiors. Some early-career pitfalls are unique to our times; some derive from the characteristics of individual students themselves; some are side effects of modern parenting; and others result from an educational system that has not kept pace with the era we live in. All have policy implications for higher-education leaders.

The problems start early. While many of today's young adults were growing up, their role models were each other. Kids today don't know or take an interest in grown-ups, apart from their parents, their teachers, and entertainers. That stands in contrast to previous generations, when young people "studied" and valued older people in the community.

Thus, a lot of contemporary college students are insatiable in their quest for social acceptance and close identification with an esteemed gaggle of peers. The commercialization of adolescence has further fueled a desire to be "cool" and accepted and respected within a kid culture. Some young adults become the victims of their own popularity, experiencing surges and spasms of immense yet highly brittle ego inflation. But that bubble is likely to burst in early career life, when their supervisors are not all that impressed by how well they play shortstop, how they express their taste through their earrings, or the direction in which they orient the brim of their baseball caps.

Life in the dormitory or the fraternity or sorority house no doubt perpetuates and even intensifies that pattern of overreliance on peer approval. It may also serve to cultivate an overwhelming preoccupation with body image and sexual and chemical bodily excitation—at times to the detriment of intellectual development and reality-based reflection on the future. We live in a period of college education in which the body may be the mind's No. 1 rival. While that tension has always existed, our culture stresses more than ever bodily perfection, self-marketing through appearance, and physical fitness over cognitive strength. Unbridled athletic fervor may reinforce such a somatically bent collegiate culture.

Meanwhile, many college students carry with them an extensive history of being overprogrammed by their parents and their middle schools and high schools—soccer practice Monday through Saturday, bassoon lessons on Tuesday evening, square dancing on Wednesday, kung fu on Saturday afternoon, on and on. That may make it hard for them to work independently, engage in original thought processes, and show initiative.

Other students were the golden girls and boys of their high schools—popular, attractive, athletic, and sometimes scholarly insofar as they were talented test takers. Yet many never had to engage in active analytic thinking, brainstorming, creative activity, or the defense of their opinions. In quite a few instances, their parents settled all their disputes with teachers, guided (or did) their homework, and filled out their college applications. As a result, such students may have trouble charting and navigating their own course in college and beyond.

Not uncommonly, start-up adults believe that everything they engage in is supposed to generate praise and fun, as opposed perhaps to being interesting or valuable. The quest for effusive verbal feedback has been a prime motivator throughout their lives, as they have sought approval from parents, teachers, and coaches. Unbridled and sometimes unearned praise may, in fact, fuel the pressure for grade inflation in college.

Similarly, students' favorite professors may well be those whose lectures are the funniest. But what if, eight years later, their bosses have no sense of humor, and their work pales in comparison to the visual and motor ecstasy of computer games and the instantaneous satisfaction of their social and sexual conquests? They might then find themselves mentally out of shape, lacking in the capacity for hard cognitive work, and unable to engage successfully in any extended mind toil that they don't feel like doing.

On top of that, some college students are afflicted with significant underlying developmental problems that have never been properly diagnosed and managed. Examples abound, including difficulties in processing language or communicating verbally (both speaking and writing), an inability to focus attention or reason quantitatively, and a serious lack of problem-solving skills. We are currently encountering far more students with learning difficulties, for a multitude of reasons. Many young adults are growing up in a nonverbal culture that makes few, if any, demands on language skills, active information processing, pattern recognition, and original thinking.

The most common learning disorder among undergraduates is incomplete comprehension. Affected students have difficulty understanding concepts, terminology, issues, and procedures. Many of them succeeded admirably in high school through the exclusive use of rote memory and procedural mimicry (known in mathematics as the "extreme algorithmic approach"). So a student may have received an A in trigonometry by knowing how to manipulate cosines and tangents yet without really understanding what they represent. Such underlying deficiencies return to haunt start-up adults striving for success and recognition on the job. A young adult may be selling a product without fully understanding it, or preparing a legal brief without perceiving its ramifications.

Trouble handling the workload is an equally prevalent, and lingering, form of collegiate dysfunction that follows students into their careers. Some college students are abysmally disorganized and have serious trouble managing materials and time, prioritizing, and handling activities with multiple components that must be integrated—like writing a term paper, applying to graduate schools or prospective employers, and preparing for a final examination. Such difficulties can manifest themselves for the first time at any academic stage in a student's life, including during law, business, or medical school. The students who are burdened with them are vulnerable to dropping out, mental-health problems, and a drastic loss of motivation.

Certainly many students leave college well prepared and well informed for careers, and not every college is affected by such negative cultural forces. But work-life unreadiness is increasingly prevalent and merits the attention of faculty members and administrators. The deterrents that I have mentioned may or may not ignite implosions of grade-point averages, but they can become crippling influences in the work lives of young adults.

Although colleges can't be expected to suture all the gaps in the culture of kids, some changes merit consideration if students are to succeed after graduation. Too many start-up adults harbor serious discrepancies between what they would like to do and what they are truly capable of doing. Often they are interested in pursuits they are not good at or wired for. They opt for the wrong careers because they are unaware of their personal and intellectual strengths and weaknesses, as well as woefully uninformed about the specific job demands of their chosen trades. That combination is a time bomb set to detonate early in a career.

Therefore, colleges should re-examine the adequacy of their career-placement or career-advisory services. Those services should be able to interview students in depth, administer vocational-interest inventories, and make use of sophisticated neuropsychological tests to help floundering students formulate career aims that fit their particular skills and yield personal gratification.

Colleges can also lessen undergraduate naïveté through formal education. Within a core curriculum, perhaps offered by the psychology department, colleges should help students get to know themselves and to think about the relationship between who they are and what they think they might do with their lives. They should provide, and possibly require, courses like "Career Studies," in which undergraduates analyze case studies and biographies to explore the psychological and political nuances of beginning a career.

Students need to anticipate the challenges and agonies of work life at the bottom rungs of a tall and steep ladder. They should be taught generic career-related skills—like how to collaborate, organize and manage projects, write proposals, and decrypt unwritten and unspoken on-the-job expectations. Colleges should also offer classes that cover topics like entrepreneurialism and leadership. Further, students should also receive formal instruction, including case studies, in the pros and cons of alternative career pathways within their areas of concentration (e.g., medical practice versus health-care administration, or teaching about real estate versus pursuing a money chase in land investment).

To elucidate the specific learning problems of students who are not succeeding, colleges need to offer up-to-date diagnostic services. Those include tests to pinpoint problems with memory, attention, concept formation, and other key brain processes that will cause a career to implode whether or not a student makes it through her undergraduate years.

Faculty members should change not only what they teach but *how* they teach, to help students make a better transition to the adult world. They should receive formal training in the latest research about brain development and the learning processes that occur during late adolescence—including such key areas as higher-language functioning, frontal-lobe performance (like planning, pacing, and self-monitoring), nonverbal thought processes, memory use, and selective attention.

Professors also should base their pedagogy on some awareness of the mechanisms underlying optimal learning and mastery of their subject matter. Chemistry professors should understand and make use of the cognition of chemistry mastery, while foreign-language instructors and those conducting political-science seminars should be aware of the brain functions they are tapping and strengthening through their coursework. Current students face complex decision-making and problem-solving career challenges, but many have been groomed in high school to rely solely on rote memory—an entirely useless approach in a meaningful career.

At the same time, professors must have keen insight into the differences in learning among the students who take their courses. They should seek to offer alternative ways in which students can display their knowledge and skills. They might discover, for instance, that their tests should de-emphasize rote recall and the spewing out of knowledge without any interpretation on the part of the student.

In short, faculty members must learn about teaching. It should not be assumed that a learned person understands how people learn.

What's more, colleges should offer opportunities for scholarly research into the cognitive abilities, political strategies, and skills needed for career fulfillment in various fields. The study of success and failure should be thought of as a topic worthy of rigorous investigation at all higher-education institutions.

Finally, every college should also strive to promulgate a campus intellectual life that can hold its own against social, sexual, and athletics virtuosity. Varsity debating teams should receive vigorous alumni support and status, as should literary magazines, guest lectureships, concerts, and art exhibitions. Undergraduate institutions reveal themselves by what gets tacked up on campus bulletin boards—which often are notices of keg parties, fraternity and sorority rush events, and intramural schedules. Colleges can work to change that culture.

Our colleges open their doors to kids who have grown up in an era that infiltrates them with unfettered pleasure, heavy layers of overprotection, and heaps of questionably justified positive feedback. As a result, childhood and adolescence may become nearly impossible acts to follow.

Higher education has to avoid hitching itself to that pleasure-packed bandwagon. Otherwise, students will view the academic side of college as not much more than a credentialing process to put up with while they are having a ball for four years. Colleges must never cease to ask themselves, "What roles can and should these young adults play in the world of our times? And what must we do to prepare them?"

"College Graduates Aren't Ready for the Real World," by Mel Levine, *The Chronicle Review*, February 18, 2005, p. 11. Reprinted by permission of the author.

▶ Reflection Questions

1. On the basis of the information you have read, what do you think you need to accomplish in order to prepare for the real world? List the three most important things and describe how they will relate to life after college. Did your high school help you prepare in any way for these three important things? If not, should they and what specifically should they have done?

2. Some college students have learning disabilities, or as Levine describes them "significant underlying developmental problems that have never been properly diagnosed and managed." He suggests that they can become apparent at any time (not necessarily diagnosed), and when they do, students can lose motivation, experience mental health problems, or drop out. Have you ever known someone who experienced this or suspected that someone you knew had? Why do you think this kind of problem was never discovered before college? What advice would you give this student?

3. Levine also indicates that many students in college have trouble managing the necessary workload. He believes that this can spill over into the world of work. What role do you think parents and teachers play in helping students manage work? Should they give more or less responsibility to the students? When and why?

Reading Three

Young adults in the mid- to late twenties are delaying decisions such as permanent career path and marriage. Presumably they are doing so to be sure that they are making the right choices for lifelong happiness. In this reading Wallis reports the results of psychologists' studies of what makes people happy—and the results may be surprising.

The New Science of Happiness

Claudia Wallis

Sugary white sand gleams under the bright yucatan sun, aquamarine water teems with tropical fish and lazy sea turtles, cold Mexican beer beckons beneath the shady thatch of palapas—it's hard to imagine a sweeter spot than Akumal, Mexico, to contemplate the joys of being alive. And that was precisely the agenda when three leading psychologists gathered in this Mexican paradise to plot a new direction for psychology. For most of its history, psychology had concerned itself with all that ails the human mind: anxiety, depression, neurosis, obsessions, paranoia, delusions. The goal of practitioners was to bring patients from a negative, ailing state to a neutral normal, or, as University of Pennsylvania psychologist Martin Seligman puts it, "from a minus five to a zero." It was Seligman who had summoned the others to Akumal that New Year's Day in 1998—his first day as president of the American Psychological Association (A.P.A.)—to share a vision of a new goal for psychology. "I realized that my profession was half-baked. It wasn't enough for us to nullify disabling conditions and get to zero. We needed to ask, What are the enabling conditions that make human beings flourish? How do we get from zero to plus five?"

Every incoming A.P.A. president is asked to choose a theme for his or her yearlong term in office. Seligman was thinking big. He wanted to persuade substantial numbers in the profession to explore the region north of zero, to look at what actively made people feel fulfilled, engaged and meaningfully happy. Mental health, he reasoned, should be more than the absence of mental illness. It should be something akin to a vibrant and muscular fitness of the human mind and spirit.

Over the decades, a few psychological researchers had ventured out of the dark realm of mental illness into the sunny land of the mentally hale and hearty. Some of Seligman's own research, for instance, had focused on optimism, a trait shown to be associated with good physical health, less depression and mental illness, longer life and, yes, greater happiness. Perhaps the most eager explorer of this terrain was University of Illinois psychologist Edward Diener, a.k.a. Dr. Happiness. For more than two decades, basically ever since he got tenure and could risk entering an unfashionable field, Diener had been examining what does and does not make people feel satisfied with life. Seligman's goal was to shine a light on such work and encourage much, much more of it.

To help him realize his vision, Seligman invited Ray Fowler, then the long-reigning and influential CEO of the A.P.A., to join him in Akumal. He also invited Hungarian-born psychologist Mihaly Csikszentmihalyi (pronounced cheeks sent me high), best known for exploring a happy state of mind called flow, the feeling of complete engagement in a creative or playful activity familiar to athletes, musicians, video-game enthusiasts—almost anyone who loses himself in a favorite pursuit. By the end of their week at the beach, the three had plans for the first-ever conference on positive psychology, to be held in Akumal a year later—it was to become an annual event—and a strategy for recruiting young talent to the nascent field. Within a few months, Seligman, who has a talent for popularizing and promoting his areas of interest, was approached by the Templeton Foundation in England, which proceeded to create lucrative awards for research in positive psych. The result: an explosion of research on happiness, optimism, positive emotions and healthy character traits. Seldom has an academic field been brought so quickly and deliberately to life.

WHAT MAKES US HAPPY

So, what has science learned about what makes the human heart sing? More than one might imagine—along with some surprising things about what doesn't ring our inner chimes. Take wealth, for instance, and all the delightful things that money can buy. Research by Diener, among others, has shown that once your basic needs are met, additional income does little to raise your sense of satisfaction with life. A good education? Sorry, Mom and Dad, neither education nor, for that matter, a high IQ paves the road to happiness. Youth? No, again. In fact, older people are more consistently satisfied with their lives than the young. And they're less prone to dark moods: a recent survey by the Centers for Disease Control and Prevention found that people ages 20 to 24 are sad for an average of 3.4 days a month, as opposed to just 2.3 days for people ages 65 to 74. Marriage? A complicated picture: married people are generally happier than singles, but that may be because they were happier to begin with. Sunny days? Nope, although a 1998 study showed that Midwesterners think folks living in balmy California are happier and that Californians incorrectly believe this about themselves too.

On the positive side, religious faith seems to genuinely lift the spirit, though it's tough to tell whether it's the God part or the community aspect that does the heavy lifting. Friends? A giant yes. A 2002 study conducted at the University of Illinois by Diener and Seligman found that the most salient characteristics shared by the 10% of students with the highest levels of happiness and the fewest signs of depression were their strong ties to friends and family and commitment to spending time with them. "Word needs to be spread," concludes Diener. "It is important to work on social skills, close interpersonal ties and social support in order to be happy."

MEASURING OUR MOODS

Of course, happiness is not a static state. Even the happiest of people—the cheeriest 10%—feel blue at times. And even the bluest have their moments of joy. That has presented a challenge to social scientists trying to measure happiness. That, along with the simple fact that happiness is inherently subjective. To get around those challenges, researchers have devised several methods of assessment. Diener has created one of the most basic and widely used tools, the Satisfaction with Life Scale. Though some scholars have questioned the validity of this simple, five-question survey, Diener has found that it squares well with other measures of happiness, such as impressions from friends and family, expression of positive emotion and low incidence of depression.

Researchers have devised other tools to look at more transient moods. Csikszentmihalyi pioneered a method of using beepers and, later, handheld computers to contact subjects at random intervals. A pop-up screen presents an array of questions: What are you doing? How much are you enjoying it? Are you alone or interacting with someone else? The method, called experience sampling, is costly, intrusive and time consuming, but it provides an excellent picture of satisfaction and engagement at a specific time during a specific activity.

Just last month, a team led by Nobel-prizewinning psychologist Daniel Kahneman of Princeton University unveiled a new tool for sizing up happiness: the day-reconstruction method. Participants fill out a long diary and questionnaire detailing everything they did on the previous day and whom they were with at the time and rating a range of feelings during each episode (happy, impatient, depressed, worried, tired, etc.) on a seven-point scale. The method was tested on a group of 900 women in Texas with some surprising results. It turned out that the five most positive activities for these women were (in descending order) sex, socializing, relaxing, praying or meditating, and eating. Exercising and watching TV were not far behind. But way down the list was "taking care of my children," which ranked below cooking and only slightly above housework.

That may seem surprising, given that people frequently cite their children as their biggest source of delight—which was a finding of a TIME poll on happiness conducted last month. When asked, "What one thing in life has brought you the greatest happiness?" 35% said it was their children or grandchildren or both. (Spouse was far behind at just 9%, and religion a runner-up at 17%.) The discrepancy with the study of Texas women points up one of the key debates in happiness research: Which kind of information is more meaningful—global reports of well-being ("My life is happy, and my children are my greatest joy") or more specific data on enjoyment of day-to-day experiences ("What a night! The kids were such a pain!")? The two are very different, and studies show they do not correlate well. Our overall happiness is not merely the sum of our happy moments minus the sum of our angry or sad ones.

This is true whether you are looking at how satisfied you are with your life in general or with something more specific, such as your kids, your car, your job or your vacation. Kahneman likes to distinguish between the experiencing self and the remembering self. His studies show that what you remember of an experience is particularly influenced by the emotional high and low points and by how it ends. So, if you were to randomly beep someone on vacation in Italy, you might catch that person waiting furiously for a slow-moving waiter to take an order or grousing about the high cost of the pottery. But if you ask when it's over, "How was the vacation in Italy?" the average person remembers the peak moments and how he or she felt at the end of the trip.

The power of endings has been demonstrated in some remarkable experiments by Kahneman. One such study involved people undergoing a colonoscopy, an uncomfortable procedure in which a flexible scope is moved through the colon. While a control group had the standard procedure, half the subjects endured an extra 60 seconds during which the scope was held stationary; movement of the scope is typically the source of the discomfort. It turned out that members of the group that had the somewhat longer procedure with a benign ending found it less unpleasant than the control group, and they were more willing to have a repeat colonoscopy.

Asking people how happy they are, Kahneman contends, "is very much like asking them about the colonoscopy after it's over. There's a lot that escapes them." Kahneman therefore believes that social scientists studying happiness should pay careful attention to people's actual experiences rather than just survey their reflections. That, he feels, is especially relevant if research is to inform quality-of-life policies like how much money our society should devote to parks and recreation or how much should be invested in improving workers' commutes. "You cannot ignore how people spend their time," he says, "when thinking about well-being."

Seligman, in contrast, puts the emphasis on the remembering self. "I think we are our memories more than we are the sum total of our experiences," he says. For him, studying moment-to-moment experiences puts too much emphasis on transient pleasures and displeasures. Happiness goes deeper than that, he argues in his 2002 book *Authentic Happiness*. As a result of his research, he finds three components of happiness: pleasure ("the smiley-face piece"), engagement (the depth of involvement with one's family, work, romance and hobbies) and meaning (using personal strengths to serve some larger end). Of those three roads to a happy, satisfied life, pleasure is the least consequential, he insists: "This is newsworthy because so many Americans build their lives around pursuing pleasure. It turns out that engagement and meaning are much more important."

CAN WE GET HAPPIER?

One of the biggest issues in happiness research is the question of how much our happiness is under our control. In 1996 University of Minnesota researcher David Lykken published a paper looking at the role of genes in determining one's sense of satisfaction in life. Lykken, now 76, gathered information on 4,000 sets of twins born in Minnesota from 1936 through 1955. After comparing happiness data on identical vs. fraternal twins, he came to the conclusion that about 50% of one's satisfaction with life comes from genetic programming. (Genes influence such traits as having a sunny, easygoing personality; dealing well with stress; and feeling low levels of anxiety and depression.) Lykken found that circumstantial factors like income, marital status, religion and education contribute only about 8% to one's overall well-being. He attributes the remaining percentage to "life's slings and arrows."

Because of the large influence of our genes, Lykken proposed the idea that each of us has a happiness set point much like our set point for body weight. No matter what happens in our life—good, bad, spectacular, horrific—we tend to return in short order to our set range. Some post-tsunami images last week of smiling Asian children returning to school underscored this amazing capacity to right ourselves. And a substantial body of research documents our tendency to return to the norm. A study of lottery winners done in 1978 found, for instance, that they did not wind up significantly happier than a control group. Even people who lose the use of their limbs to a devastating accident tend to bounce back, though perhaps not all the way to their base line. One study found that a week after the accident, the injured were severely angry and anxious, but after eight weeks "happiness was their strongest emotion," says Diener. Psychologists call this adjustment to new circumstances adaptation. "Everyone is surprised by how happy paraplegics can be," says Kahneman. "The reason is that they are not paraplegic full time. They do other things. They enjoy their meals, their friends. They read the news. It has to do with the allocation of attention."

In his extensive work on adaptation, Edward Diener has found two life events that seem to knock people lastingly below their happiness set point: loss of a spouse and loss of a job. It takes five to eight years for a widow to regain her previous sense of well-being. Similarly, the effects of a job loss linger long after the individual has returned to the work force.

When he proposed his set-point theory eight years ago, Lykken came to a drastic conclusion. "It may be that trying to be happier is as futile as trying to be taller," he wrote. He has since come to regret that sentence. "I made a dumb statement in the original article," he tells TIME. "It's clear that we can change our happiness levels widely—up or down." Lykken's revisionist thinking coincides with the view of the positive-psychology movement, which has put a premium on research showing you can raise your level of happiness. For Seligman and like-minded researchers, that involves working on the three components of happiness—getting more pleasure out of life (which can be done by savoring sensory experiences, although, he warns, "you're never going to make a curmudgeon into a giggly person"), becoming more engaged in what you do and finding ways of making your life feel more meaningful.

There are numerous ways to do that, they argue. At the University of California at Riverside, psychologist Sonja Lyubomirsky is using grant money from the National Institutes of Health to study different kinds of happiness boosters. One is the gratitude journal—a diary in which subjects write down things for which they are thankful. She has found that taking the time to conscientiously count their blessings once a week significantly increased subjects' overall satisfaction with life over a period of six weeks, whereas a control group that did not keep journals had no such gain.

Gratitude exercises can do more than lift one's mood. At the University of California at Davis, psychologist Robert Emmons found they improve physical health, raise energy levels and, for patients with neuromuscular disease, relieve pain and fatigue. "The ones who benefited most tended to elaborate more and have a wider span of things they're grateful for," he notes.

Another happiness booster, say positive psychologists, is performing acts of altruism or kindness—visiting a nursing home, helping a friend's child with homework, mowing a neighbor's lawn, writing a letter to a grandparent. Doing five kind acts a week, especially all in a single day, gave a measurable boost to Lyubomirsky's subjects.

Seligman has tested similar interventions in controlled trials at Penn and in huge experiments conducted over the Internet. The single most effective way to turbocharge your joy, he says, is to make a "gratitude visit." That means writing a testimonial thanking a teacher, pastor or grandparent—anyone to whom you owe a debt of gratitude—and then visiting that person to read him or her the letter of appreciation. "The remarkable thing," says Seligman, "is that people who do this just once are measurably happier and less depressed a month later. But it's gone by three months." Less powerful but more lasting, he says, is an exercise he calls three blessings—taking time each day to write down a trio of things that went well and why. "People are less depressed and happier three months later and six months later."

Seligman's biggest recommendation for lasting happiness is to figure out (courtesy of his website, reflectivehappiness.com) your strengths and find new ways to deploy them. Increasingly, his work, done in collaboration with Christopher Peterson at the University of Michigan, has focused on defining such human strengths and virtues as generosity, humor, gratitude and zest and studying how they relate to happiness. "As a professor, I don't like this," Seligman says, "but the cerebral virtues—curiosity, love of learning—are less strongly tied to happiness than interpersonal virtues like kindness, gratitude and capacity for love."

Why do exercising gratitude, kindness and other virtues provide a lift? "Giving makes you feel good about yourself," says Peterson. "When you're volunteering, you're distracting yourself from your own existence, and that's beneficial. More fuzzily, giving puts meaning into your life. You have a sense of purpose because you matter to someone else." Virtually all the happiness exercises being tested by positive psychologists, he says, make people feel more connected to others.

That seems to be the most fundamental finding from the science of happiness. "Almost every person feels happier when they're with other people," observes Mihaly Csikszentmihalyi. "It's paradoxical because many of us think we can hardly wait to get home and be alone with nothing to do, but that's a worst-case scenario. If you're alone with nothing to do, the quality of your experience really plummets."

But can a loner really become more gregarious through acts-of-kindness exercises? Can a dyed-in-the-wool pessimist learn to see the glass as half full? Can gratitude journals work their magic over the long haul? And how many of us could keep filling them with fresh thankful thoughts year after year? Sonja Lyubomirsky believes it's all possible: "I'll quote Oprah here, which I don't normally do. She was asked how she runs five miles a day, and she said, 'I recommit to it every day of my life.' I think happiness is like that. Every day you have to renew your commitment. Hopefully, some of the strategies will become habitual over time and not a huge effort."

But other psychologists are more skeptical. Some simply doubt that personality is that flexible or that individuals can or should change their habitual coping styles. "If you're a pessimist who really thinks through in detail what might go wrong, that's a strategy that's likely to work very well for you," says Julie Norem, a psychology professor at Wellesley College and the author of *The Positive Power of Negative Thinking*. "In fact, you may be messed up if you try to substitute a positive attitude." She is worried that the messages of positive psychology reinforce "a lot of American biases" about how individual initiative and a positive attitude can solve complex problems.

Who's right? This is an experiment we can all do for ourselves. There's little risk in trying some extra gratitude and kindness, and the results—should they materialize—are their own reward.

"The New Science of Happiness" by Claudia Wallis, *Time,* January 17, 2005. © 2005 TIME Inc. reprinted by permission.

▶ Reflection Questions

1. According to this reading, what really makes us happy? Is it money? Jobs? Marriage? Do you agree with what the researchers discovered? How does this relate to your own life?

2. In research done on twins, Lykken found that about 50 percent of our happiness comes from our genes. Some people are simply born with a predisposition to deal well with stress and to have an easygoing personality. The other 50 percent of our happiness comes from what happens to us in life. Explain why you think that studies done on people who have won the lottery show they do not end up any happier than individuals in a control group who did not.

3. Peterson suggests that "giving makes you feel good about yourself." Do you agree? Describe a situation where you did something for someone else and felt good about it.

 # Final Writing Assignment

audience: A friend

purpose: To reflect back on your first semester in college and share with a friend whether what you predicted would happen did

length: Minimum of five typed pages, double-spaced

You will write a final assignment using the envelope you gave your instructor at the start of the semester. (Your instructor will return the sealed envelope to you that you turned in during the first week of class.) After rereading your letter, reflect back on your first semester and write responses to these questions. How have you changed? What have you learned? Did your letter anticipating your first semester in college accurately reflect what happened? Why or why not? What advice would you now give to your friend? What are your expectations for the remainder of your college experiences? Include suggestions that you have learned from each chapter. Quote articles where appropriate, using either the MLA or the APA method of citation.

 ## Journal Entries: DISCOVERY AND INTENTION STATEMENTS

The final journal entry is one that you will not share with anyone. This entry is simply for you to put down things you learned about yourself this semester that you may not have wanted to put in the letter you wrote to your friend. Be honest. What did you learn this semester that surprised you about yourself? Are you planning on doing anything about it? If so, what? Also, it's very important to note your accomplishments.

Ask yourself if you think you will be ready to face the real world at graduation time. Describe what you think the first three years after graduation will be like for you. Is it what you want? If not, is there anything you could do now to change it?

Make a list of the strides your have made this semester, and take a moment to think about what you do that makes you special. Pat yourself on the back for all of those good things. Congratulate yourself for a job well done.

Mastering Vocabulary

List five words that were new to you (more or less if necessary). For each, include which reading you found the word in, the definition, and where you got the definition from, as well as a time or place you might use the word again.

1. _____

_____

2. _____

_____

3. _____

_____

4. _____

_____

5. _____

_____

 ## Additional Activities

Go to your college's Career Center and get information on how to develop a résumé. Then create a résumé listing your accomplishments to date. Share it with the class. While you are sharing, listen for statements other students make that are true for you too, but you forgot to add to your résumé. Then make a list of things you would like to accomplish in the upcoming semester. Consider revising your résumé at the end of each semester in college.

Photo Credits

Chapter Opening Photos:

Discover What You Want, p. 1	© PhotoDisc
Ideas Are Tools, p. 24	© PhotoDisc
Be Here Now, p. 50	© Comstock
Love Your Problems, p. 72	© PhotoDisc
Notice Your Pictures, p. 97	© Royalty Free
I Create It All, p. 117	© Corbis
Detach, p. 132	© Elektra Vision/AG/PictureQuest
Find a Bigger Problem, p. 155	© Digital Vision/Getty
Employ Your Word, p. 178	© Brand X/Wonderfile
Choose Your Conversation, p. 196	© PhotoDisc
Risk Being a Fool, p. 212	© Corbis
Surrender, p. 224	© Ron Chapple/Thinkstock/ PictureQuest
Be It, p. 249	© Digital Vision/Wonderfile

Readings List

272

Index

Italicized page numbers indicate a figure or table.

SCNT. *See* Somatic cell nuclear transfer
"Secrets of Sleep, The" (Boyce and Brink), 142–148
Self-awareness, stress reduction and, 138
Self-discovery, through literature, 150–152
Self-image, equations for, 135
Self-monitoring, stress management and, 137
Seligman, Martin, 261, 262, 263, 264, 266
Senility, 89. *See also* Alzheimer's disease
"September 11, 2001: Answering the Call" (Moon), 127–129
September 11, 2001 terrorist attacks
  leadership during, 64–65
  loved ones and aftermath of, 158–161
Service learning, 176
Sex and Race (Rogers), 104
Shakespeare, William, 139
Sherwood, Kaitlin Duck, 184
Shipp, Drew, 57
Shipp, Gregg, 57, 59
Siegel, Jerry, 145
Simonton, Dean, 58
Singer, Peter, 173
Sleep
  brain and, 87
  importance of, 142–148
Sleep apnea, 147
Sleep-learning theory, 144–145
Smart drugs, 80–81
Smith, Carlyle, 87, 143
Snowdon, David, 88, 89
Social service, demand for college graduates in, 18
Social skills, 263
Socrates, 107
Somatic cell nuclear transfer, 167
Somers, Virend, 147
Souls of Black Folk (Du Bois), 103
Speakers Unlimited, 77, 78
Speaking
  overcoming fear of, 76–79
  powerful, 181
Spellings, Margaret, 191
Spirituality, 89
Sports, flow in, 8
Statistics, trouble with, 13
Status anxiety, 61
Steinfeld, Trudy, 255
Stem cell controversy
  biochemist's perspective on, 174–175
  ethicist's perspective on, 171–174
  neurobiologist's perspective on, 166–169
  political scientist's perspective on, 169–171
"Stem Cell Controversy" (Condic, Ellison, Coulehan, and Gergen), 166–175
Stereotypes, 100

Steven, Richard, 145
Stevenson, Adlai, 106
Stewart, Barbara, 83
Stewart, Martha, 218
Stickgold, Robert, 144
Story of Civilization (Durant), 103
Story of Oriental Civilization, The (Durant), 105
Stress
  causes of, 137, 140–141
  check-up, 141
  excessive ambition and, 58
  sources of, 138
  warning signs of, 140
"Stress Management: Rolling with the Punch" (Hook), 137–141
Stress management program, integrated, *138*
Stressors, dealing with, 152–153
Student loans, 243
Students with learning disabilities, 203–207
SuÃjrez-Orozco, Marcelo, 62
Subjective knowledge, 34–35
Success
  conversations and, 199
  detachment and, 136
"Summer I Discovered Coltrane, The" (Marsalis), 38–39
Summers, Lawrence H., 207
Support systems, stress reduction and, 138, 139–140
Surrender, 224–247
  detachment and, 227
  power of, 226
  releasing control and receiving help, 225–226
  true source of control and, 226–227
Swayne, Ian, 206
Sweeney, Amy, 159, 161
Sweeney, Mike, 159, 160, 161
Swinney, James, 146

Tapp, Dwight, 83
Tardiness, in classroom, 200, 201
Tasks, prioritizing, 241
Tate, Angela, 183, 184
Temperamental determinism, 59
Tenet, George, 160
Term-paper sites, plagiarizing and, 218
Terrorism
  conflicting emotions in wake of, 158–161
  heroes and, 127–129
Thoreau, Henry David, 157
Thoughts, choosing, 120
"3 Years after Attacks, Conflicting Emotions" (Aucoin), 158–161